Putting Children First
a guide for immigration practitioners

Jane Coker is a solicitor and partner in the London firm of Coker Vis Partnership. She specialises in immigration, asylum and nationality law. She has lectured and trained for, among others, the Immigration Law Practitioners' Association, the Law Society and Legal Action Group. She is a contributor to *Cohabitation: Law and Precedents* (Sweet & Maxwell) and also published articles on various topics in this area. She is the Chief Assessor of the Law Society's Immigration Law Panel and founder member of the Refugee Women's Legal Group.

Nadine Finch is a barrister at 2 Garden Court in London and specialises in immigration, asylum and nationality law. She is a contributor to *Macdonald's Immigration Law and Practice* (Butterworths, 5th edn, 2001), Halsbury's *Immigration and Nationality volume* (Butterworths), *Human Rights Practice* (Sweet & Maxwell) and *Cohabitation: Law and Precedents* (Sweet & Maxwell). She regularly trains for the Immigration Practitioners' Association.

Alison Stanley is a solicitor and partner in the London firm of Bindman and Partners. She specialises in immigration, asylum and nationality law. She has lectured and trained for, amongst others, the Immigration Law Practitioners' Association, the Joint Council for the Welfare of Immigrants and UKCOSA: The Council for International Education. She is Deputy Chair of the Law Society's Immigration Law Committee and a founder member of the Refugee Women's Legal Group.

The Legal Action Group is a national, independent charity which campaigns for equal access to justice for all members of society. Legal Action Group:
- provides support to the practice of lawyers and advisers
- inspires developments in that practice
- campaigns for improvements in the law and the administration of justice
- stimulates debate on how services should be delivered.

Putting Children First

a guide for immigration practitioners

Jane Coker, Nadine Finch and
Alison Stanley

 Legal Action Group
2002

This edition published in Great Britain 2002
by LAG Education and Service Trust Ltd
242 Pentonville Road
London
N1 9UN

© Jane Coker, Nadine Finch and Alison Stanley 2002

Apart from any fair dealing for the purposes of research or private study, or criticism or review, as permitted under the Copyright, Designs and Patents Act 1988, this publication may only be reproduced, stored or transmitted, in any form or by any means, with the prior permission in writing of the publishers, or in the case of reprographic reproduction in accordance with the terms and licences issued by the CLA. Enquiries concerning reproduction outside these terms should be sent to the publishers.

British Library Cataloguing in Publication Data
A CIP catalogue record for this book is available from the British Library

ISBN 1 903307 11 2

Typeset by Regent Typesetting, London
Printed in Great Britain by Biddles Ltd, Guildford, Surrey

Introduction

This book grew out of a course on family law issues for immigration practitioners which had been run for many years by the Immigration Law Practitioners' Association. The chronic delays experienced by asylum-seekers and those seeking to remain in the United Kingdom for other reasons has meant that almost inevitably families are started or expanded before most applications are finally determined. Equally the intricacies of nationality law mean that members of one family can find themselves with very different entitlements to British nationality. Individuals then face the prospect of being separated, sometimes indefinitely from partners or children as a result of immigration and nationality decisions. In addition, the stress of long drawn out immigration proceedings leads to family breakdown. As a result many immigration practitioners now need to be aware of family law and human rights jurisprudence which protects the right to enjoy family and private life. The aim of the book is to provide immigration practitioners with the tools needed to argue family law issues successfully in an immigration context. It is assumed that the adviser will have a basic grounding in immigration law.

The authors are aware that this is a rapidly expanding area of the law and that the Nationality, Immigration and Asylum bill presently before parliament will introduce further changes which will affect children and their families. They intend to update the book by holding regular training sessions based on its contents.

Jane Coker
Nadine Finch
Alison Stanley

April 2002

Contents

Introduction v
Table of cases xi
Table of statutes xv
Table of statutory instruments xix
Table of European legislation xxi
Abbreviations xxiii

1 **Family law: concepts and principles** 1
Introduction 3
Family law definitions and concepts 3
Orders that can be made 16
Local authority responsibility for children 23
Complaints procedure under CA 1989 s26 31
Effect of court orders made in the UK 31

2 **Adoption** 33
Non-British children adopted in the UK by British parents 34
Non-British children 'adopted' abroad 36
Where adoption abroad was not possible 38
Adoptive children of EEA nationals 39

3 **Support** 41
Access to financial support and public services 42
Access to other services 51

4 **Human rights** 55
The relevance of human rights law 56
European Convention on Human Rights 56

5 **Family aspects of asylum** 77
Introduction 79
The family 79
Divorce 80
Domestic violence 81
Unaccompanied children 81

vii

Where sponsor is an asylum-seeker   88
Mixed applications   89
Where sponsor is a refugee   89
Where sponsor has exceptional leave   92
Where a person is recognised as a refugee in another country   94
Unmarried partners   94
Divorce and separation   94
Failed asylum-seekers and exceptional leave to remain or enter   95
Family aspects of immigration   96

6   Applications outside the rules: Home Office practice and general principles   99
Introduction   101
Sources of policies   101
Legal position of Home Office policies and concessions   102
Home Office policies outside the rules regarding children   103
Marriage concession relating to the 'one year' rule and domestic violence and widowed partners   114
The domestic violence concession and EU law   116
Separated spouses and EU law   116
AIDS, HIV infection and other serious illnesses   117
Psychiatric illness   121
Long residence concessions   122
Administrative removal and deportation   126
Citizenship issues   141

7   Interviewing   147
Introduction   148
Taking instructions   149
Issues that may have to be addressed by experts   156
Obtaining reports in support of the application   158

8   Making the application   161
Introduction   162
Assessing the claim   162
When to approach the Home Office   166
Use of family court orders   167
How to make the application   170
Preparing an application   171
Appeal rights   175

APPENDICES

A   Immigration Directorate Instructions on adoption   179
B   Extract from Entry Clearance General Instructions Vol 1 Chapter 16 and Annex 16   205
C   Extract from Asylum Policy Instructions   209
D   Some relevant Concessions   215
E   Extracts from European Convention on Human Rights   227
F   International Covenant on Civil and Political Rights (selected articles)   233
G   Other International Conventions   237
H   Convention of the Rights of the Child   243
I   Universal Declaration of Human Rights 1948 (selected articles)   255
J   Practice Notes   257
K   Letter from Barbara Roche to Lord Archer of Sandwell QC, 30 June 2000   263
L   Extracts from Marriages Handbook for Registration Officers (produced by General Register Office)   265
M   Useful resources   269

Index   275

Table of cases

A (a minor) (wardship: immigration), Re [1992] 1 FLR 432	8.34
A (children: UN Declaration 1959), Re [1998] 1 FLR 354	4.1
A v A (contact: representation of child's interests) [2001] 1 FLR 715	1.34
Abdi v Home Secretary [1996] Imm AR 148	6.10
Abdulaziz v UK (1985) 7 EHRR 471	4.55
Associated Provincial Picture House v Wednesbury Corporation [1948] 1 KB 223	3.30, 4.10, 4.53
B, Re [1999] 2 AC 136	2.5, 2.7
B v Home Secretary [2000] INLR 361; [2000] Imm AR 478, CA	4.53, 6.98, 6.108
Belgian Linguistic Case (No 2) (1979-80) 1 EHRR 252	4.60, 4.63
Bensaid v UK [2001] INLR 325	4.31, 6.64
Berrehab v Netherlands (1989) 11 EHRR 322	4.51
Brind v Home Secretary [1991] 1 AC 696, HL	4.2, 4.7
Chahal v UK (1997) 23 EHRR 413	4.29, 4.30
Chief Adjudication Officer v Bath [2000] 1 FLR 8	1.11
Ciliz v Netherlands [2000] 2 FLR 469	4.51
Costello-Roberts v UK (1995) 19 EHRR 112	4.57
D v UK (1997) 24 EHRR 423	6.61, 6.63
Diatto v Land Berlin [1986] 2 CMLR 164, ECJ	6.57
E, Re [1995] Imm AR 475	1.27
Elsholz v Germany [2000] 2 FLR 486	4.49
F (childcare: disclosure of documents), Re [1995] 1 FCR 589	1.41, 8.18, 8.19
Fitzpatrick v Sterling Housing Association Limited [2001] 1 AC 27	4.57
G (Secure Accommodation), Re [2000] 2 FLR 259	1.6
Gillick v West Norfolk and Wisbech Area Health Authority and the DHSS [1986] 1 AC 112	1.29, 1.31
H (a minor) (adoption: non-patrial), Re [1996] 2 FCR 597	2.4

xii   *Putting children first / Table of cases*

H (Parental Responsibility,) Re [1998] 1 FLR 855	1.56
Holub & Holub v Home Secretary [2001] INLR 219	4.63
Home Secretary v Hastrup [1996] Imm AR 616, CA	6.9
Home Secretary v Kacaj [2001] INLR 354	4.23, 4.30
Ireland v UK (1979–80) 2 EHRR 25	4.32
J (adoption: non-patrial), Re [1998] FCR 125	2.10
K (a minor) (adoption order: nationality), Re [1995] Fam 38	2.7
K (adoption and wardship), Re [1997] 2 FLR 221	2.4
KD (a minor) (access: principles), Re [1988] 2 FLR 139	1.37
K and S (minors), Re [1992] 1 FLR 432	8.34
Kaya v Haringey LBC [2001] EWCA Civ 677	3.24, 3.40
Keegan v Ireland (A/290) (1994) 18 EHRR 342; [1994] 3 FCR 165	1.4, 4.51
Khan (Asif Mahmood) v IAT [1984] Imm AR 68	6.9
Kroon v Netherlands 19 EHRR 263	1.4
Kumarakuraparan v Secretary of State for the Home Department [2002] EWHC 112	4.12
Lamuratur Mbatude v Home Secretary [1996] Imm AR 184	8.35
Lustig Prean v UK (2000) 29 EHRR 548	4.57
MNM v Home Secretary [2000] INLR 576	4.48
Maaouia v France (2001) 9 BHRC 205	4.48
Matondo , Re [1993] Imm AR 541	8.34
Marcks v Belgium (1979) 2 EHRR 330	1.4
Niemietz v Germany (1993) 16 EHRR 97	4.58
Nhundu & Chiwera (01/TH/0613)	4.19
Nuruwa (00/TH/2345)	4.20, 4.53
Osman v UK (2000) 29 EHRR 245	4.25
Pardeepan v Home Secretary [2000] INLR 447	4.22
Payne v Payne [2001] 1 FCR 424; (2001) *Times* 22 February	1.67, 4.20, 4.54
R (Care Proceedings: Jurisdiction), Re [1995] 3 FCR 305	1.27
R on the application of A v Lambeth LBC [2001] EWCA Civ 1624; (2001) 4 CCLR 486; [2001] 3 FCR 673; (2001) *Times* 20 November, CA	1.79, 3.30
R on the application of J and Enfield LBC v Secretary of State for Health [2002] EWHC 432	3.30

Table of cases xiii

R on the application of Kariharan v Home Secretary [2001] EWCA Admin 1004	4.12, 4.21
R on the application of Mahmood v Home Secretary [2001] INLR 1	4.9, 4.20, 4.56
R on the application of Mario Montano v Home Secretary [2001] INLR 148	4.62
R on the application of Westminster City Council v NASS [2001] EWCA Civ 512; (2001) 33 HLR 83; (2001) 4 CCLR 143, CA	3.26
R v DPP ex p Dianne Pretty and Home Secretary [2002] 1 All ER 1	6.63
R v Governor of Durham Prison ex p Hardial Singh [1984] 1 WLR 704	4.46
R v Home Secretary ex p Abdullah Turgut [2000] INLR 292	4.8
R v Home Secretary ex p Ahmed and Patel [1998] INLR 570	4.2
R v Home Secretary ex p Amankwah [1994] Imm AR 240	6.9
R v Home Secretary ex p Arman Ali [2000] INLR 89	4.3
R v Home Secretary ex p Begum [1996] Imm AR 582	4.54, 8.35
R v Home Secretary ex p Daly [2000] 2 AC 532, HL	4.10
R v Home Secretary ex p Gangadeen [1998] INLR 206, CA	6.9, 6.68
R v Home Secretary ex p Isiko [2001] INLR 175	4.9
R v Home Secretary ex p K [2001] Imm AR 11	4.32, 6.63
R v Home Secretary ex p Sandhu [1983] 3 CMLR 131	6.58
R v Home Secretary ex p Zakrocki [1996] COD 304	8.8
R v Home Secretary ex p Zighem [1996] Imm AR 194	4.19
R v Immigration Officer ex p Quaquah [2000] INLR 196	4.50
R v Lambeth LBC ex p Caddell [1998] 1 FLR 253	1.88
R v Ministry of Defence ex p Smith [1996] 1 All ER 257, CA	4.2, 4.7, 4.8
R v North and East Devon Health Authority ex p Coughlan (1999) 2 CCLR 284	4.58
R v Wandsworth LBC ex p O [2000] 4 All ER 590; (2000) 3 CCLR 237, CA	3.26
Raninen v Finland (1998) 26 EHRR 563	4.57
SSC v Sweden App 46553/99 (2000) 29 EHRR CD245	4.33, 6.63
Saadi v Home Secretary [2001] EWCA Civ 1512; [2001] 4 All ER 461	4.42
Selmouni v France (2000) 7 BHRC 1	4.33
Sorabjee App 239938/93 (1995) unreported	4.55
T, Re [1994] ImmAR 368	1.27, 8.35
Tan Te Lam v Superintendent of Tai A Chau Detention Centre [1997] AC 97	4.46
Thlimmenos v Greece (2001) 31 EHRR 15	4.61
Thomas, Re (2000) 1 September, NI HC	4.25

W and B (children: care plan), Re [2001] 2 FLR 582   1.99

X v Secretary of State for the Home Department [2001]
    INLR 205   6.74
X and Y v Netherlands (1986) 8 EHRR 235   4.57

Table of statutes

Adoption Act 1976		Children Act 1989 *continued*	
s1	2.1	s5(6)	1.55
s6	1.21, 2.4	s7(1)(b)	1.32
Adoption (Intercountry Aspects) Act		s8	1.22, 1.46, 1.48,
1999	2.2, 2.8, 2.14,		1.49, 1.64, 8.23
	2.15	s10	1.48
Anti-Terrorism, Crime and Security		s10(b)	1.65
Act 2001		s12	1.57
s23	4.47	s13	1.67, 8.24
British Nationality Act 1981		s13(1)(b)	1.67
	6.136, 6.146	s17	1.75, 3.27–3.31
s1(1)	6.136	s17(1)(a)	1.78
s1(3)	5.33, 6.137,	s17(1)(b)	3.28
	6.145	s17(5)	3.27
s1(4)	2.9, 6.112,	s17(6)	1.79
	6.114, 6.124,	s17(10)	1.76, 1.79
	6.137, 7.4	s19	1.100
s1(5)	2.1	s20	1.80, 1.81,
s3(1)	6.138, 6.142,		1.83, 1.84,
	6.146		3.19, 3.31
s47	6.146	s20(5)	1.6
s50(9)	6.146	s22	1.81
Children Act 1989	1.2, 1.6, 1.18,	s22(1)	1.81
1.24, 1.27, 1.41, 1.43, 1.77, 1.81,		s24	1.82, 1.84
1.82, 1.94, 1.105, 1.106, 3.34, 8.7,		s24B	3.20
8.19, 8.34, 8.36		s25	1.74
Pt IV	1.28	s26	1.105
s1	1.20, 1.67, 6.25	s31	1.45, 1.73, 1.80,
s1(1)	1.90		1.89, 6.21
s1(2)	1.20, 1.24	s31(3)	1.6
s1(3)	1.22, 1.90	s34	1.96
s2	1.54	s37	1.92
s2(9)	1.60	s55	1.61
s3	1.54	s70(1)(a)	2.14
s3(1)	1.54	s100	1.62
s4	1.22, 1.54, 1.57	Sch 2	1.100
s5	1.26	Sch 2, para 19A	3.19

xv

Putting children first / Table of statutes

Act	References
Children (Leaving Care) Act 2000	1.82, 1.84, 1.86, 1.87, 3.19, 6.128, 8.36
County Courts Act 1984	
s38	1.18
Criminal Justice and Courts Service Act 2000	
s11	1.30
Domicile and Matrimonial Proceedings Act 1973	1.13
Education Act 1996	
s10	3.32
s512(3)	3.32
Education (Fees and Awards) Act 1983	
s1	3.33
Family Law Act 1986	1.13
ss1, 3	1.27
Family Law Act 1996	
Pt IV	1.14, 1.18
s11	1.35
ss33–38	1.14
s42	1.14
s47	1.17
Human Rights Act 1998	4.5, 4.9, 4.11, 4.21, 4.22, 5.40, 6.63, 6.75
s2	4.20
Immigration Act 1971	6.74, 6.116, 6.121
s3(5)(a)	6.92, 6.96
s3(5)(aa)	6.95
s3(5)(b)	6.92, 6.95, 6.116, 6.120
s3(5)(c)	6.94, 6.119, 6.121
s3(6)	6.92, 6.95
s5	6.91
s5(3)	6.116, 6.121
s5(4)	6.116
s19	6.10
s30	6.72
Immigration and Asylum Act 1999	3.5, 3.26, 3.34, 5.26, 5.51, 6.11, 6.121, 6.122
Immigration and Asylum Act 1999 *continued*	
Pt VI	3.22, 3.30
s10	6.92
s10(1)(c)	6.122
s10(3)	6.122
s10(5)	6.116
s24	1.9
s65	4.11, 4.12, 4.15, 4.21, 5.26, 5.42, 5.49, 8.40
s73	4.12, 4.15
s74	4.12, 4.13, 6.131
s75	4.12, 4.15, 6.133
s76(3)	4.15
s77	4.24
s94(1)	6.65
s96(2)	3.8
s115(9)	3.23
s116	3.26
s118	3.40
ss160–163	1.9
Sch 14	1.9
Sch 14, para 44(2)	6.92
Sch 14, para 46	6.116, 6.119
Sch 14, para 117	3.32
Local Government Act 2000	
s2	3.30
Marriage Act 1949	1.9
Marriage Act 1970	1.9
Marriage Act 1983	1.9
Marriage Act 1994	1.9
Mental Health Act 1983	3.36
s86	6.72, 6.74
Mental Health (Scotland) Act 1960	
s82	6.72
National Assistance Act 1948	3.31, 3.34
s21	3.4, 3.26
National Health Service Act 1977	3.38
s21	3.37
Powers of the Criminal Courts Act 1973	3.36
Protection from Harassment Act 1997	1.18

Table of statutes xvii

Race Relations (Amendment) Act 2000   6.128
Recognition of Divorce and Legal Separations Act 1971   1.13

Rehabilitation of Offenders Act 1974   6.87
Supreme Court Act 1981
   s37   1.18

Table of statutory instruments

Adoption (Designation of Overseas Adoptions) Order 1973
    SI No 19   2.8
Adoption of Children from Abroad Order 2000 S1 No 1251   2.2
Adoption of Children from Overseas Regulations 2001
    SI No 1251   2.12
Allocation of Housing (England) Regulations 2000
    SI No 702
    reg 4   3.40
Asylum Support Regulations 2000 SI No 704   3.8
Asylum Support (Amendment) Regulations 2000
    SI No 3053   3.8
Civil Procedure Rules
    Pt 35   7.24
Education (Fees and Awards) Regulations 1997 SI No 1972   3.33, 3.34
Education (Mandatory Awards) Regulations 1997 SI No 431
    reg 13   3.33
Homelessness (England) Regulations 2000 SI No 701
    reg 3(f)   3.40
Immigration and Asylum Act 1999 (Commencement
    No 6 and Transitional Provisions) Order 2000
    SI No 2444   4.21
Immigration Asylum Appeals (Procedure) (Amendment)
    Rules 2001 SI No 4014   3.18
Immigration (European Economic Area) Regulations 2000
    SI No 2326
    reg 6(4)   1.7
Immigration Rules (HC 395 as amended)   1.3, 2.3, 2.9, 5.7,
    5.29, 5.36, 5.44, 5.45, 5.50, 6.1, 6.2, 6.10, 6.59, 6.60, 6.86, 6.93, 6.98,
    6.100, 6.110, 6.115, 7.2, 8.22, 8.30
    para 101(ii)   1.7
    paras 246–248   1.26
    para 246   5.50, 8.22
    para 255   6.60
    paras 277–289   6.100
    paras 295A–295M   5.45
    para 297   1.3
    para 297(e), (f)   6.14

Immigration Rules (HC 395) *continued*

para 298(ii)(b)	1.7
para 302	6.23
para 310	2.9
para 311	2.9, 2.10
para 316A	2.11
para 316B	2.11
para 317	6.38
paras 327–352F	5.1
paras 349–352	5.9
para 349	5.23
paras 350–352	5.9
paras 352A–352F	5.1
para 352A(ii)	5.2
para 349	1.6, 5.1, 5.9
para 364	6.97, 6.117
paras 365–368	6.94
paras 366–367	6.117
para 366	6.117
para 367	6.118
para 368	6.123
para 395A	6.92
para 395B	6.93
r246	1.69
r257	1.7
rr295A–295I	5.29
r349	5.29, 5.31
Marriage Regulations 1986	1.9
National Health Service (Charges to Overseas Visitors) Regulations 1989 SI No 306	3.36, 3.37
reg 4	3.37
National Health Service (Charges to Overseas Visitors) (Amendment) Regulations SI 1991 No 438	3.36
National Health Service (Charges to Overseas Visitors) (Amendment) Regulations SI 1994 No 1535	3.36
Social Security (Immigration and Asylum) Consequential Amendments Regulations 2000 SI No 636	
reg 2(4)(a)	3.25
reg 2(4)(b)	3.25
Sch, Pt 1, para 1(b)	3.24
Sch, Pt 1, para 2	3.24
Sch, Pt 1, para 3	3.2, 3.24
Sch, Pt 1, para 4	3.24

Table of European legislation

Treaties and Conventions

Council of Europe Social Charter	3.24, 3.40
European Convention on Establishment 1969	
art 3(3)	6.76
European Convention on Social and Medical Assistance	3.24, 3.40
European Convention on the Protection of Human Rights and Fundamental Freedoms	1.4, 3.7, 4.1, 4.2, 4.4–4.9, 4.11–4.16, 4.18, 4.19, 4.21–4.23, 4.33, 4.60, 5.26, 5.38, 6.65, 6.89, 6.97, 6.98, 8.28, 8.29, 8.39
art 2	4.25, 4.28
art 3	4.8, 4.17, 4.24, 4.28, 4.29, 4.31, 4.33, 4.57, 5.49, 6.55, 6.65, 6.134
art 4	4.17, 4.34
art 5	4.42, 4.46, 4.47
art 5(1)	4.42
art 6	4.48–4.50
art 7	4.17
art 8	4.18, 4.49, 4.51–4.58, 5.6, 5.9, 5.17, 5.24, 5.26, 5.38, 5.40, 5.43, 5.49, 6.11, 6.89, 6.98, 6.108, 6.134
art 8(2)	1.67
art 14	4.17, 4.59, 4.62
art 15	4.17
European Convention on the Protection of Human Rights and Fundamental Freedoms Protocol 1	
art 2	4.46, 4.63
art 77	4.35
European Convention on the Protection of Human Rights and Fundamental Freedoms Protocol 6	4.25
European Convention on the Protection of Human Rights and Fundamental Freedoms Protocol 11	
art 4	4.35

EC Treaty	
art 250(2)	1.8
Geneva Convention 1949	4.35
Hague Convention on the Protection of Chil;dren and Co-operation in Respect of Intercountry Adoptions 1993	2.3
International Convention on Civil and Political Rights	4.1
Treaty of Rome	5.50, 6.58, 6.59, 6.99
UN Convention on the Rights of the Child	1.35, 4.1, 4.41, 5.11
art 32	4.37, 4.41
art 34	4.37, 4.41
art 35	4.37, 4.41
art 38	4.35
UN Convention Relating to the Status of Refugees 1951	4.12, 5.2, 5.32, 5.47, 8.29
Universal Declaration of Human Rights 1948	4.1, 4.4

Directives

64/221	
art 4	6.71
68/360	
art 1	6.56
73/1148	
art 1(1)	6.56

Regulations

1612/68/EEC	
art 7(2)	6.55
art 10	1.7
art 10(1)	6.56
art 11	1.7
1408/71/EEC	3.39

Abbreviations

API	Asylum Policy Instructions
BMA	British Medical Association
BNA 1981	British Nationality Act 1981
CA 1989	Children Act 1989
CAFCASS	Children and Family Court Advisory and Support Service
CLCA 2000	Children (Leaving Care) Act 2000
EC	European Commission
ECHR	European Convention on Human Rights
ECO	entry clearance officer
ECtHR	European Court of Human Rights
EU	European Union
FLA 1996	Family Law Act 1996
GP	general practitioner
HRA 1998	Human Rights Act 1998
IA 1971	Immigration Act 1971
IAA 1999	Immigration and Asylum Act 1999
IAT	Immigration Appeal Tribunal
ICCPR	International Convention on Civil and Political Rights
IDI	Immigration Directorate's Instructions
ILPA	Immigration Law Practitioners Association
IND	Immigration and Nationality Department
IR	Immigration Rules (HC 395 as amended)
LSC	Legal Services Commission
MHRT	Mental Health Review Tribunal
NAA 1948	National Assistance Act 1948
NASS	National Asylum Support Service
NI	Nationality Instructions
NSPCC	National Society for the Prevention of Cruelty to Children
SBSH	*Secure Borders, Safe Haven*
SSIA Regs 2000	Social Security (Immigration and Asylum) Consequential Amendments Regulations 2000 SI No 636
UDHR	Universal Declaration of Human Rights 1948
UN	United Nations
UNCRC	United Nations Convention on the Rights of the Child
UNHCR	United Nations High Commission for Refugees

CHAPTER 1

Family law: concepts and principles

1.1	Introduction
1.2	Family law definitions and concepts
1.9	Marriage
1.12	Divorce: void/voidable marriages
1.14	Domestic violence
1.20	Welfare principle
1.24	Delay
1.26	Presumption of no order
1.27	Who can make an application?
1.30	Representation of children's views in court
1.37	Importance of birth family
1.38	Confidentiality and disclosure
1.42	Community Legal Service Funding (Legal Aid)
1.43	Medical and psychiatric experts
1.45	Distinction between private law and public law
1.53	**Orders that can be made**
1.54	Parental responsibility
1.61	Guardianship
1.62	Wardship
1.64	Custodianship
1.65	Section 8 orders
	Residence order • Contact order • Prohibited steps order • Specific issue order

continued

1.72	Emergency protection order
1.73	Supervision orders under CA 1989 s31
1.74	Secure accommodation orders under CA 1989 s25
1.75	**Local authority responsibility for children**
1.80	Children looked after by a local authority
1.83	Accommodation under CA 1989 s20
1.89	Care orders under CA 1989 s31
1.96	Contact with children in care under CA 1989 s34
1.98	Care plans
1.100	Removal of child to live abroad when looked after by a local authority
1.105	**Complaints procedure under CA 1989 s26**
1.106	**Effect of court orders made in the UK**

Introduction

1.1 This chapter outlines and defines basic family law concepts and principles to give immigration practitioners an overview of the issues relating to family law that may affect their clients.

Family law definitions and concepts

1.2 The Children Act (CA) 1989 sets out the law relating to children and the relationship between children and their parents, whether married or unmarried. The general principles apply whether the parents are married or unmarried, although there are some significant differences in application where the parents are not married. There is no definition of 'family' in the Act.

1.3 Immigration law does not define 'family' for the purposes of entry and stay in the United Kingdom. 'Family' is determined by dependency: this requires a responsibility on the part of the adult for the child and is set out in the relevant Immigration Rule.[1]

1.4 The position is rather more complex in European Convention on Human Rights (ECHR) jurisprudence. A number of cases[2] indicate that the expression 'family life' extends to relationships that exist in social terms rather than only those relationships that are recognised by the relevant countries' domestic law. ECHR jurisprudence still refers to the relationship that exists between a homosexual couple as private rather than family life.[3] However, any children of either partner would have a right to enjoy family life with their biological parent and, arguably, the parent's partner, as the relationship would be akin to that with an unmarried step-parent. In a recent article, Linda Hantrais[4] describes the breadth of meanings accorded to 'family' in European law.[5] She

---

1 See, eg, Immigration Rules (IR) (HC 395 as amended) para 297.
2 Eg, *Marcks v Belgium* (1979) 2 EHRR 330; *Keegan v Ireland (A/290)* (1994) 18 EHRR 342; *Kroon v Netherlands* 19 EHRR 263.
3 See chapter 4, note 64 and para 4.57.
4 'What is a family or family life in the European Union' in *The legal framework and social consequences of free movement of persons in the United Kingdom* (Kluwer Law International, 1999).
5 'The UN definition presents the family as a subcategory of a household. Accordingly, a family is said to be composed of couples who are or are not related as man and wife, or of singles and their biological or adoptive children, generally for so long as these children remain unmarried.' 'Lone parenthood is often a transitional phase into a new relationship, generally involving a reconstituted family.' (Ibid).

gives examples of the differing ways in which such families are treated by different European states. For example, 'The concept of 'living under the same roof ... would not ... be recognised in some countries (Belgium and Germany) as a sufficient reason to justify the legal responsibility of a step-parent towards the children of a new partner, unless they are married, whereas in the Netherlands the social responsibility of the step-parent takes precedence over that of the biological parent.'

1.5 The different nature of family relationships was recognised by the UK in the formulation of the family reunion policy for Somali refugees, when it was stated that, 'given the nature of the Somali family we are prepared to be flexible and if a refugee is able to show that a person not covered by that policy was a dependant member of the refugee's immediate family unit ... prepared to consider exceptionally extending the refugee family reunion provision to cover that person'.[6]

1.6 For the purposes of the CA 1989, a child is an individual under the age of 18. Orders made in the family courts remain valid until the individual reaches the age of 18. The family court will not generally make an order if the child is approaching 18, but there is no prohibition to an order being made save that a care order cannot be made if a child is 17, or is 16 and over and also married.[7] Nor can a court make a secure accommodation order in relation to a child who is over 16 and had previously been accommodated under CA 1989 s20(5) and nor can such a child be placed in secure accommodation.[8] There is no definition of 'child' for the purposes of immigration legislation save that for asylum purposes a child is defined as a person who is or appears to be under 18.[9] Children can remain dependent as family members even where they are over the age of 18, and thus eligible, provided they comply with the requirements of the relevant immigration rules.

1.7 The age at which a child is deemed no longer to be dependent, depends on the particular nationality or category of leave being sought. For example:

- For European nationals exercising free movement the upper age of children entitled to seek entry as dependants is 21.[10]

---

6 *Butterworths Immigration Law Service* 2B [4]; [1993] Imm AR 40.
7 CA 1989 s31(3).
8 *Re G (Secure Accommodation)* [2000] 2 FLR 259.
9 HC 395 as amended para 349.
10 EEC Regulation 1612/68, arts 10 and 11; IR r257; Immigration (European Economic Area) Regulations 2000 SI No 2326 para 6(4).

Family law: concepts and principles 5

- Merely because an applicant for leave to enter has a child does not mean that the child will also be granted leave to enter. A working holiday-maker may only bring a dependent child into the UK with him/her if that child is under the age of five and will remain under five during the course of the working holiday.[11]
- A child who attains 18 while his or her parent seeks to remain in the UK, will continue to be eligible to remain provided he or she remains dependent and has not established an independent life.[12]

1.8 There is presently a European Commission proposal for an EC Directive on the rights of citizens of the Union and their families to move and reside freely within the territory of the member states.[13] The proposal consolidates and extends the free movement rights of EU citizens and their family members, defining 'family member' as encompassing all ascending and descending relatives within its scope (provided there remains some element of dependency), although it does not include unmarried partners. It is unlikely that the UK will opt in to this proposal, but it is an example of good practice.[14]

Marriage

1.9 A marriage[15] that takes place in the UK[16] is valid in English law provided it has been carried out in accordance with the requirements of the Marriage Act 1949 as amended by the Marriage Acts of 1970, 1983 and 1994, the Marriage Regulations of 1986 and some other related Acts. If a marriage takes place in accordance with the various Marriage Act requirements a marriage certificate will be issued. A certified copy of a marriage certificate can be obtained either from the local registrar's office where the marriage was celebrated[17] or from

11 HC 395 as amended para 101(ii).
12 HC 395 as amended para 298(ii)(b).
13 Amended proposal for a Council Directive on the right to family reunification (presented by the Commission pursuant to art 250(2) of the EC Treaty). The ILPA response (October 1999) can be found on their website: www.ilpa.org.uk.
14 Council Directives are proposed either by the Commission or particular countries. The UK has reserved the power to opt in or out. For more information, see *Macdonald's Immigration Law and Practice* (5th edn, Butterworths, 2001) Ch 7.
15 Marriage may give rise to an asylum claim, eg, forced marriage. See Heaven Crawley, *Refugees and Gender: Law and Process* (Jordans, 2001).
16 Immigration and Asylum Act 1999 ss24, 160–163 and Sch 14; see also Appendix L.
17 Address available from the relevant local authority.

the Superintendent Registrar.[18] To be valid the marriage must be, amongst other things, monogamous and not between prohibited relatives, for example, stepmother and son. A marriage undergone according to religious or other custom or tradition is not valid in English law as a marriage, unless the parties have also undergone a ceremony valid in accordance with the legislation.

1.10 A marriage that took place overseas is recognised according to English law if it is the type of marriage that is recognised in the country in which it took place, was properly executed in accordance with the legal requirements of that country, and there was nothing in law that prevented the lawful marriage taking place, for example, the marriage was not prevented from being lawful because of the domicile of one of the parties to the marriage. This includes polygamous marriages.

1.11 Religious ceremonies or customary marriages that take place in the UK are not lawful marriages according to English law unless they have complied with the requirements of UK legislation. However this is not as straightforward as it seems. In some circumstances, if the couple underwent a ceremony intending it to be a lawfully binding marriage and were unaware that it was not legally binding this may be considered to be legally binding and the couple may require a divorce before they can remarry.[19] Couples may have problems undergoing a civil ceremony if, after a religious ceremony, the registrar considers that they genuinely, albeit erroneously, believe they were married and that the marriage was valid under English law.[20]

Divorce: void/voidable marriages

1.12 To divorce[21] in the UK, a decree absolute has to be obtained from a civil court. No other divorce, undergone in the UK, is valid in the UK.

1.13 A divorce obtained abroad is valid if recognised in the UK in accordance with the Family Law Proceedings Act 1986. If the divorce is not recognised under this legislation, it is still valid if it is recognised under the provisions of the Domicile and Matrimonial Proceedings Act 1973 or the Recognition of Divorce and Legal Separations Act 1971. In brief terms, a divorce will be recognised in the UK on two bases:

18 See Appendix M for contact addresses and Appendix L for marriage registrar instructions.
19 *Chief Adjudication Officer v Bath* [2000] 1 FLR 8.
20 See also Gerald Wilson, 'The status of religious weddings in English law' [2000] Fam Law 437.
21 Divorce may give rise to an asylum claim. See Heaven Crawley, see note 15.

- If it was obtained by way of proceedings, it has to be valid in the country in which it was obtained and either party must have been habitually resident or domiciled or a national of that country.
- If it was obtained without proceedings (for example, a talaq), it has to be valid in the country in which it was obtained, and at the date of the divorce both parties must have been domiciled in the country from which it was obtained or one was and the other was in a country that recognised the divorce and neither party had been habitually resident in the UK for the preceding year.

There are however complex rules and if there is any doubt as to the validity of a divorce, detailed research should be undertaken and, possibly, an expert's report obtained.

Domestic violence[22]

1.14 The law of domestic violence is dealt with in Part IV of the Family Law Act (FLA) 1996. There are two main orders that can be applied for: a non-molestation order[23] and an occupation order.[24] A non-molestation order is to prevent violence, threats of violence or other anti-social behaviour. It can be directed at specific or general behaviour, and be made for a specified period of time or until further order. Virtually any unpleasant behaviour can amount to molestation but each situation turns on its own facts – what may be molestation for one couple is not molestation for another. The court can make a 'without notice' order if the circumstances render it 'just and convenient to do so'.

1.15 An occupation order used to be called an 'ouster' or 'exclusion order' and deals with entitlement to remain in occupation of the whole or part of the dwelling and can require a respondent to leave the whole or part of a dwelling:

> If a couple is or has been married or the applicant has an interest in the dwelling house (legal or beneficial) then in certain circumstances the court has a duty (albeit rebuttable) to make an occupation order in the applicant's favour ... if the applicant is or has been a cohabitant who does not have a legal or beneficial interest in the dwelling house then the court will only have a discretion to make an occupation order.[25]

22 See also para 6.56 and Heaven Crawley, see note 15.
23 FLA 1996 s42.
24 Ibid ss33–38.
25 *Cohabitation Law and Precedents*, Craig and Pearson, eds (Sweet and Maxwell, 2001) para 3-005.

1.16　Orders can be applied for within other family proceedings or as freestanding applications. In determining what order to make the court also has to take into account that a cohabiting couple has not given the same commitment to each other as if they were married.

1.17　There is a presumption that a power of arrest[26] will be added to orders where there has been violence or a threat of violence save in without notice cases where there must also be a risk of significant harm.

1.18　There are some people who will fall outside FLA 1996 Pt IV, for example, those who have never cohabited. Injunctions may be obtained in these cases using the court's inherent jurisdiction, under:
- Supreme Court Act 1981 s37 and County Courts Act 1984 s38 when associated with an action in tort, for example, assault (includes threatening behaviour);
- CA 1989 (prohibited steps order – see paragraph 1.70); or
- Protection from Harassment Act 1997.

1.19　Criminal proceedings may also be brought. While these are pending, bail conditions may be imposed. The Home Office operates a concession in marriage cases where there has been domestic violence.[27]

Welfare principle[28]

1.20　Children Act 1989 s1(1) determines that the welfare of the child is the family court's 'paramount consideration' in determining any matter with 'respect to the upbringing of the child'. Any dispute about residence or contact is to be considered and decided by the court on the basis of the child's best interests even where that conflicts with the wishes or desires of the adults concerned. This test does not apply where the child's upbringing is not concerned. So where the issue is concerned with, for example, financial provision, the welfare of the child is not the paramount consideration.

1.21　In adoption law, the questions which the family court should now ask are:
- Will the adoption bring about a genuine transfer of parental responsibility?
- Will the adoption, taking into account all the child's personal circumstances, confer real benefits on the child throughout his/her childhood?

26　FLA 1996 s47.
27　See para 6.56.
28　CA 1989 s1.

Welfare is a first consideration rather than a paramount consideration.[29]

1.22 There is no definition of 'welfare' in the Act, but CA 1989 s1(3) sets out a checklist of factors that are to be taken into account when considering whether an outcome is in a child's best interests:

- the ascertainable wishes and feelings of the child concerned (considered in the light of his/her age and understanding);
- his/her physical, emotional and educational needs;
- the likely effect on him/her of any change in his/her circumstances;
- his/her age, sex, background and any characteristics which the court considers relevant;
- any harm which he or she has suffered or is at risk of suffering;
- how capable each of his/her parents (or any other person in relation to whom the court considers the question to be relevant) is of meeting his/her needs;
- the range of powers open to the court in the proceedings in question.

This checklist is to be applied when the court determines applications under CA 1989 s8, care and supervision.[30]

1.23 Where a court is considering whether to make one or more orders with respect to the child, it shall not make any order(s) unless it considers that doing so would be better for the child than making no order at all. [31]

Delay

1.24 It is a general principle of the CA 1989 that any delay in reaching a decision in relation to a child is likely to be detrimental to that child's welfare.[32] Therefore, the courts are very resistant to applications for adjournments and practitioners should be aware of the need to ensure that directions are complied with and witnesses and statements are available.

1.25 Reports from Children and Family Court Advisory and Support Service (CAFCASS)[33] and the relevant local authority are often required. Other expert reports are more likely to be relevant in public

---

29 Adoption Act 1976 s6.
30 CA 1989 s4.
31 See para 1.26.
32 CA 1989 s1(2).
33 See para 1.30.

law cases.[34] In most cases, the matter is unlikely to be resolved in less than about six months and others, in particular care cases, may take very much longer. This is particularly so when the final hearing is likely to take a number of days or weeks, as the courts have long waiting lists for trials of such length. However, the length of delay will vary considerably from court to court and depending where in England and Wales the application is made. Local family practitioners should be able to advise immigration practitioners of the length of likely delay.

Presumption of no order

1.26 No order should be made unless it provides a positive benefit to the child.[35] The lack of need for an order in family law terms does not preclude the court making an order for other reasons. For example, if parents consent to arrangements for contact, an order would not usually be made, but if an order is required to facilitate entry of a parent to exercise contact, the court will facilitate this.[36]

Who can make an application?

1.27 Applications can be made in relation to any child who is either habitually resident or merely present on a temporary basis in the jurisdiction.[37] Any adult present in the UK, even if he or she is on temporary admission, is in detention or has been served with a notice of illegal entry, can apply for an order relating to a child.[38] In this case the applicant for a residence order in relation to his younger siblings was a failed asylum-seeker and the Court of Appeal held that it could hear an application under the CA 1989 or in wardship from a person liable to be removed or deported.

1.28 Applications under CA 1989 Pt IV (care and supervision orders) can also be made in similar situations.[39] Even so, the family court will be anxious to avoid making orders which may only be effective for a matter of months or weeks, fearing that this disruption will not be in

---

34 For definition of 'public law cases' see para 1.45.
35 CA 1989 s5.
36 HC 395 as amended paras 246–248.
37 FLA 1986 ss1 and 3.
38 *Re T* [1994] Imm AR 368.
39 *Re R (Care Proceedings: Jurisdiction)* [1995] 3 FCR 305.

the child's best interests. However, the court does accept that there are cases where it is in the best interests of a child to make a short-term order, so that parental responsibility could be identified, even though such an order would not prevent the child's removal from the UK.[40]

1.29 In private law cases, a child may also apply for an order. However, leave from the High Court is required and will only be given if he or she is deemed to have sufficient understanding to participate as a party in the proceedings.[41]

Representation of children's views in court

1.30 On 1 April 2001, the Children and Family Court Advisory and Support Service (CAFCASS), created under Criminal Justice and Courts Service Act 2000 s11, came into being. This reorganised the way in which children and their views are presented to the family courts.[42] Representation of children and adults under a disability is now divided between the Official Solicitor and CAFCASS. CAFCASS will not act for adults under a disability. CAFCASS officers now represent children in most public law cases, and CAFCASS Legal[43] represents children in the cases that were previously handled by the Official Solicitor (mainly private law, ie, wardship, adoption and private law Children Act cases). The Official Solicitor continues to act for parents and other adults who are under a disability where no other willing and suitable next friend or guardian ad litem is available. The Official Solicitor remains the first port of call to act for children who are not the subject of proceedings, for example, if advice is needed on taking instructions where there are mental health problems.

1.31 A 'children's guardian' (formerly 'guardian ad litem') is appointed by the court to safeguard the interests of the child in public law proceedings. His or her role is to ensure that the interests of the child are

---

40 *Re E* [1995] Imm AR 475.
41 'It will be a question of fact whether a child seeking advice has sufficient understanding of what is involved to give a consent valid in law.' Lord Scarman in *Gillick v West Norfolk and Wisbech Area Health Authority and the DHSS* [1986] 1 AC 112 – 'Gillick competence'.
42 CAFCASS and the Official Solicitor have both issued practice notes dated March 2001 and April 2001 respectively – see Appendix J. More information is available from the CAFCASS website: www.cafcass.gov.uk and from the Official Solicitor's website: www.offsol.demon.co.uk.
43 Officers of CAFCASS Legal Services and Special Casework.

protected where the local authority and the parents may have interests which are distinct from those of the child. He or she does not actually act for the child but will usually appoint a solicitor to act for him/her in proceedings before the court. There may, on occasion, be conflict between the children's guardian's view about the interests of the child and the child's instructions, if he or she were of an appropriate age or competence.[44] In such a case the child would usually seek to instruct his/her own solicitors. A children's guardian has access to local authority records or records held by any other person to produce his/her report for the court.

1.32 A 'welfare officer' (formerly a 'court welfare officer') prepares a report[45] at the request of the court, to assist the court in taking a decision in private law proceedings. Occasionally, the court may invite the local authority to prepare a report, particularly where the local authority has been involved previously.[46]

1.33 In the family court, it has been established that children can be and are separately represented in public law proceedings but there has been no acknowledgement that children in private law proceedings should be separately represented.

1.34 This view was challenged in a case where the National Youth Advisory Service successfully sought leave to intervene and act as guardian ad litem in a contact dispute. Following a successful appeal, the President of the Family Division said:

> ... in the light of the particular problems facing both parents of the allegations of sexual abuse and the potential conflict of interests between each parent and the child, it was appropriate to add the child as a party and to appoint a guardian ad litem for her. The National Youth Advisory Service was a well-known and respected service. In principle, there was no objection to such a service representing a child when separate representation was justified.[47]

1.35 Although FLA 1996 s11 enables the Lord Chancellor to draw up court rules, so that children's views can be represented in family courts in accordance with the UN Convention on the Rights of the Child, such rules have not yet been compiled. The drawing-up of court rules has been postponed by the Lord Chancellor, but the principles are still

---

44 Gillick competence – see note 41 above.
45 CA 1989 s7(1)(b).
46 'Family Court Practice' [2001] Fam Law 497.
47 *A v A (contact: representation of child's interests)* [2001] 1 FLR 715.

of relevance to the manner in which family court proceedings are pursued.

1.36   A report by Ann O'Quigley[48] summarises the findings of researchers on how children's views are currently ascertained in private law proceedings.[49]

Importance of birth family

1.37   It is recognised that it will be in the interests of a child to be brought up by its birth parents.[50]

Confidentiality and disclosure

1.38   Family courts are not open to the public and only the parties, legal representatives, experts and (when required) witnesses are entitled to be in the courtroom. All papers connected with the proceedings are confidential. In private law cases, they can only be shown to the parties, their legal representatives, CAFCASS, or the Legal Services Commission. In public law cases, they can also be disclosed to the local authority.

1.39   If anyone wishes to disclose any evidence to anyone who is not involved in the family proceedings, he or she must seek the leave of the court. It may well be that the evidence before the court in the family case will be of great importance in relation to applications being made for leave to remain in the UK and an application for disclosure should be made to the family court in those cases.

1.40   If it is likely that documents will need to be relied upon in the immigration case, an early application should be made for disclosure.

1.41   It must be remembered that documents and statements, whether favourable or not, obtained in the course of CA 1989 proceedings have to be disclosed to all the parties involved.[51] Thus, for example, medical or other expert reports will be disclosed, even if not supportive in terms of the arguments being put forward in the immigration case.

---

48 *Listening to children's views: The Findings and recommendations of recent research* (York Publishing Services, Joseph Rowntree Foundation, March 2000).
49 See June [2000] Fam Law which does a summary.
50 *Re KD (a minor) (access: principles)* [1988] 2 FLR 139.
51 *Re F (childcare: disclosure of documents)* [1995] 1 FCR 589.

Community Legal Service Funding (Legal Aid)

1.42 Legal aid is automatically available in care or supervision order proceedings, to parents or those with parental responsibility. They do not have to satisfy the merits or means tests. Others who become parties, for example, grandparents, to such proceedings will also be deemed to have met the merits test. In private law cases, the grant of legal aid will be subject to the usual merits and financial eligibility tests.

Medical and psychiatric experts

1.43 If reports are required in the course of public law proceedings under the CA 1989, the named expert is agreed between the parties. The instructions sent requesting the report are agreed between the parties and the report, once obtained, is disclosed to all parties.

1.44 In private law cases, consideration should be given to the appointment of a single joint expert if it is considered that one should be appointed at all. If agreement is not reached, the leave of the court can be sought for separate experts. Directions may be made for the issues in dispute to be identified prior to trial.

Distinction between private law and public law

1.45 There is a distinction between public and private law applications. Public law applications are made by local authorities, the police or the National Society for the Prevention of Cruelty to Children (NSPCC) when it is believed that any child under 17 (or under 16, if married) is suffering or is likely to suffer significant harm from his/her parents or carers or is beyond parental control. They include applications for care orders, supervision orders, education supervision orders and emergency protection orders.[52] Children, no matter how young, are entitled to have their own representatives.[53] The application can result in orders:

- directing removal of a child from the family home;
- for supervision of the care provided at home;
- for detention of the child in secure accommodation;
- for control of contact between a child in the state's care and a parent.

---

52 CA 1989 s31.
53 See para 1.30.

1.46 Private law applications are made by individuals, including children of sufficient capacity to conduct their own cases, for orders contained in CA 1989 s8 in relation to a child under 16, (or themselves, if the child is the applicant). Section 8 orders are:
- residence;
- contact;
- prohibited steps;
- specific issue orders.

1.47 It has not been the practice in such applications between parents, for children to have their own representation, though there have been occasions when a child has been separately represented and this may become more frequent. It is unlikely that the current dichotomy between public and private law will be sustainable.[54]

1.48 The parents or guardians, an adult with a residence order or parental responsibility, a step-parent or a person with whom the child has lived for three years or any other adult who has the consent of an adult with a residence order or parental responsibility in relation to a child or a local authority with care of a child can apply as of right (ie, without the leave of the court) for any CA 1989 s8 order. Other individuals, including grandparents and other siblings, or the child him/herself, who do not fall within the above categories, have to apply to the court for leave to make an application. When deciding whether to grant leave, the court will take into account their connection with the child, any risk that the child's life may be disrupted by such an application, the nature of the application and any future plans a local authority may have for the child.[55]

1.49 Applications can be made in any family-related proceedings, not just proceedings specifically issued for a CA 1989 s8 order.

1.50 It is important to note that, in general, a court will be unwilling to make such orders if there is no practical need for them. For example, if it has already been agreed between the parties that there should be contact at specified times and specified places.[56]

1.51 The courts may also make residence orders even where the parties have consented, in order to give the child an added sense of security and permanence.

1.52 The consequence of an order is that leave of the court is required

---

54 Judith Timms OBE, 'Best Interests and Best Practice: improving outcomes for children', *Seen and Heard*, Vol 11, issue 2, p23.
55 CA 1989 s10.
56 See para 1.26.

Orders that can be made

1.53 The court determines what order to make by an analysis of what is in the best interests of the child, taking all the circumstances into account. The order is not determined by what the adult wants, although that will be a matter that is taken into account. In determining whether a child should visit or stay with a particular adult, it will be the court's view as to what is best for the child that prevails. This analysis can be utilised in immigration cases. The potential conflict between the need to maintain immigration control and the interests of the child and the consequences to public policy can be exploited in submissions to the Home Office.

Parental responsibility[57]

1.54 Parental responsibility amounts to all the rights, powers, duties, responsibilities and authority, which, by law, a parent of a child has in relation to the child and his/her property.[58] There is no exhaustive definition. It includes claims to contact, the duty to provide a home and financial support, discipline and the right to take decisions in connection with education and medical treatment. All mothers and married fathers have parental responsibility automatically.

1.55 A testamentary guardian has parental responsibility for a child upon the death of a parent.[59]

1.56 An unmarried father can obtain parental responsibility either by:
- registering the written agreement of the mother with the Principal Registry, or
- obtaining an order from a family court.

In the latter case, the court will take into account the degree of commitment the father has shown towards his child, the degree of attachment between him and the child and the reasons why he is applying for the order and all other relevant considerations, bearing in mind that the child's interests will be paramount.[60]

---

57 CA 1989 ss2, 3, 4.
58 CA 1989 s3(1).
59 CA 1989 s5(6).
60 *Re H (Parental Responsibility)* [1998] 1 FLR 855.

1.57 A person who obtains a residence order also obtains parental responsibility for the child for the duration of the residence order. However, if the person is the child's unmarried father, the court must also make a parental responsibility order under CA 1989 s4.[61]

1.58 Where a child has been born as a result of a surrogacy arrangement, in the UK (unlike other jurisdictions) the woman who gives birth is the mother and has parental responsibility whether or not it was her egg. Her husband is the father and has parental responsibility. Anyone else who wishes to obtain parental responsibility has to make an application to the court.

1.59 Parental responsibility on the part of a non-biological parent or local authority can also be acquired through a care order, supervision order, adoption order and guardianship.

1.60 CA 1989 s2(9) provides for a person with parental responsibility to delegate by arranging for some or all of the responsibilities, duties, etc, to be met by one or more persons acting on his/her behalf.

Guardianship[62]

1.61 Any parent who has parental responsibility for a child, or the court, can appoint a guardian to take over parental responsibility on the death of that parent. It only becomes operative if there is no one with parental responsibility. If there is a remaining parent with parental responsibility, the appointment of the guardian will not take effect until that parent no longer has parental responsibility. Guardians are usually appointed by will.

Wardship

1.62 CA 1989 s100 sets out the circumstances where wardship proceedings can be issued, but this happens very rarely. Leave of the court is always required and leave will only be granted where the court is satisfied that, if the court's inherent jurisdiction is not exercised with respect to the child, the child will suffer significant harm. If the relevant court order can be obtained through other means, for example, where a care order can protect a child, the High Court's inherent jurisdiction is not to be exercised. The circumstances in which it is appropriate to issue would be, for example, where there is an international law element (for example, 'internet' babies) or treatment

---

61 CA 1989 s12.
62 CA 1989 s55.

issues (for example, conjoined twins). A child becomes a ward of court as soon as wardship proceedings are issued and cannot be removed from the jurisdiction without the leave of the court.

1.63 The court acquires parental responsibility. The final order in wardship proceedings will generally cover care, supervision, parental responsibility and residence.

Custodianship

1.64 'Custodianship' is referred to in DP 3/96.[63] There was a short period of time when custodianship orders could be applied for, but this form of order no longer exists.

Section 8 orders

Residence order

1.65 This defines where and with whom a child will live and gives the person in whose favour the order is made the power to make day-to-day decisions about the child. Residence orders can be made in favour of individuals who are not the child's parents, even if they are not parties to the proceedings. The court can make an order even if there has been no application.[64] Such an order will give parental responsibility to that person during the course of the order.

1.66 Orders can be made in favour of more than one person, such as a parent and partner. In immigration cases, such an order might be viewed as a measure of the strength of the relationship between an adult and a child which was not biologically his/hers. Residence orders are rarely made in favour of two individuals who do not live together, as it is thought that it is in a child's interest to be certain where his/her main home is and that the more appropriate orders are a residence order to one parent or party and a contact order, allowing extensive contact, to the other. Joint residence orders tend to be appropriate where the parents are thought to be capable of co-operating together or where the couple is unmarried.

1.67 If there is a residence order in force, no other person may cause the child to be known by a new surname. The child cannot be removed from the jurisdiction of England and Wales for one month

---

63 See Appendix D.
64 CA 1989 s10(b).

> **Example: Residence order**
>
> A five-year-old Jamaican child, Sandra, arrives in the UK, alone, to visit Grandma for one month, Grandma has been here for 25 years. Sandra's mother remains in Jamaica as do Sandra's seven and ten-year-old siblings. Sandra's father is not on the scene. Sandra is given leave to enter the UK for six months as a visitor. After she has been here for two months word is received that her mother has died in a car crash. Sandra's siblings are being looked after by their paternal grandmother in Jamaica – who is not Sandra's paternal grandmother. Grandma in the UK is quite elderly but reasonably fit. Grandma makes an application for a residence order, disclosing all the family details, which is granted. An application is submitted on Form SET(O) for Sandra to be granted indefinite leave to remain. The Home Office grants indefinite leave.

or more without either the written consent of every person who has parental responsibility or the leave of the court.[65] Where there is an application to remove the child from the jurisdiction, the rights of the child, and either of the parents could be:

> ... in conflict and had, under article 8(2) ECHR to be balanced against the rights of others. In addition and of the greatest significance was the welfare of the child which, according to European jurisprudence, was of crucial importance and, where in conflict with a parent, was overriding ... Section 13(1)(b) of the 1989 Act did not create any presumption in favour of the applicant parent, and the criteria in section 1 of the Act clearly governed an application under section 13(1)(b).[66]

When the Home Secretary sets removal directions, this is frequently overlooked by him/her and can form part of representations requiring the Home Secretary to obtain the leave of the court to remove the child along with the parent.[67]

---

65 CA 1989 s13.
66 *Payne v Payne* [2001] 1 FCR 424.
67 See also para 1.100. Reference to these criteria can be made to challenge the decision-making process of the Home Office – see chapter 8.

Contact order

1.68 A contact order requires the person with whom the child lives or is to live:
- to allow the child to visit or stay with the person named in the order; or
- for that person and the child to have contact with each other in some way which may be defined, for example, at a contact centre.

The latter is called 'supervised contact' and is usually appropriate where there is a fear that the adult may attempt to harm or abduct the child or where he or she has had very little previous contact with the child. Even such limited contact may give rise to a successful application for leave to remain in the UK.

1.69 Where one parent is not resident in the UK and wishes to return to the UK on a periodic basis to see his/her child, a contact order will enable an application to be made for entry clearance in accordance with IR r246 as amended.

Prohibited steps order

1.70 An order may be made that no step which is of a kind specified in the order (for example, taking to a specified place, behaving in a particular way, meeting particular people) shall be taken by a parent with parental responsibility for a child or by any person without the consent of the court. This can be of some use in immigration matters depending on the circumstances. For example, a prohibition on meeting grandparents if the grandparents are in a country to which the Home Office proposes to remove the child/adult.

Specific issue order

1.71 This is an order giving directions for the purpose of determining a specific question which has arisen or which may arise in connection with any aspect of parental responsibility for a child, for example, the school to be attended by the child, or medical treatment to be received by the child. If this order will not or cannot be enforced in the country to which it is proposed that the child should be removed, this can be a useful addition to representations to the Home Office.

Emergency protection order

1.72 Care proceedings may be commenced by a local authority, the NSPCC or a police officer, who is designated for such purposes, applying in the family court for an emergency protection order to remove the child from his/her present accommodation. An order will only be made where there is reasonable cause to believe that the child is likely to suffer immediate significant harm.[68] An emergency protection order will be effective for up to eight days and will provide the applicant with parental responsibility for the child. During this period, investigations into the child's treatment can be undertaken and if necessary a care order can be applied for.

Supervision orders under CA 1989 s31

1.73 The court may make a supervision order where it considers that there is a continuing requirement for local authority involvement,[69] the 'threshold criteria'[69a] are met and that it is in the best interests of the child to place him/her at home subject to the supervision order. A supervision order will be made for a year. Consideration will be given to extensions thereafter but it is unusual for a supervision to order to be extended for a further year. The existence of a supervision order can be useful in submissions to the Home Office requiring a family to remain in the UK to enable effective supervision.

Secure accommodation orders under CA 1989 s25

1.74 Where a child is considered to be at risk to him or herself or others, the court will be asked to make an order restraining the child to secure accommodation. Secure accommodation requires a child to comply with particular regulations regarding attendance or can prevent a child from leaving the accommodation without permission. Restrictions can vary and may include locking children in the accommodation. Such orders are frequently used where a child has been accused of serious crimes, for example, multiple burglaries or assault.

---

68 The threshold criteria must be met.
69 See para 1.75.
69a See below, para 1.89 for a definition.

Example: Care proceedings versus supervison order

Mrs Robin arrived in the UK with her two children aged four and six and claimed asylum. She became severely depressed and tried to commit suicide by jumping, with her two children, off a bridge onto a main road. She was not severely injured. Her two children survived with broken limbs. Care proceedings were issued. During the course of the care proceedings her husband arrived in the UK to look after the children. He also claimed asylum but made it clear during the course of his asylum interview that he was only doing that to enable him to remain in the UK to look after his wife and children and that he did not fear persecution.

Both Mr and Mrs Robin were refused asylum. Removal directions were postponed pending the outcome of the care proceedings. The family, including the children, wanted to remain in the UK. The local authority during the course of the care proceedings returned the children to the parents. Mrs Robin attempted to commit suicide three more times, slashing her wrists while the father was at the park with the children. The local authority did not remove the children from the care of the parents. It was not known what their long-term views were likely to be as to the future care of the children.

At the time of the final care hearing the children were aged ten and eight. The children were represented by family solicitors, Mr Robin had a family solicitor and Mrs Robin had a family solicitor. Mr and Mrs Robin had separate immigration solicitors, as did the children. The family solicitors for Mr and Mrs Robin wanted to argue that there should be no order – Mr Robin was looking after the children who were showing no signs of trauma; any local authority involvement carried with it the risk of the children being removed from the parents' care, despite Mr Robin's parenting skills; they considered that there was very little risk of the local authority wanting a supervision or care order at this time now that Mrs Robin was responding to treatment. The children's family solicitors were undecided. Mr and Mrs Robin's immigration solicitors took the view that if there were no local authority involvement there would be no reason for the Home Office to defer removal any longer. In all the circumstances, a decision was taken to argue for a supervision order. This was the order made by the court, valid for one year. The family were given exceptional leave for one year. An argument was put to the court a year later for a further, exceptional extension to the supervision order at the end of the year which was granted. The family were subsequently granted indefinite leave to remain.

Local authority responsibility for children

1.75 Under CA 1989 s17, all local authorities owe a general duty to all children, who are living within their area:

(a) to safeguard and promote their welfare; and
(b) so far as it is consistent with (a), to promote their upbringing by their own families.

1.76 CA 1989 s17(10) further defines 'children in need' as those:

(i) who are unlikely to achieve or maintain, or to have the opportunity of achieving or maintaining, a reasonable standard of health or development without the provision of services by the local authority;
(ii) whose health or development is likely to be significantly impaired, or further impaired, without provision of such services; or
(iii) who are disabled.

1.77 In the context of the CA 1989, 'development' means physical, intellectual, emotional, social or behavioural development and 'health' means both physical and mental health.

1.78 The fact that a child is not a British citizen, is not settled, and does not even have leave to remain in the UK, does not provide a local authority with a lawful basis to ignore his/her needs, as CA 1989 s17(1)(a) imposes a general duty in relation to all children within the geographical area covered by that authority.

1.79 The local authority may, at times, exercise this duty by providing assistance, including, in exceptional circumstances, cash assistance, to the child's family.[70] 'Family' for these purposes, includes anyone with parental responsibility for the child or any other person with whom he or she has been living.[71] However, it is now not possible for the local authority to provide accommodation for children and their families using the powers under this section.[72]

Children looked after by a local authority

1.80 It is important to realise that a distinction is drawn in law between children accommodated by the local authority, as children in need

---

70 CA 1989 s17(6).
71 CA 1989 s17(10).
72 *R on the application of A v Lambeth LBC* [2001] EWCA Civ 1624; (2001) 4 CCLR 486; (2001) *Times* 20 November, and see also para 3.30 but also note para 3.31.

under CA 1989 s20, and children taken into care, because they are suffering or are likely to suffer significant harm.[73]

1.81 Children Act 1989 s22(1) first introduced the concept of children who were 'being looked after by a local authority', to include all children who were being provided with accommodation by the local authority, whether or not they were subject to a care order at the time. The Act also imposed certain duties on local authorities in relation to all children being looked after and those who were under 21 who had previously been looked after. The requirement of local authorities to provide for children means that many local authorities do not formally acknowledge that the children whom they are looking after *are* accommodated under CA 1989 s20. Some local authorities may try to assert that since no formal decision to accommodate under CA 1989 s20 has been taken, there is no duty to provide assistance.[74] Local authorities will, in practice, be 'looking after' the child in accordance with CA 1989 s22. If a decision had not been taken to look after a child in accordance with the Act *any* expenditure under the Act would be ultra vires.

1.82 The Children (Leaving Care) Act (CLCA) 2000 amends the CA 1989 to require local authorities to assess the needs of children they have accommodated or taken into care for more than 13 weeks to determine what advice, assistance and support is appropriate, initially in the period up to their 18th birthday and secondly in the period from their 18th birthday until their 21st birthday. Once assessed, the local authority is under a duty to provide a 'pathway plan' and a 'personal adviser' for each eligible child. CA 1989 s24, as amended by the CLCA 2000, requires local authorities to have continuing responsibilities to those young people who were previously accommodated, ie, looked after at any time between the ages of 16 and 18, to assess and to meet the needs of 16 and 17-year-old care leavers, to maintain contact with care leavers up to the age of 21, and to provide funding for education and training for care leavers up to the age of 24.

Accommodation under CA 1989 s20

1.83 A local authority accommodates a child if he or she is provided with accommodation for more than 24 hours and is not also subject to a care order or emergency protection order. There is some argument that there has to be a formal decision for a child to be accommodated

---

73 For instance, the threshold criteria have been met as set out in CA 1989 s31 – see para 1.89.
74 See para 3.17.

under CA 1989 s20. This is not the case, given that the power of the local authority to provide accommodation and assistance would not otherwise arise.[75] Section 20 places a duty on local authorities to provide accommodation for any child in need within their geographical area who appears to require it because:

- no one has parental responsibility for him/her;
- he or she is lost or abandoned;
- the person who had been caring for him/her was prevented, temporarily or permanently, from providing him/her with suitable accommodation or care.

1.84 This is the section that should be used to provide for unaccompanied minors who arrive in the UK alone or are brought in by adults and then left at social services departments or community centres or with other members of the same community. Some local authorities attempt to argue that they are not looking after unaccompanied children in accordance with their obligations under CA 1989 s20 and try to evade responsibilities after the child reaches the age of 18.[76] An attempt by a local authority to assert this should be challenged, as the consequences for longer-term support can be dramatic.

1.85 Accommodation for children up to the age of 16 is likely to be provided in a children's home or with foster carers. If the child is over 16 years old and the authority believes that his/her welfare will be seriously prejudiced if he or she is not provided with accommodation, he or she is likely to be placed with foster carers or in a community home until he or she reaches the age of 21.

1.86 The authority will also maintain accommodated children and provide them with the necessary resources to attend school and further education. The CLCA 2000 has improved the position of older children and young people, empowering local authorities to provide funding for their education and training, including vacation and term-time accommodation, up to the age of 24.

1.87 Many local authorities are currently considering the impact of the CLCA 2000 in relation to unaccompanied minor asylum-seekers who have since reached the age of 18 but are still awaiting a decision on their application. It is possible to argue that the continuing duty extends to these young people and to argue that education and training should be funded.[76a]

---

75 See para 3.17.
76 CA 1989 s24 as amended by the CLCA 2000.
76a *Secure Borders, Safe Haven* Cm 5387 Home Office, February 2002, paragraph 4.60.

1.88 It is often the case that a child who has been accommodated by one local authority up until the age of 18 may be placed, or him/herself find accommodation outside that local authority's area between the ages of 18 and 21. In addition, local authorities are actively dispersing children under 18.[76b] If that is the case, it will be the local authority into whose area he or she has moved who will become responsible for providing him/her with advice and assistance.[77] If a child has been in education for over a year there is a strong argument, in accordance with government policy as set out in the National Asylum Support Service guidelines,[78] that he or she should not be moved.

Care orders under CA 1989 s31

1.89 Children, up to the age of 17 if unmarried, or 16 if married, can only be taken into care where a local authority, or in a minority of cases the NSPCC, can establish in a family court that:

(a) she or he is suffering, or is likely to suffer, significant harm; and
(b) that the harm, or likelihood of harm, is attributable to –
  (i) (the care given to him/her, or likely to be given to him/her if the order is not made, not being what it would be reasonable to expect a parent to give to him/her; or
  (ii) she or he is beyond parental control.

Paragraphs (a) and (b) are commonly referred to as the 'threshold criteria'.

1.90 The threshold criteria have to be met before the court will make a care order, but the court is not obliged to make a care order, even if the threshold criteria are met. The court will consider the matters set out in the checklist provided in CA 1989 s1(3).[79] Depending on all the circumstances the court may make a care order, a supervision order, a residence order or no order. The interests of the child are of paramount importance in coming to a decision.[80] The court will only make an order if it believes that making an order would be better for the child than making no order at all.

1.91 Care proceedings are usually the result of a multi-disciplinary case conference of professionals involved with the child, such as social

---

76b The government plans to assist this process, see *Secure Borders, Safe Haven*, para 4.60.
77 *R v Lambeth LBC ex p Caddell* [1998] 1 FLR 253.
78 See para 3.00.
79 See para 1.22.
80 CA 1989 s1(1).

> **Example: Care proceedings, unidentified child**
>
> Alain is nine years old and the subject of care proceedings. His father and stepmother are separated. There is no mention in the father's asylum papers of a child called Alain, but there is mention of a child called Hubert by his first wife who remains in the country of origin but is untraceable. The stepmother confirms that Alain is not her child but is the child of her husband. There is reference in her asylum papers to her looking after a child called Alain. The date of birth as given in the stepmother's papers and in the care proceedings of Alain is the same. There is a birth certificate for Hubert showing the date of birth as given by the father. There is no birth certificate for Alain. The date of birth of Hubert in the father's papers shows him as one year older. The stepmother has indefinite leave to remain. Her papers refer to her three other children and to Hubert as having indefinite leave. There is no mention of Alain either in her indefinite leave papers or in the father's indefinite leave papers. Alain says he used to be called Hubert.
>
> **Action:** family court to be asked to declare that so far as it is concerned Alain and Hubert are the same person. Application to be made to the Home Office for Alain to be given papers in the name of Alain. The full story should be set out in the application.

workers, teachers, health professionals and police advising the local authority that this would be the preferred course of action. The Immigration Service may sometimes be invited, in which case there is a strong argument for the immigration adviser to be present.[81]

1.92 A court dealing with other family applications may also direct a local authority to investigate and report back on the need for care proceedings, when it appears appropriate to it that this should be done.[82]

1.93 A care order is usually only applied for on an interim basis, as it can take weeks or months before sufficient evidence is gathered to justify a full care order.

1.94 Once a care order has been granted, either on an interim or full basis, the local authority will have parental responsibility for the child concerned and will assume all the rights and duties connected with this. Those who previously had parental responsibility retain it and will be consulted, but will not be entitled to take any steps in relation

---

81 In such cases it is advisable to obtain prior authority from the LSC for costs of attendance to be covered under Legal Help.
82 CA 1989 s37.

to the child, which may be incompatible with the care order or other orders made under the CA 1989.

1.95 While a care order is in force no other person may cause the child to be known by a new surname, or remove him/her from the UK without either the written consent of every person who has parental responsibility for the child or the leave of the court.

Contact with children in care under CA 1989 s34

1.96 While children are in care, the local authority should allow and promote reasonable contact with their parents and those who previously had care of them.[83] A family court can also make an order in relation to the amount and type of contact that should take place. Specific reference to contact will ensure not only that contact is defined and should take place, but reference to it can be made in representations to the Home Office. The court will make a contact order if it is persuaded that contact is in the best interests of the child even where there is a care order. It can then be argued that removal of a parent would interfere with the court's intentions.[84]

1.97 The amount of contact likely to be ordered will depend largely on the care plan[85] formulated by the local authority and later approved by the court. If the care plan is for rehabilitation with a parent or parents, or if the child is older and is likely to be placed with alternative carers on a medium or long-term basis, but contact with the family is thought to be beneficial, contact is likely to be fairly generous. However, if the child has suffered severe harm, is young, and the care plan indicates that he or she will be placed with alternative carers on a permanent basis, contact is likely to be much less generous and is likely to be decreased as the case moves towards its conclusion and eventually be terminated altogether.

Care plans

1.98 The local authority must provide a care plan, which is satisfactory to the court, outlining where it proposes to place the child and the plans it may have for his/her future. Guidance about what should be included in such a plan is provided in paragraph 2.62 of the CA 1989 Guidance and Regulations Vol 3, Family Placements:

---

83 CA 1989 s34.
84 See chapter 8.
85 See para 1.98.

The plan should be recorded in writing and contain the child's and his family's social history and the following key elements:
- the child's identified needs (including needs arising from race, culture, religion or language, special educational or health needs);
- how those needs might be met;
- aim of plan and timescale;
- proposed placement (type and details);
- other services to be provided to child and or family either by the local authority or other agencies;
- arrangements for contact and reunification;
- support in the placement;
- likely duration of placement in the accommodation;
- contingency plan if the placement breaks down;
- arrangements for ending the placement (if made under voluntary arrangements);
- who is to be responsible for implementing the plan (specific tasks and overall plan);
- specific detail of the parent's role in day to day arrangements;
- the extent to which the wishes and views of the child, his parents and anyone else with a sufficient interest in the child (including representatives of other agencies) have been obtained and acted upon and the reasons supporting this or explanation of why wishes/views have been discounted;
- arrangements for input by parents, the child and others into the ongoing decision-making process;
- arrangements for notifying the responsible authority of disagreements or making representations;
- arrangements for health care (including consent to examination and treatment);
- arrangements for education; and
- dates of reviews.

1.99 The requirements are extensive and cover the child's identified needs, arising from race, culture, religion or language, special educational or health needs, the specific role of the parents and the wishes of the child and others involved with the child. Those with parental responsibility should also have been consulted about this plan. This can be useful in immigration cases where the child/family are awaiting a decision or where the care plan may depend on the implementation of a residential placement plan. The court has no continuing supervisory responsibility for care plans.[86]

---

86 *Re W and B (children: care plan)* House of Lords, 14 March 2002.

Removal of child to live abroad when looked after by a local authority

1.100 A child who is subject to a care order or supervision order may be considered for removal abroad.[87] A child who lacks a right to remain or enter the UK, or a child who has other potential carers abroad may be the subject of an investigation by the local authority to establish whether there are alternative carers and the authority may then seek leave of the court to place them there. Such investigation may arise at the instigation of the local authority, or at the request of carers in the UK who wish to leave the UK and take the child with them. Leave of the court is required where the child is subject to a court order in connection with residence, care or supervision. If the local authority has responsibilities by virtue of the order it should always be remembered that the child in question may lack any right to remain or, in the case of those on temporary admission, to enter the UK. Removal could also, therefore, in practice, operate to prevent any return in the future. A local authority may well decide to investigate whether there are alternative carers for the child in his/her country of origin and then seek leave from the court to place the child there.

1.101 A local authority may well feel that this would be the most appropriate course to take given the difficulties faced by most local authorities in finding adoptive parents or even foster carers which match the race, religious and cultural profile of many children coming into their care. Local authorities will also look to paternal or maternal grandparents or the parents' siblings as alternative carers in the first instance and they will often be in the country of the child's origin.

1.102 Before any such placement is finalised, the local authority will have to make the necessary inquiries through International Social Services or other sources. Increasingly, they are also financing their own social workers to travel abroad to do home visits and make the necessary arrangements to place a child in his/her country of origin.

1.103 Before any such placement can be made, the local authority will have to satisfy the family court that:

- such a move would be in the child's best interests;
- suitable arrangements had been made for the child's reception and welfare;
- the child had consented; and
- everyone with parental responsibility had consented.

87 CA 1989 Sch 2, s19.

1.104 The child's consent can be dispensed with if he or she is not deemed to have sufficient understanding and a parent's consent can be dispensed with if he or she is held to be withholding it unreasonably.

Complaints procedure under CA 1989 s26

1.105 Complaints procedures exist under the CA 1989 and under community care and social services legislation, but implementation varies between local authorities and can be lengthy and cumbersome. It has become common for judges to inquire about whether the complaints procedure has been instigated and it is likely that this will become more common due to the pre-action protocol in judicial review. Use of the complaints procedure requires considerable effort to maintain momentum.[88] In some circumstances, where an urgent review of a decision is required, such as on financial matters or accommodation, it may well be preferable to consider an action in the Administrative Court. But care needs to be exercised to ensure that other remedies have been exhausted or are unsuitable because, for example, of unconscionable delay or if there is no proper remedy or the remedy would merely result in the disciplining of a member of staff rather than resolving the issue in question.

Effect of court orders made in the UK

1.106 Court orders under the CA 1989, whether in conjunction with other orders, for example, divorce, or on their own, determine the relationship between the child and the adults who were party to the proceedings and/or the local authority. If there is a court order the future of the child's relationship with those adults will be governed in legal terms by the parameters of that order. Rights and responsibilities referred to in court orders can only be added to or taken away by the court. Such amendment will be subject to the same considerations as at the time of the making of the original order.[89]

---

[88] Provided the complaint forms a legitimate part of the conduct of the case, there is no reason why it should not be funded under Legal Help.
[89] See also paras 6.18–6.21.

> **Example: Use of family law orders**
>
> Eta was two years old when her mother, who had exceptional leave to remain, died of AIDS. In the months leading up to her death Eta's mother gave Eta to her very close friend Betty who continued to care for her. The Home Office accepted that Eta had exceptional leave to remain. Betty unfortunately had lost her appeal against her asylum refusal and removal directions were made. These were deferred when the Home Office was informed that Betty was looking after Eta and was threatened with judicial review if it proceeded with removal having been informed of this.
>
> The local authority wrote to the Home Office asserting that Eta's 'father', James, who was looking after Eta's four siblings, would be able to look after Eta and tried to persuade James, and Betty, that Eta would be better off with James. Betty said that James was not Eta's father. Eta's mother had been separated from James for many months before she became pregnant with Eta and Eta's mother had made her promise always to look after Eta. Betty had no relatives in her country of origin and had no prospects of employment. Eta was currently receiving prophylactic drugs as the hospital was unable to test her because so far as it was concerned no one had parental responsibility to authorise testing.
>
> Betty applied for a residence order. James was served with the proceedings but did not participate. A residence order was made that Eta live with Betty. The Home Office set removal directions for both Betty and Eta. Its attention was drawn to the need to obtain the leave of the court to remove Eta from the UK, that Eta had exceptional leave to remain and that her leave had to be curtailed to enable removal directions to be set and that the court had been aware of these matters when making the residence order. Eventually indefinite leave to remain was granted to Eta and Betty.

CHAPTER 2
Adoption

2.1	Non-British children adopted in the UK by British parents
2.8	Non-British children 'adopted' abroad
2.9	Adoption in a designated country
2.11	Adoption in a non-designated country
2.13	Where adoption abroad was not possible
2.15	Adoptive children of EEA nationals

Non-British children adopted in the UK by British parents

2.1 If British parents adopt a non-British child in the UK, he or she automatically becomes a British citizen as soon as the order is made.[1] A couple can only adopt a child together if they are married.[2] Therefore, an unmarried couple cannot confer British nationality on their child, if the non-British partner adopts the child alone.

2.2 It is now an offence to bring a child to this country for the purposes of adoption if the prospective adopters have not been approved by a local authority social services department or an approved adoption society. The Home Secretary also has to issue a certificate of eligibility.[3] Prospective adopters will no longer be able to rely on private home study reports, but will have to apply to be considered as prospective adopters alongside those wishing to adopt in this country. Although the regulations do impose a duty on local authorities to treat the prospective adopters of non-British children with the same priority as those involved in domestic adoptions, the new process may well be slower. Prospective adopters should note that it is possible to seek approval from any local authority, not just the one in whose area they live.

2.3 These new requirements have been adopted to enable the UK to comply with the provisions in the Hague Convention on Protection of Children and Co-operation in Respect of Intercountry Adoptions 1993 and may lead to amendments to the Immigration Rules HC 395 in the future.

2.4 When the application for adoption is filed in the UK, the prospective adopters must also inform the Home Secretary, so that he or she has the opportunity to apply to be joined as a respondent.[4] At one time, the family court gave great weight to the need to maintain efficient immigration controls and the first test which it would apply was whether the adoption was just an arrangement which would facilitate a child being granted British nationality in order to be able to study and work in the UK or whether it really necessary for an order to be made in order to safeguard and promote that child's welfare

1 British Nationality Act (BNA) 1981 s1(5).
2 Adoption Act 1976 s1.
3 Adoption of Children from Abroad Order 2000 S1 No 1251, Adoption (Intercountry Aspects) Act 1999 and Immigration Directorate Instructions (IDI) Ch 8, s5, Annex Q.
4 *Re K (adoption and wardship)* [1997] 2 FLR 221.

Adoption 35

> **Example: Adoption**
>
> Mr and Mrs Adler wanted to adopt a child. They went through a reputable agency in a Latin American country. A child was found whose mother had put him into a children's home as she was unable to care for him. The birth mother subsequently died. Mr and Mrs Adler started to support the child financially, and went to see him on a number of occasions. But matters moved very slowly. Eventually, the child was brought into the UK by an intermediary. He was granted leave to enter as a visitor (although he was clearly an illegal entrant). Adoption proceedings were initiated in the UK. An application for an extension of stay was submitted and the Home Office was kept informed of the progress of the adoption proceedings. The family court asked if the Home Office intended to intervene. It did not, and an adoption order was made in Mr and Mrs Adler's favour. The child therefore became a British citizen. Since the coming into force of the Adoption (Intercountry Aspects) Act 1999 the couple could now face prosecution. There are significant numbers of prospective adopters in this position, who have already started the adoption process, who face potential prosecution.

throughout his/her childhood.[5] Even if it decided that there was no obvious abuse, it would still go on to balance the welfare of that child against the public interest involved in maintaining strict immigration controls.[6]

2.5 However, the House of Lords has recently adopted a more purposive approach.[7] The questions that the family court should now ask are:

- Will the adoption bring about a genuine transfer of parental responsibility and not only be motivated by a wish to assist the child to obtain a right of abode?
- Will the adoption, taking into account all the child's personal circumstances, confer real benefits on the child throughout her/his childhood?

2.6 It then went on to state that although the views of the Home Office should be taken into account, it is very unlikely that general concerns

---

5 This test is to be applied by the family court when considering making any adoption order and is found in Adoption Act 1976 s6.
6 *Re H (a minor) (adoption: non-patrial)* [1996] 2 FCR 597.
7 *Re B* [1999] 2 AC 136.

relating to the maintenance of immigration controls could justify the rejection of an order which met both these tests.

2.7 In *Re B*,[8] the child in question was 16 years old and was being adopted by her grandparents. Her mother had returned to Jamaica to a life of destitution and her grandparents wanted to be able to provide her with a secure home and educational opportunities. Evidential difficulties may arise in establishing that sufficient benefits will accrue to a child who is very close to becoming 18 years old.[9]

> **Example: Adoption**
>
> A 17-year-old Peruvian boy living in the UK with his mother and her new husband was the subject of adoption proceedings by the stepfather and mother. The boy had lived with them for three years. The mother was a failed asylum-seeker who was due to be removed. Her ex-husband, the boy's father, whom she was in the process of divorcing, was also a failed asylum-seeker and facing removal. The boy saw his father about once a month. The boy, mother and father had been in the UK for about four years. The boy was bright and doing well at school. The stepfather was a British citizen, working in the UK but with no other family in the UK. A report on the immigration consequences was sought by the solicitors acting for the adopting couple. Any written advice would have had to have been disclosed to the court. No written report was provided. The adoption hearing proceeded without an immigration opinion, perhaps fortunately, as if one had been provided, it would not have been helpful to the prospective adopters: the immigration advice was that the length of time spent by the boy in the UK, together with the other circumstances, was unlikely to result in the Home Office granting him and his mother leave to remain in the UK. An adoption order was made.

Non-British children 'adopted' abroad

2.8 If British parents adopt a non-British child abroad, he or she will not become British automatically.[9a] The parents will have to seek entry clearance for him/her and then make further applications. The nature of the applications which need to be made depend upon:

---

8 [1999] 2 AC 136.
9 *Re K (a minor) (adoption order: nationality)* [1995] Fam 38.
9a This may change when, and if, the full provisions of the Adoption (Intercountry Aspects) Act 1999 come into force.

- whether the adoption was one which was in accordance with a decision taken by a competent administrative authority abroad (ie, a legal adoption) in one of the countries designated by the Home Secretary under the Adoption (Designation of Overseas Adoptions) Order 1973;[10]
- whether it was made by a competent authority in any other country;
- whether it was a de facto adoption;
- whether the country from which the child comes recognises adoption as a legal concept.

Adoption in a designated country

2.9 Where a child has been adopted in a designated country, the Immigration and Nationality Directorate will accept the validity of the adoption and the fact that he or she is now legally a child of the family. As long as the other requirements of the Immigration Rules (IR) can be met,[11] he or she will be admitted for settlement and can subsequently apply for British citizenship.[12] He or she can also apply for settlement, if he or she is already in the UK with limited leave in another capacity.[13]

2.10 Where the adoption involves an infertile couple adopting a close relative's child, it can be difficult to show that he or she has broken all ties with his/her natural family and, therefore, some children do not fit neatly within IR para 311. This creates something of an anomaly, as in cases based on similar facts, where there was no adoption in a designated country, the family court has shown itself willing to make an adoption order and thus enable the child to become a British citizen.[14]

10 SI No 19: Anguilla, Australia, Bahamas, Barbados, Belize, Bermuda, Botswana, British Virgin Islands, Canada, Cayman Islands, Cyprus, Dominica, Fiji, Ghana, Gibraltar, Guyana, Hong Kong, Jamaica, Kenya, Lesotho, Malaysia, Malawi, Malta, Mauritius, Montserrat, New Zealand, Nigeria, Pitcairn Islands, Zimbabwe, St Christopher and Nevis, St Vincent, Seychelles, Singapore, Sri Lanka, Swaziland, Tanzania, Tonga, Trinidad and Tobago, Uganda, Zambia, Austria, Belgium, Denmark, Finland, France (including Reunion, Martinique, Guadeloupe, and French Guyana), Germany, Greece, Iceland, Ireland, Israel, Italy, Luxembourg, Netherlands (including the Antilles), Norway, Portugal (including the Azores and Madeira), South Africa, Namibia, Spain, Switzerland, Turkey, USA, Yugoslavia.
11 HC 395 as amended para 310.
12 BNA 1981 para 1(4).
13 HC 395 as amended para 311.
14 *Re J (adoption: non-patrial)* [1998] FCR 125.

Adoption in a non-designated country

2.11 Where a child has been adopted in a non-designated country, the adoption will not be recognised here and an application will have to be made to bring the child to the UK to be legally adopted.[15] The requirements to be met are similar, but not identical, to those to be met by a child who has been adopted in a designated country, but the child will initially be admitted for 12 months to enable the adoption order to be made.[16] If the adoption order has not been made within 12 months, further leave will usually be granted on application.

2.12 In addition, prior approval as prospective adopters must have been obtained, as outlined above at para 2.2, and the local authority must be informed of the intention to apply for an adoption order in this country within 14 days of bringing the child into this country.[17]

Where adoption abroad was not possible

2.13 The requirement that the adoption must be by a court or administrative authority (for instance, in some countries a board made up of social services and medical staff) is obviously a very useful safeguard at a time when many children are being put up for adoption by agents, who seek to gain from a ready market for babies in the western world. However, many countries do not recognise adoption as a legal concept. For instance, many Islamic countries do not, but children do become part of families other than the one they were born into and de facto adoption occurs.

2.14 If there is no intention to apply to adopt the child in the UK, but an intention that the child will live as part of the family, entry clearance and immigration officers can use their discretion and admit such a child for settlement.[18] As no question of adoption arises, the Adoption (Intercountry Aspects) Act 1999 does not apply and the child's presence in the family is treated as a private fostering arrangement. Once the child has been admitted, his/her de facto adoptive parents must inform their local authority of his/her presence in the family. If they do not they will be committing an offence.[19]

---

15 HC 395 as amended para 316A.
16 Ibid para 316B.
17 Adoption of Children from Overseas Regulations 2001 SI No 1251.
18 IDI Ch 8, s5, Annexe S.
19 Children Act 1989 s70(1)(a).

Adoptive children of EEA nationals

2.15 The previous policy in relation to EEA nationals was that an EEA national could bring an adopted child to the UK as a dependant, if that child had been adopted in a designated country. Otherwise, the child would have to comply with all the usual requirements for a child who has not been adopted in a designated country and make an application for leave to enter for the purposes of adoption, unless the immigration officer concerned decided to exercise his/her discretion outside the IR. An application for the purpose of adoption had to be made even when an application to adopt was being made in the EEA national's home country.[20] It is not yet clear how this policy has been modified by the Adoption (Intercountry Aspects) Act 1999, but the old policy should be read in the light of the new changes to the law.

---

20 Letter from the Home Office to Bindman & Partners dated 5 February 1996 and letter to Goodman Ray dated 5 June 1998.

CHAPTER 3
Support

3.1	**Access to financial support and public services**
3.2	Support for those who are destitute
	Refugees and those with indefinite or exceptional leave to remain • Asylum-seekers • Unaccompanied minors (or separated children) • Those who are subject to immigration control • Those who are destitute for other reasons
3.27	Families which include children
3.30	**Access to other services**
3.30	Education
3.36	National Health Service
3.40	Public housing

Since this chapter was written the voucher system has been abolished. Other changes to the support system are currently under discussion in parliament.

Access to financial support and public services

3.1 This is a very complex area and immigration lawyers and advisers may need to seek further advice from welfare rights specialists. The White Paper *Secure Borders, Safe Haven*, published by the Home Office in February 2002, proposes far reaching changes which are in the process of being implemented. However, a brief overview of current possible entitlements has been included in this book, because the need to provide for his/her children's physical needs will often be uppermost in an adult's mind and may prevent him/her paying sufficient immediate attention to the question of immigration status and the need to make the necessary applications and representations.

Support for those who are destitute[1]

Refugees and those with indefinite or exceptional leave to remain

3.2 Anyone[2] who falls within any of these three categories will be entitled to claim welfare benefits and apply for public housing if he or she meets the usual conditions attached to entitlement under the relevant social security and housing legislation. Immigration status will be no bar to such entitlement.

Asylum-seekers

3.3 Prior to 4 February 1996, all asylum-seekers were entitled to claim income support, which was 90 per cent of the amount usually available to claimants. They were also entitled to claim housing benefit and to have some access, although diminishing over the years, to public housing. Most tended to settle in London or near to the seaports where they had arrived, which tended to be in the south east of England. The main attraction of London was that there were often established refugee or other immigrant communities there. The settlement around most ports was more coincidental.

3.4 From 4 February 1996, entitlement to income support was restricted to those who claimed asylum immediately on arrival at ports

---

1 For further details of the support scheme see Willman, Knafler and Pierce, *Support for asylum-seekers* (LAG, 2001); *Macdonald's Immigration Law and Practice* (5th edn, Butterworths, 2001) Ch 13; and *Migration and Social Security Handbook* (3rd edn, CPAG, 2001).
2 Except where there is a sponsorship declaration, which prevents access to benefits for five years: Social Security (Immigration and Asylum) Consequential Amendments Regulations 2000 SI No 636 Sch, Pt 1, para 3.

of entry. This was a response to the government's belief that the fact that asylum-seekers were entitled to such support attracted a large number of would-be economic migrants posing as asylum-seekers. The effect of this change was to create an underclass of destitute asylum-seekers, who may have had no option but to enter the UK illegally or who had only realised that they were entitled to claim asylum once they were in the country. After lengthy legal controversy, it was held that if asylum-seekers in this category were actually destitute, local authorities had a duty to support them.[3]

3.5 On 6 December 1999, everything changed again. The Immigration and Asylum Act (IAA) 1999 created a new National Asylum Support Service (NASS) within the Home Office, which would in future support all destitute asylum-seekers. For an initial transitional period, it did this by arrangement with local authorities through the Interim Support scheme, but now NASS itself is responsible for all new asylum-seekers. A number of asylum-seekers who made an application prior to 6 December 1999 remain within the Interim Support scheme. This scheme has recently been extended to April 2004.

3.6 By the end of 2001, NASS was providing 50 per cent of asylum-seekers with accommodation and maintenance support in the form of vouchers. It was providing a further 20 per cent with vouchers only.[4]

3.7 When asylum-seekers make an application for asylum or if an application is made for leave to enter or remain on the basis that removal would be a breach of European Convention on Human Rights (ECHR) art 3, and they have no means to support themselves, they are referred to a reception assistant, who is an employee of a voluntary sector organisation, acting under a contract from NASS. This assistant helps them fill in the long and complex NASS application form, which has to be completed in English, and also finds them temporary accommodation.

3.8 NASS then considers whether they are destitute and, therefore, entitled to support. If it decides that they are, they are allocated accommodation and provided with vouchers. The vouchers are worth around 70 per cent of current income support rates, and £10 per person is redeemable as cash.[5] Vouchers stigmatise asylum-seekers and

---

3 NAA 1948 s21.
4 David Blunkett, Home Secretary, HC Debates col 640, 29 October 2001.
5 An adult over 25 was given £36.54 per week; an adult between 18 and 24, £28.95; a couple £57.37; a child under 16, £30.95 and a child of 16 or 17, £31.75: see Asylum Support Regulations 2000 SI No 704 as amended by SI 2000 No 3053.

restrict the variety of food and other goods that can be bought, as only a limited number of retailers accept them. The widespread criticism of the voucher system led to a review[6] and it is being phased out by the autumn of 2002 and replaced with a system whereby those with an application registration card (ARC)[7] can access cash from a post office. *Secure Borders, Safe Haven* (SBSH) also confirms in the interim the value of the vouchers will be increased by 1.67% and the cash element will increase from £10 to £14.[8] The government states that this increase will bring vouchers to 70% of income support for adults and 100% for children. The government is amending IAA 1999 s96(2) to enable the Secretary if State for the Home Department to provide cash not vouchers. But the government is also considering abolishing the right to claim support only and not accommodation thus avoiding dispersal.[9]

3.9 The vast majority of the accommodation provided is outside London with private sector landlords with whom NASS has entered into a contract. If asylum-seekers are receiving treatment from the Medical Foundation for the Care of Victims of Torture or other medical or psychiatric treatment, not available outside London, or has a child who has been settled in school for more than a year so that they are able to argue successfully against dispersal, they should be housed within London or the south east of England.[10]

3.10 Dispersal is often very problematic for people with children, especially if they are single parents. The majority of the established refugee communities are in the greater London area and historically have been able to offer much-needed support and advice to newly-arrived asylum-seekers from their own communities. Different nationalities or ethnic groupings have tended to establish themselves in different parts of the capital. As they have done so, community centres and support groups have been established, local law firms have developed their expertise in immigration and asylum law and interpreters have become available to liaise with doctors, landlords and schools. Most importantly, individual parents and their children have a community to relate to and, to some extent, be protected by.

---

6 It resulted in a report: *Report of the Operational Reviews of the Voucher and Dispersal Schemes of the National Asylum Support Scheme*, 29 October 2001 ('Operational Review Report').
7 *Secure Borders, Safe Haven*, (SBSH) paras 4.25 and 4.26.
8 SBSH para 5.2.
9 SBSH para 4.53.
10 See *Dispersal Guidelines*, NASS Policy Bulletin 31. The individual's needs should be set out in the NASS application form.

3.11 Outside London it has been a very different story. Asylum-seekers have been dispersed at random to cities chosen primarily because there were landlords willing to enter into a contract with NASS. Despite there being much talk about asylum-seekers being sent to 'cluster areas', where expertise and community support would develop and their language was spoken, this has not happened. Instead, many families have been housed in sub-standard accommodation in isolated locations and have suffered social exclusion and, all too often, racist abuse and attack.[11]

3.12 Despite the government providing extra resources for health and education, these services are still often unable to meet the needs of asylum-seekers and their families. On a very basic level, interpreters are not available, teachers have no experience of dealing with often traumatised children and the nearest experieced immigration solicitor may be a hundred miles away. Initially there was no attempt to ensure that there were firms of solicitors with contracts to provide immigration advice and representation in the areas to which asylum-seekers were dispersed. More recently, the Legal Services Commission (LSC) has taken steps to encourage new firms to start up in these areas, but provision is still limited.

3.13 In 2000, the Audit Commission[12] produced a report on dispersal under the Interim Scheme operated by local authorities before the NASS national scheme became operational. It was extremely critical of the failure to create an infrastructure capable of coping with the rapid dispersal of asylum-seekers.

3.14 The government published the results of a review of the dispersal and voucher system in October 2001.[13] It stated that there had been great shortcomings in the system and a Bill was published in April 2002, which will radically alter the support system.

3.15 It is proposed[14] that in future most asylum-seekers will initially be sent to an induction centre[15] for between one and seven days, where they will be assisted to apply for asylum and to seek NASS support, if they need it. There will be four options:

- after about one day if not relying on NASS support they may be free to live with friends of relatives; or

11 See note 6 above.
12 *Another Country: implementing dispersal under the Immigration and Asylum Act 1999*, Audit Commission, June 2000.
13 Operational Review Report.
14 'Radical Reform Unveiled for More Robust Asylum System', Home Office News Release, 29 October 2001.
15 SBSH paras 4.20–4.24.

- they will be dispersed to approved accommodation outside London and the South East; or
- they will be required to go to an accommodation centre; or
- they will be detained.

If allocated to an accommodation centre[16] they will be required to stay overnight. Educational facilities for children will be provided, as will health and legal services. Adults will be expected to take part in purposeful activities. In addition to board and lodging, they will be given pocket money. For an initial pilot period, there will only be 3,000 bed spaces available in these centres. However, if the pilot is successful, further such centres will be opened. The asylum decision will be served at the accommodation centres.

3.16 Dispersal will continue to be 'one offer' only but will be to cluster areas based on language.[17] NASS will also develop a regional structure to administer support and monitor delivery.[18] Regulations will also be introduced to change the notice period for ending asylum support from 14 to 21 days for failed asylum-seekers and 21 days for those granted leave to remain.[19]

3.17 Oakington Reception Centre will continue to be used as a detention centre for those who are deemed appropriate to be dealt with under the Oakington procedure.

3.18 The support system will also be closely linked to the enforcement of immigration control in two main ways. First, all asylum-seekers, who are not in induction, accommodation, Oakington Reception Centre or removal centres, will have to report on a regular basis to a reporting centre,[20] as a condition of any support and in order to pursue their application. Second, any decision in their case, whether it is a decision by the Home Secretary or the Immigration Appellate Authority, will be given to them at one of these centres. If the decision is adverse, they are likely to be detained with a view to removal. Regulations have already been made requiring the Immigration Appellate Authority to inform the SSHD but not the appellant of the determination of cases where no appeal lies from an adjudicator to the Immigration Appeal Tribunal (IAT) or where leave to appeal to the IAT has been refused.[21] A network of removal centres will be

16 SBSH paras 4.28–4.41.
17 SBSH para 4.41.
18 SBSH paras 4.47–4.48.
19 SBSH para 4.48.
20 SBSH paras 4.42–4.46.
21 Immigration Asylum Appeals (Procedure) (Amendment) Rules 2001 SI No 4014.

established so that those who have been refused asylum and who have exhausted their appeal rights can be swiftly removed from the UK. These centres will contain family accommodation. Children will be detained along with their parents.[22]

Unaccompanied minors (or separated children)

3.19 NASS is not responsible for supporting unaccompanied children who have claimed asylum. They should be accommodated by the social services department of the local authority area where they arrive or where they are when they make an asylum application. That local authority will have a duty to accommodate and maintain them as children in need in their geographical area if no one has parental responsibility for them or they have been lost or abandoned.[23] This duty will continue until they reach 18 years old. At that point, if they still have an outstanding asylum application or appeal, they will become the responsibility of NASS. The local authority will retain a duty to advise and assist them until they are 21 years of age, if it has looked after them at any point between the ages of 16 and 18.[24] Local authorities are now under a duty to prepare a pathway plan, having undertaken an assessment of their individual needs, for all 16- and 17-year-olds they look after. They must also appoint a personal adviser to keep in contact with them, and to review the suitability of their pathway plan at regular intervals between the ages of 18 and 21.

3.20 The local authority may also provide the child or young person with assistance in the form of a contribution towards the expenses of living near to the place where he or she is being educated or trained and actually undertaking the course. It may also provide assistance with obtaining accommodation during vacations or accommodation in an area where he or she has found or is looking for employment. The authority retains this responsibility until the young person is 24 years old.[25]

3.21 If he or she is still studying at age 18, it would be unreasonable to disperse him/her and any attempt to do so should be challenged and it should be argued that his/her situation is similar to the one where a family has a child who has been in school for more than one year, as the local authority is fulfilling a parental role towards him/her. This may be very important as the government is planning to support local

---

22 See SBSH February 2002, chapter 4.
23 CA 1989 s20.
24 Ibid Sch 2, para 19A, as amended by the Children (Leaving Care) Act 2000.
25 Ibid s24B.

authority plans to disperse 16- to 18-year-old unaccompanied asylum-seekers outside London and the South East.[26]

Those who are subject to immigration control

3.22 Immigration and Asylum Act 1999 Pt VI deals primarily with support for asylum-seekers. However, it also clarifies that no one who is subject to immigration control is entitled to claim:

- attendance allowance;
- severe disablement allowance;
- invalid care allowance;
- disability living allowance;
- income support;
- working families' tax credit;
- disabled person's tax credit;
- a social fund payment;
- child benefit;
- housing benefit; or
- council tax benefit.

3.23 This means that if a person is not a national of an EEA member state *and*:

- requires leave to enter or remain in the UK and does not have it; or
- has leave to enter or remain in the UK, which is subject to a condition that he or she does not have recourse to public funds; or
- has leave to enter or remain given as a result of a maintenance undertaking which has not expired; or
- is subject to conditions attached to previous leave while appealing against a decision to refuse to grant asylum or variation of that leave,

he or she will not be entitled to any of these benefits, as he or she will be classified as a person subject to immigration control.[27]

3.24 However, there will be a limited number of people who are subject to immigration control, but who are entitled to benefit in certain circumstances. If a person has leave to enter or remain, which is subject to a prohibition on reliance on public funds and is temporarily without funds, because, for example, he or she is a student and a grant has not arrived, he or she may seek assistance.[28] A person who

---

26 SBSH paras 4.59–4.60.
27 IAA 1999 s115(9).
28 Social Security (Immigration and Asylum) Consequential Amendments Regulations (SSIA Regs) 2000 SI No 636 Sch, Pt 1, para 1(b).

has leave to enter or remain under a maintenance agreement can claim benefits if his/her sponsor dies or if he or she has been resident in the UK for more than five years under the agreement.[29] Nationals of states which have ratified either the European Convention on Social and Medical Assistance or the Council of Europe Social Charter[30] and who are lawfully present[31] in the UK will also be entitled to benefit.

3.25 Transitional provisions also protect entitlement to benefit for some of those who claimed asylum before 6 February 1996[32] or 3 April 2000.[33] There may also be others who have been permitted to work, for example, as an asylum-seeker, and have accrued sufficient National Insurance contributions to qualify for entitlement to contribution-based benefits, such as:

- contribution-based job-seeker's allowance;
- incapacity benefit;
- maternity allowance;
- widow's payment;
- widowed mother's allowance;
- widow's pension; or
- category A or B retirement pension.[34]

Those who are destitute for other reasons

3.26 The IAA 1999 sought to remove from local authorities the power under National Assistance Act (NAA) 1948 s21 to provide residential accommodation to those who were in need of care and assistance, if the person concerned was subject to immigration control.[35] However, the Court of Appeal has held that local authorities still have this power if it can be shown that the need for care and assistance does not arise solely because the person is without the financial resources to obtain accommodation and sustenance.[36] Where a person qualifies

---

29 SSIA Regs 2000 Sch, Pt 1, paras 2 and 3.
30 Ibid Sch, Pt 1, para 4. These are the EEA member states, Cyprus, Czech Republic, Hungary, Malta, Poland, Slovakia, Turkey and Ukraine.
31 For instance, those who have leave to enter or remain for temporary purposes, but not those on temporary admission. See *Kaya v Haringey LBC* [2001] EWCA Civ 677.
32 SSIA Regs 2000, reg 2(4)(a).
33 Ibid reg 2(4)(b).
34 See, generally, *Migration and Social Security Handbook* (3rd edn, CPAG, 2001).
35 IAA 1999 s116.
36 *R v Wandsworth LBC ex p O* [2000] 4 All ER 590, CA.

for assistance both from NASS and under NAA 1948 s21, the Court of Appeal has further held that the local authority should be the body to provide support.[37]

Families which include children

3.27 Additional assistance may also be available from social services departments of the family's local authority if there is a child under 18 years old in the family. If there is a likelihood that the child will not achieve or maintain, or have the opportunity of achieving or maintaining, a reasonable standard of health or development without that local authority's assistance or if he or she is disabled, the local authority will be under a general duty to provide assistance to the family.[38] The local social services department can provide assistance in kind, which could be a place at a day nursery or playcentre or the provision of toys, books or additional vouchers. In exceptional circumstances, it can even provide cash to assist the child and his/her family.[39]

3.28 Children Act (CA) 1989 s17 also makes it clear that unless there is a risk that the family are responsible for the child's failure to thrive, the assistance should be given with a view to ensuring that the child can continue to live with his/her family.[40]

3.29 Until recently, most social services departments were giving CA 1989 s17 a purposive interpretation and families who were subject to immigration control, and who could not access any other assistance, were being housed and maintained under CA 1989 s17. In doing so they were following advice given to them by the Immigration and Nationality Department (IND).[41]

3.30 However, the Court of Appeal has recently held that local authorities cannot use CA 1989 s17 to provide housing, as their power to do so derived solely from housing legislation.[42] Lambeth LBC also

---

37 R on the application of Westminster City Council v NASS [2001] EWCA Civ 512; (2001) 33 HLR 83; (2001) 4 CCLR 143. A petition to the House of Lords is pending.
38 CA 1989 s17.
39 Ibid s17(5).
40 Ibid s17(1)(b).
41 '... the families of those persons who are here unlawfully ... will continue to be entitled to claim assistance from local authorities under the Children Act until such time as they are removed from the country.' Letter to all Chief Executives of Local Authorities in England and Wales from the IND, 19 November 1999.
42 R on the application of A v Lambeth LBC [2001] EWCA Civ 1624; [2001] 3 FCR 673; (2001) 4 CCLR 486.

successfully argued that the duty being imposed in CA 1989 s17 was a 'target' duty, which merely required the authority to assess a child's need and decide whether or not to meet it. An individual child and his/her family cannot, therefore, assert that a local authority is obliged in law to house and support them under CA 1989 s17. However, the Court of Appeal did confirm that a decision to provide assistance, or to decline to do so, would still be open to challenge on the ground of *Wednesbury* unreasonableness or in relation to issues of natural justice. This case has wide implications and is already affecting non-migrant families.[43]

3.31 The court did not accept that CA 1989 s17 acted as a safety-net for children who were without accommodation and support and who, because they were under 18 years old, could not be assisted under the NAA 1948. This, it believed, was already provided by CA 1989 s20, which imposed a specific duty on local authorities to provide accommodation for a child if his/her parents were not able to do so. This decision leads to the prospect of parents being faced with no choice but to ask a local authority to accommodate their child and the child in question knowing that although he or she is being fed and has a roof over his/her head, the rest of his/her family will be on the streets. It raises questions about whether a local authority may be in breach of its fiduciary duties to its council tax payers when it pays large sums to place children in foster care when it would have been cheaper to provide accommodation and support for the child within his/her own family. Elias J recently held that local authorities did have a power under Local Government Act 2000 s2 to provide financial assistance to a person who is subject to immigration control to enable them to acquire accommodation.

Access to other services

Education

3.30 Any child present in the UK, who is under 18 years old, is entitled to free education at a local state school, as long as his/her education in the UK started before he or she was age 16.[44] Children of asylum-

---

43 *R on the application of J and Enfield LBC v Secretary of State for Health* [2002] EWHC 432.
44 Education Act 1996 s10 for the general duty and DfEE Code of Practice on School Admissions, Annex B.

seekers are also entitled to free school meals, if the asylum-seeker is in receipt of income support, income-based job-seeker's allowance or support under IAA 1999 Pt VI.[45]

3.33 Colleges of further and higher education are entitled to charge higher fees to students who do not qualify as 'home' students.[46] To qualify as a 'home' student, it is necessary to prove settled status and ordinary residence in the UK for the previous three years for a reason other than attendance at a full-time educational establishment. This requirement does not, however, apply to recognised refugees. Local authorities may lawfully impose eligibility criteria for awards to meet a student's maintenance or tuition fees, which exclude those subject to immigration control.[47]

3.34 An asylum-seeker is usually treated as an overseas student in higher and further education. The Learning and Skills Council (formerly the Further Education Funding Council) has published the *Guidance on further education funding eligibility and rates 2001/2002*.[48] The Learning and Skills Council will fund any student who is entitled to 'home' fees under the Education (Fees and Awards) Regulations 1997.[49] Paragraph 47 gives details of categories of students who are eligible for funding (whether or not they are entitled to 'home' fees under the Regulations) if the institution charges 'home' fees. These concessionary categories include asylum-seekers and their dependants in receipt of a means-tested benefit or support under IAA 1999, CA 1989 or NAA 1948. The LSC will also consider other exceptional circumstances, the approach for funding to be made by the institution concerned.

3.35 UKCOSA (Council for International Education)[50] is a useful source of information and support to students who are subject to immigration control.

---

45 IAA 1999 Sch 14, para 117 amends Education Act 1996 s512(3).
46 Education (Fees and Awards) Act 1983 s1 and Education (Fees and Awards) Regulations 1997 SI No 1972.
47 Education (Mandatory Awards) Regulations 1997 SI No 431 reg 13.
48 This can be downloaded from www.lsc.gov.uk/news_docs/funding_guidance_01–02.pdf. For further information see also the *UKCOSA Manual 2001: A guide for regulations and procedures for international students*.
49 SI No 1972.
50 See Appendix M, Useful resources.

National Health Service

3.36 Treatment in accident and emergency and casualty departments is free irrespective of immigration status, as is the diagnosis and treatment of certain diseases, including malaria, tuberculosis and whooping cough, family planning services, the treatment of sexually transmitted diseases and the diagnosis of Human Immunodeficiency Virus (HIV) and AIDS and any related counselling and the treatment of those detained under the Mental Health Act 1983 or the Powers of the Criminal Courts Act 1973.[51]

3.37 Charges can be made for any other treatment for anyone who is not ordinarily resident in the UK.[52] Anyone who has lived here for more than a year is likely to be treated as being ordinarily resident. The National Health Service (Charges to Overseas Visitors) Regulations 1989 do not apply to general practitioners (GPs),[53] as they are self-employed. GPs may decide to treat overseas visitors without charge. Asylum-seekers and those in immigration or prison service detention are entitled to treatment no matter how long they have been living here.[54] NASS will supply asylum-seekers with an HC2 certificate on application, which will entitle the asylum-seeker and his/her dependants to free prescriptions, dental treatment, sight tests, wigs and fabric supports. They may also be entitled to vouchers towards the cost of glasses or contact lenses or travel to hospital for NHS treatment.[55]

3.38 The NHS has adopted directions[56] which prioritise the inclusion of certain groups on transplant programmes. Those in Group 1 include persons ordinarily resident in the UK, members of the armed forces or Crown servants working abroad and employees of the British Council and the Commonwealth War Graves Commission, who are working abroad but were recruited in the UK, and non-British nationals who are entitled to medical treatment under EEC regulations or bilateral health agreements. Everyone else falls under

---

51 National Health Service (Charges to Overseas Visitors) Regulations 1989 SI No 306 as amended by SI 1991 No 438 and SI 1994 No 1535.
52 National Health Service Act 1977 s21.
53 SI No 306. Those subject to immigration control sometimes have difficulties being accepted onto GPs' lists. Any complaint about such discrimination should be raised with the British Medical Association.
54 Ibid reg 4 as amended.
55 See notes to NASS application form.
56 Directions on the Allocation of Human Organs for Transplantation, 12 February 1996, made under the National Health Service Act 1977.

Group 2 and will only be included in a programme if there is no suitable Group 1 recipient. Even if a person is ordinarily resident in the UK, a hospital may be reluctant to admit a person to a programme unless he or she has indefinite leave to remain in case he or she is removed before the necessary follow-up treatment and monitoring is completed.

3.39 Nationals of EEA member states who are temporarily working or studying in the UK, in possession of a Form E128, and their dependants are also entitled to free non-emergency treatment.[57] There are also a number of reciprocal arrangements with EU and EEA states and with Cyprus and Turkey.[58]

Public housing

3.40 As a general rule, anyone who is subject to immigration control cannot register for public housing or be provided with accommodation if he or she is homeless, even if he or she is in priority need due to the presence of children.[59] There are exceptions:

- refugees;
- those with exceptional leave to remain;
- those who have indefinite leave to remain and who are habitually resident here;
- those who fled Montserrat after 1 November 1995 because of the volcanic eruption; and
- nationals of a state which has ratified the European Convention on Social and Medical Assistance or the Council of Europe Social Charter who are lawfully present and habitually resident.[60]

Asylum-seekers who claimed asylum on arrival in the UK before 3 April 2000 and whose applications have not yet been recorded as having been decided are still eligible for temporary accommodation if they are homeless and in priority need and not intentionally homeless.[61]

---

57 Reg 1408/71/EEC; Health Services Circ HSC 1999/018
58 For further details of NHS entitlement, see *Macdonald's Immigration Law and Practice*.
59 IAA 1999 s118.
60 Allocation of Housing (England) Regulations 2000 SI No 702 reg 4; *Kaya v Haringey LBC* [2001]EWCA Civ 677.
61 Homelessness (England) Regulations 2000 SI No 701 reg 3(f).

CHAPTER 4
Human rights

4.1	The relevance of human rights law
4.4	European Convention on Human Rights
4.11	Immigration appeals
4.16	How to apply the ECHR
4.25	Substantive rights

Article 2 • Article 3 • Article 4 • Article 5 • Article 6 • Article 8 • Article 14 • Protocol 1, article 2

The relevance of human rights law

4.1 There are a number of international human rights instruments that are of relevance to cases involving children. These include the Universal Declaration of Human Rights 1948 (UDHR), the International Convention on Civil and Political Rights (ICCPR), European Convention on Human Rights (ECHR) and the UN Convention on the Rights of the Child (UNCRC). As the ECHR has direct effect in courts in the UK, it will be the starting point in most cases.[1] However, other human rights conventions and treaties are useful indications of international standards and good practice[2] and, if they are ignored, can lead to a challenge to the rationality of the decision reached by the Home Secretary or an immigration officer.

4.2 Cases such as *Brind*[3] and *ex p Smith*[4] are relevant when it is necessary to rely on provisions contained in international human rights instruments other than the ECHR. The Court of Appeal has held that when the UK has ratified a treaty, a legitimate expectation will then arise that the government will fulfil its obligations, under that treaty, unless it indicates otherwise by, for instance, publishing a specific policy.[5]

4.3 Furthermore, if the Home Secretary asserts that he or she has taken a treaty into account and has misinterpreted it, this could form the basis for a successful allegation of irrationality.[6]

European Convention on Human Rights

4.4 The ECHR was adopted by the member states of the Council of Europe in 1951, in the wake of the atrocities committed during the Second World War. It meant that its citizens were given the range of rights contained in the UDHR 1948 and could expect these rights to be protected under international public law within Europe.

4.5 Over the next five decades, the European Commission and the

---

1 Keir Starmer, *European Human Rights Law* (LAG, 1999); Jessica Simor and Ben Emmerson QC (eds), *Human Rights Practice* (Sweet & Maxwell, 2001); *Human Rights: The 1998 Act and the European Convention*, Stephen Grosz, Jack Beaston and Peter Duffy (Butterworths, 2000).
2 *Re A (children: UN Declaration 1959)* [1998] 1 FLR 354.
3 *Brind v Home Secretary* [1991] 1 AC 696, HL.
4 *R v Ministry of Defence ex p Smith* [1996] 1 All ER 257, CA.
5 *R v Home Secretary ex p Ahmed and Patel* [1998] INLR 570.
6 *R v Home Secretary ex p Arman Ali* [2000] INLR 89.

European Court of Human Rights created a great deal of case-law, which clarified the practical extent of these rights. This case-law and the ECHR was of direct effect in many other member states, as they had incorporated the ECHR into their domestic law. It is instructive to see how they dealt with a particular situation. The UK declined to incorporate the ECHR until the Human Rights Act (HRA) 1998 was passed, and the convention was incorporated into UK domestic law with effect from 2 October 2000.

4.6 Prior to incorporation, breaches of the ECHR could not be relied upon in appeals against an adverse immigration or asylum decision. But, over time, breaches became a relevant consideration in judicial review cases.

4.7 The developments in European human rights law inevitably influenced domestic common law in areas such as immigration and asylum law where freedom of expression, the right to family life or fear of persecution were often involved. Many judges also believed that many of the rights and freedoms contained in the ECHR were already protected by the domestic common law. This was acknowledged by the House of Lords in 1991 when it stated that although it could not give direct effect to the ECHR when deciding a case, it could find that a decision by a secretary of state had been unreasonable if he or she had not taken into account the breaches of the ECHR which could occur as a result of a decision.[7] It also found that the ECHR could be used to interpret a provision of a statute if there appeared to be an ambiguity in it. This approach was further developed by the Court of Appeal in 1996, in a case which involved the prohibition on homosexuality in the armed forces.[8] There it was stated that the more a decision would lead to a substantial interference with a person's human rights, the greater the need for a decision-maker to justify him or herself.

4.8 However, as the Court of Appeal pointed out in *ex p Smith*, the range of possibly reasonable responses by a secretary of state is very wide and, therefore, judicial review was of limited value as a forum to challenge adverse decisions, which led to a clear breach of an individual's human rights. In practice, the courts were usually only willing to quash a decision when it was not just unreasonable but also perverse. For example, in *Turgut*,[9] Simon Brown LJ stated that although he had a lingering sense of unease about a failed asylum-seeker being returned to Turkey without a passport, in the light of that country's

---

7 *Brind v Home Secretary* [1991] 1 AC 696, HL.
8 *R v Ministry of Defence ex p Smith* [1996] 1 All ER 257, CA.
9 *R v Home Secretary ex p Abdullah Turgut* [2000] INLR 292.

grave human rights record, the Home Secretary was not irrational in finding that there had been no breach of ECHR art 3. In the same case, Schiemann LJ concluded that the Home Secretary would not have been perverse to have concluded that there had been a breach of ECHR art 3 on the evidence before him.

4.9 In terms of judicial review, the incorporation of the ECHR has not resulted in radical changes. The Court of Appeal is still prepared to permit the executive to retain a large measure of discretion in relation to policy decisions.[10] It has also stated that the HRA 1998 does not authorise it to substitute its own decision for that of the decision-maker.[11]

4.10 However, the House of Lords has held that courts must now ensure that decisions taken by the executive are proportionate, not merely reasonable in the *Wednesbury* sense.[12] This requires them to assess the balancing exercise carried out by the decision-maker and the relative weight given to the different interests and considerations at play.

Immigration appeals

4.11 Prior to the HRA 1998 coming into force, the ECHR could only be relied on as the basis upon which to challenge the rationality of a decision by way of an application for judicial review. It could not be relied upon in any way in the Immigration Appellate Authority courts. This changed on 2 October 2000, when the HRA 1998 and Immigration and Asylum Act 1999 s65 came into force.

4.12 Since 2 October 2000, if the Home Secretary refuses to grant a person leave to remain, that person can appeal on the usual immigration grounds to the Immigration Appellate Authority (or, if relevant, to the Special Immigration Appeals Commissioner).[13] He or she will,

---

10 *R v Home Secretary ex p Isiko* [2001] INLR 175.
11 *R on the application of Mahmood v Home Secretary* [2001] INLR 1.
12 *R v Home Secretary ex p Daly* [2000] 2 AC 532, HL.
13 Attempts are being made to preclude applicants from appealing under IAA 1999 s73 as a result of *R on the application of Kariharan v Home Secretary* [2001] EWCA Admin 1004. There is conflicting judicial opinion in *Kumarakuraparan v Secretary of State for the Home Department* [2002] EWHC 112 Admin. The SSHD appears to believe there is a right as he proposes to restrict the right of appeal under IAA 1999 s65 to certain specified immigration cases. See SBSH para 4.63. There is also no right of appeal against any decision taken by airline liaison officers or airline officials. This is a serious lacuna given the use of airline liaison officers in preventing foreign nationals from travelling to the UK to seek protection under the Refugee Convention or entry in accordance with the ECHR, for example, the special operation in the Czech Republic, which effectively prevents Roma from travelling to the UK.

4.13 at the same time, be served with an Immigration and Asylum Act (IAA) 1999 s74 or s75 notice requiring him/her to set out details of any alleged breach of the ECHR.

4.13 The process is different for port applicants. Apart from asylum-seekers (who will be served with an IAA 1999 s74 notice at the same time as being served with a notice of refusal of asylum), those alleging a breach of their ECHR rights have to make a formal written assertion, the response to which generates the appeal.[14]

4.14 Where an application for entry clearance has been refused, the alleged breach of ECHR rights should be incorporated in the grounds of appeal. The grounds should briefly particularise the factual basis of the alleged breach and how this amounts to a breach of an identified article of the ECHR. Subsequent skeleton arguments, witness statements and any examination in chief should amplify this. If this is not done, it is very difficult to appeal against any dismissal of the appeal or contend that any decision was disproportionate.

4.15 If the existence of an alleged breach of the ECHR is not raised in a response to an IAA 1999 s74 or s75 notice, this does not mean that the appellant is automatically barred from raising it at the appeal hearing.[15] However, if a breach is not raised within the appeal process at all and that appeal has been determined, the Home Secretary can prevent any further appeal on human rights grounds by issuing a certificate.[16]

How to apply the ECHR

4.16 The ECHR provides individuals with two very different types of rights. They have an *absolute* right to protection in relation to some of the rights, and a *qualified* right to protection in relation to the others.

4.17 The Home Secretary cannot apply to derogate absolute rights, even in times of war or other public emergency threatening the lives of those in the UK.[17] There is an absolute prohibition on:

- torture and the infliction of inhuman and degrading treatment (article 3);
- slavery (article 4); and
- prosecuting a person for an act or omission which occurred before such behaviour amounted to a criminal offence (article 7).

14 This procedure is cumbersome. SBSH para 4.62 proposes simplification.
15 IAA 1999 s76(3).
16 Ibid s73.
17 Under ECHR art 15.

4.18 The other rights contained in the ECHR can be proscribed in certain specific circumstances and are, therefore, only qualified rights. For example, in relation to ECHR art 8, a decision-maker may be able to justify a breach of the right to family or private life, if he or she can show that the breach is in the interests of national security, public safety or the economic well-being of the country, for the prevention of disorder or crime, for the protection of health or morals, or for the protection of the rights and freedoms of others. Even then, the state will have to show that the breach was necessary in a democratic society and proportionate.

4.19 It is important that the decision-maker considers qualified rights in a methodical manner. He or she must first decide whether a breach of the ECHR will occur and then consider whether the breach can be justified in the light of the qualifications given to the breadth of that right in the convention.[18]

4.20 When considering a case, a court or tribunal must take into account any relevant decisions made by the European Court of Human Rights or the Commission, but does not necessarily have to follow them.[19] However, it is likely that great weight will be given to previous relevant decisions by these two bodies. There is also a growing body of authority now being developed in the Court of Appeal in both immigration and family cases which is of direct relevance.[19a]

4.21 The HRA 1998 enables an individual, whose ECHR rights have been breached, to use the convention as both a sword and a shield, either by bringing proceedings against a public authority on this ground or by defending any action that might be brought. In immigration cases, when enforcement action is taken, an asserted breach of an ECHR right generally gives rise to a right of appeal to the Immigration Appellate Authority.[20] The mechanism for using the Act as a sword is more cumbersome. For example, a child who wishes to come to the UK as a dependant must first make an application for entry clearance. If he or she does not meet the requirement of the Immigration Rules then he or she will be refused and will have to assert the breach of ECHR rights in the grounds of appeal.

4.22 In immigration cases, there is no right to use the ECHR as a

---

18 *R v Home Secretary ex p Zighem* [1996] Imm AR 194; *Nhundu & Chiwera* (01/TH/0613).
19 HRA 1998 s2.
19a *R on the application of Mahmood v Secretary of State for the Home Department* [2001] INLR 1; *Nuruwa* (00/TH/2345); *Payne v Payne* [2001] 1 FCR 424.
20 IAA 1999 s65 but see also note 13 above.

4.23 defence against enforcement action or any other adverse decision, unless that decision was made after the HRA 1998 came into force.[21]

4.23 The Home Secretary has often asserted that rights under the ECHR have no extra-territorial effect, and has argued that the Immigration Appellate Authority does not need to consider whether a breach of the ECHR will occur once the appellant has left or been removed from the UK. However, there is a wealth of authority in the European Court of Human Rights which suggests this is not the case. The Immigration Appeal Tribunal takes the same view as the ECtHR.[22]

4.24 Evidence of post-decision facts is admissible in an ECHR art 3 case if the evidence is relevant. In relation to other articles, it is admissible only if it relates to facts which were relevant and available at the date of the decision.[23]

Substantive rights

Article 2

4.25 Member states are required to protect an individual's right to life. The European Court of Human Rights has held that ECHR art 2 imposes a positive duty on states.[24] The use of the death penalty is also now prohibited except in times of war or imminent threat of war.[25] The High Court in Northern Ireland has also quashed a decision of the Home Secretary to remove an applicant to his country of origin, when this was likely to lead to an attempt to commit suicide.[26]

4.26 This article is likely to be relevant when a child is going to be returned to a country where there is a real risk that he or she will be killed. One example would be returning children, who have been separated from their families, to Colombia, where street children are regularly rounded up and killed by paramilitaries working closely with government forces to clear the street of 'undesirables'.

4.27 It would also be relevant where a child was being returned to a country which not only still used the death penalty, but also did not prohibit the execution of minors.

---

21 IAA 1999 (Commencement No 6 and Transitional Provisions) Order 2000 SI No 2444; *Pardeepan v Home Secretary* [2000] INLR 447.
22 *Home Secretary v Kacaj* [2001] INLR 354. An appeal to the Court of Appeal on another ground was dismissed and the IAT's other findings were not overturned.
23 IAA 1999 s77.
24 *Osman v UK* (2000) 29 EHRR 245.
25 Optional protocol 6, which was ratified by the UK on 17 January 1999.
26 *Re Thomas* (2000) 1 September, NI HC.

4.28 Cases where ECHR art 2 is relevant will usually also engage ECHR art 3. As a result, case-law on this article is limited, as the European Court of Human Rights has tended to consider ECHR art 3 first and, if it has found that there will be a breach, does not go on to consider ECHR art 2.

Article 3

4.29 Article 3 imposes an absolute prohibition on torture and inhuman and degrading treatment.[27] Such treatment can arise in two ways. First, as the result of action which is taken by a government or other state body, or second, on account of the circumstances in which an individual will live if returned to another country.

4.30 In either case, it will be necessary for the individual concerned to establish that there are substantial grounds for believing that there is a real risk that such treatment will occur.[28] This standard of proof has been held to be comparable to that applied in an asylum appeal.[29]

4.31 When the treatment will not occur as a result of state action, the European Court of Human Rights has held that the court must subject the circumstances surrounding the case to rigorous scrutiny and, in particular, look at the applicant's personal situation in the expelling state.[30] In the same case, it held that ECHR art 3 imposed a high threshold and that the evidence that he or she would be subjected to inhuman and degrading treatment needed to be more than speculative. As it is more likely that children will claim the protection of ECHR art 3 when they are faced with removal to a country where their circumstances would of themselves arise to inhuman and degrading treatment, this is an unfortunate decision. Practitioners must therefore be aware of the need to produce very persuasive evidence when seeking to rely on ECHR art 3.

4.32 For example, where a child has HIV positive status and is to be returned to a country where there is no retro-viral or palliative treatment available, it would not be sufficient to rely on medical evidence from doctors here doubting the availability of treatment abroad. Expert evidence will need to be produced on exactly what would be available to that child and the effect of withdrawal of anti-retroviral

---

27 *Chahal v UK* (1997) 23 EHRR 413.
28 Ibid.
29 *Home Secretary v Kacaj* [2001] INLR 354. The standards of proof required in medical cases appear to be higher.
30 *Bensaid v UK* [2001] INLR 325.

treatment or lack of palliative care. In one case, the Court of Appeal also commented that the UK could not be expected to provide facilities for anyone who could not afford the medical treatment in their country of origin.[31] However, this comment was made in the course of a renewed application for judicial review, not a full appeal. The Home Secretary also relies on a decision by the European Court of Human Rights, which reached a similar conclusion.[32] However, again, this was just an admissibility determination and not the result of a full hearing. Prohibited treatment can take the form of mental, as well as physical, ill-treatment.[33]

4.33 The courts should now expect a greater appreciation of the need to prohibit a range of forms of ill-treatment, which may once have been thought to be acceptable. For instance, the interrogation techniques used in Northern Ireland, which were the subject of the application to the European Court, may now be thought to be forms of torture, not merely inhuman treatment. It is also important to note that the ECHR is to be interpreted as a living instrument, which responds to increasingly high standards in relation to the protection of an individual's human rights.[34]

Article 4

4.34 Slavery and servitude is absolutely prohibited by ECHR art 4 and forced or compulsory labour is only permissible in very limited circumstances, such as when an individual is serving a prison sentence, completing military service or performing a civic obligation.

4.35 Many children are presently enslaved or being forced to undertake forced labour in many parts of the world and, therefore, this article may become increasingly useful. One example is where children have been forced to join the army or militia in their country of origin. It is a violation of international law for an army to recruit any child under the age of 15.[35] For example, in Angola young men have been being press-ganged into the army even though they are under age. In other African states, there is no minimum age limit for military service.[36] These children have usually been separated from their families or

---

31 *R v Home Secretary ex p K* [2001] Imm AR 11.
32 *SSC v Sweden* App 46553/99 (2000) 29 EHRR CD245.
33 *Ireland v UK* (1979–80) 2 EHRR 25.
34 *Selmouni v France* (2000) 7 BHRC 1.
35 UNCRC art 38, protocol 1, art 77 and Geneva Convention 1949 protocol II, art 4.
36 See *Human Rights Watch World Report* 2000 on child soldiers.

their families have been killed and, therefore, if they were returned to their country of origin, they are likely to be forced to rejoin the army.

4.36 Young girls (and sometimes boys) are vulnerable to traffickers who are working for the sex industry in European cities. Like the child soldiers they will often be children who are living alone or who are particularly vulnerable. This means that even if they escape from the traffickers in Europe, they are likely to be vulnerable to the trafficking gangs if returned to their country of origin. This will particularly be the case for Nigerian children, due to the large number of trafficking gangs operating there and also to children in the Baltic and Eastern European states, where the mafia's influence is particularly strong.

4.37 Children[37] are not capable of giving informed consent to involvement in prostitution. Their participation can be classified as forced labour. It is also a breach of international law to coerce or induce a child to take part in unlawful sexual activity, prostitution or pornography.[38] In most cases, it will not be necessary to raise this argument, because there will be clear evidence of the children being coerced into taking part in these activities.

4.38 The experience of minors being brought in from the Baltic and Eastern European states is that if they do not comply with the traffickers they will be subjected to severe physical punishment. Traffickers in the Nigerian rings rely on psychological coercion. They pick on vulnerable young women and, often, young women who are trying to escape from one of the many cults which exist in Nigeria. The girls' beliefs are used to control them, threatening that if they try to escape or tell anyone what they are being asked to do, they will die or be injured.

4.39 Many other children are being brought in as unpaid domestic slaves. A recent report has identified children being trafficked into domestic slavery through a ring operating from Nigeria via Ireland.[39] They are expected to work all day every day caring for young children and doing the housework. They are often forced to live on the floor and are given the minimum in terms of food and clothing. Again, these children will be vulnerable even if they are removed from the

---

37 However, in practice the police treat children involved in the sex industry aged between 16 and 18 as adults and, depending on the circumstances, they may be treated as culpable at an even younger age, rather than as the victims of crime. This is illustrated by the police approach to the well publicised raids in Soho, London in February 2002. Some of the victims were aged under 18 but were not referred to Social Services.

38 UNCRC arts 32, 34 and 35.

39 *Today*, BBC Radio 4, 19 December 2001.

> **Example: Trafficking**
>
> Both of Lula's parents died of AIDS-related illnesses in her country of origin in Africa and she became involved in a violent and sexually abusive cult. She was 'rescued' by an older man, who said that he would take her to Europe where she could obtain a good job. He told her that as long as she did everything he told her and did not tell anyone who she had travelled to the UK with, she would be safe and the spirits invoked by the cult could not harm her.
>
> She entered the UK illegally and was imprisoned in a house in London with a number of other teenagers and forced to act as a prostitute. She escaped some months later and was taken into care by a London local authority. Some months later, she told her caseworker the full story of her arrival and life in London. The next day, she slipped and fell down the stairs, at the children's home where she was living, and believed that she was being punished by the spirits for revealing her past.
>
> She made contact with the people who had brought her to London and they arranged for her to move to Italy to 'work'. However, she was stopped at Dover, in the company of an older man, and placed with supportive foster carers. She was subsequently granted exceptional leave to remain on the basis that, if she were returned to her country of origin, she may again fall into the hands of the traffickers who had brought her to London. The man who had been taking her to Italy was released without charge.

household enslaving them and returned to their country of origin. This is because these children have sometimes been sold into servitude by their families in order to provide for other members of the family or in order to provide an income in remittances to the family in the future.

4.40 *Secure Borders, Safe Haven* (SBSH) chapter 5 recognises the increased incidence of people trafficking for sexual exploitation and proposes introducing a new offence of trafficking for the purpose of sexual exploitation with a maximum sentence of 14 years. There is also recognition of the need to protect and assist the victim but there are not as yet any proposals to grant leave to remain to the victims of trafficking in recognition of their trauma and vulnerability. In practice many trafficked children are granted exceptional leave to remain.

4.41 The UNCRC places a duty on signatories to take steps to prevent

Article 5

4.42 Article 5 prohibits unlawful arrest and detention but art 5(1)(f) does permit the lawful arrest and detention of a person to prevent him/her from effecting an unauthorised entry into the UK or of a person against whom action is being taken with a view to deportation or removal.[42]

4.43 The lawfulness of any such detention may be fatally undermined if the person in question is a minor. The UN Commissioner for Refugees' view is that detention of an unaccompanied asylum-seeker can never be justified and that where a child is accompanied by a parent, an appropriate alternative to detention should be sought.[43] It is not policy or practice to detain minors who have claimed asylum or have sought leave to enter or remain. Unlike in the United States for instance, such children are seen to be the responsibility of the appropriate local authority social services department, not the Immigration Service.

4.44 Nevertheless, because of the Home Secretary's belief that many asylum-seekers pretend to be minors in order to avoid being interviewed or dispersed, many children have been held unlawfully in a number of prisons and detention centres. The burden of proof lies on the child to prove that he or she is not an adult and as it may be very difficult to obtain papers confirming their age, children will often spend quite a long time in detention. It is the understanding of the British Medical Association that it is extremely difficult to assess accurately the age of a child and almost impossible to do so when a child is between 15 and 18 years old.[44] Therefore, reports from paediatricians are of limited value.

---

40 UNCRC arts 32, 34 and 35.
41 See www.europa.eu.int/eur-lex/en/com/pdf/2002/en-502PC0071.pdf. Council directive on the short-term residence permit issued to victims of actions to facilitate illegal immigration or trafficking in human beings who co-operate with the competent authorities (2002/0043(CNS)).
42 *Saadi v Home Secretary* [2001] EWCA Civ 1512; [2001] 4 All ER 461.
43 Guideline 6 of the *UNHCR Revised Guidelines on applicable Criteria and Standards Relating to the Detention of Asylum-Seekers*, February 1999.
44 Letter from the BMA to Association of Visitors to Immigration Detainees, 28 May 1998. See also para 5.15.

4.45   It was previously the policy of the Home Secretary only to detain children who were accompanied by parents or carers for a very short time after all appeal rights had been exhausted and their deportation or removal was to occur within the next few days.[45] Even then, very few children were detained, as there was only very limited family accommodation. A change to this policy was announced on 25 October 2001:

> ... the increase in family detention accommodation [at Harmondsworth, Yarl's Wood and Dungavel] will allow the detention of those families whose circumstances justify this (ie, a risk of absconding, identities and claims that need to be clarified pre-removal) but who are not detained at present because they fall outside the detention criteria as qualified for families.[46]

4.46   There will initially be 200 bed spaces for families, excluding accommodation at Oakington, and it is clear from the criteria that children and their families could be detained at any point during the asylum process, not merely the period immediately before removal. Families will be held in a separate part of the detention centre from that used for adults without children, but this will still expose them to possible abuse from adults outside their own family.[47] School-rooms have been provided within the detention centres but, at present, it does not appear that funds have been made available to provide the necessary interpreters and translators to make education in any real sense possible.[48] This may lead to challenges under ECHR protocol 1, art 2. Challenges may also be possible under ECHR art 5 if the period of detention becomes unreasonable.[49]

4.47   The UK has derogated from ECHR art 5 in relation to those certified by the Home Secretary as international terrorists, which means that such individuals can be detained indefinitely.[50] These detainees are being held in high security prisons (category A) and family members visiting them are being subjected to intensive strip-searching, with visits only taking place in closed conditions.

---

45 *Fairer, Faster and Firmer – A Modern Approach to Immigration and Asylum*, Cm 4018, White Paper, para 12.5.
46 Letter from the IND to 'Bail for Immigration Detainees', 25 October 2001. SBSH para 4.71 confirms that it is now Home Office policy that children may be detained for longer periods.
47 In practice this has exposed children to all the dangers contingent in being placed with traumatised and desperate adults who may resort to violence, as has been seen by the fire at Yarlswood on 15 February 2002.
48 Home Office Detention User Group, 12 November 2001.
49 *R v Governor of Durham Prison ex p Hardial Singh* [1984] 1 WLR 704 and *Tan Te Lam v Superintendent of Tai A Chau Detention Centre* [1997] AC 97.
50 Anti-Terrorism, Crime and Security Act 2001 s23.

Article 6

4.48 Article 6 provides a right to a fair and public hearing in both criminal courts and in other courts where an individual's civil rights and obligations are being decided. The European Court of Human Rights has held that ECHR art 6 does not apply to administrative decisions relating to entry into or removal from a member state because there is no civil right to enter or remain in a country of which the individual is not a national.[51] However, the Immigration Appeal Tribunal has stated that when it is considering any complaint that an adjudicator has not conducted an appeal hearing fairly, it would apply the same tests as those contained in ECHR art 6.[52]

4.49 If a case engages issues of family life and, therefore, ECHR art 8, the ECHR art 6 will apply. For example, in a recent case in the European Court of Human Rights, the court held that there had been a breach of ECHR art 6 when a father in a contact matter had not been permitted to obtain expert evidence or adduce oral evidence on appeal.[53]

4.50 It has been held that an individual should be allowed to remain in the UK in order to bring a civil action for malicious prosecution against the Home Secretary on the basis that removal would interfere with his/her right to have the proper time and facilities to prepare for a hearing.[54] One practical application of ECHR art 6 is when, for example, a parent is involved in care or private law family proceedings and is served with removal directions or is subject to a deportation order. It can be asserted that such removal would be in breach of ECHR art 6, as it would prevent him/her from attending the hearing, giving evidence or giving instructions. In general, the Home Secretary permits parents to remain in order to attend such proceedings, but there may be problems when a parent has a particularly poor immigration history or when his/her chance of success in the family court is very low.

Article 8

4.51 Article 8 is the right to respect for private or family life and home and moral and physical integrity. This article is the one of most obvious relevance to cases involving families. The European Court of Human

---

51 *Maaouia v France* (2001) 9 BHRC 205.
52 *MNM v Home Secretary* [2000] INLR 576.
53 *Elsholz v Germany* [2000] 2 FLR 486.
54 *R v Immigration Officer ex p Quaquah* [2000] INLR 196.

Example: Contact

Ali, a Kenyan, entered the UK illegally in 1995 and was removed in 1996, after being discovered working illegally in a supermarket. He returned again illegally in 1997. Two months later he met Joan at a nightclub, and they started a relationship. He soon realised that she was suffering from some form of mental illness, as she had periods when her speech was disordered. However, the relationship developed and he believed that she was improving because of this.

Six months later, she became pregnant and her condition deteriorated. He then learnt that she had been diagnosed with schizophrenia some years before and had previously spent time in a series of psychiatric hospitals. It was decided to re-admit her to one of these one week later. Shortly afterwards, Ali was discovered working illegally in a clothing warehouse and detained. He was only subsequently granted temporary admission because of Joan's illness. However, he was not permitted to work and was dependent on support in the form of vouchers from his local authority. Their child, Ryan, was subsequently born four months later. By that time, Joan's condition had not improved and social services had become involved and had decided to apply for an interim care order.

An interim order was granted and the local authority informed Ali that he could have one hour's supervised contact with Ryan each week, as they were concerned about his uncertain immigration status. He maintained this contact with Ryan for the next nine months even though he had to walk five miles to the contact centre and found it very depressing and limiting. Joan's mother, Dora, who was sixty years old, put herself forward as an alternative permanent placement for Ryan. Ali applied for a contact order, but was in no position to apply for a residence order, as he was living in a hostel. Dora opposed Ali having continuing contact with Ryan.

At the final care hearing, Dora was granted a residence order for Ryan, but the judge was impressed by Ali's commitment to Ryan and ordered that he have unsupervised contact with him for three hours per week. In making the order, he stressed the need for Ryan, as a mixed-race child, to know and have contact with both his birth families. He also noted Dora's age and stated that it may be that in the future Ali would need to play a larger part in Ryan's life.

An order for disclosure of this very positive judgment was obtained and forwarded to the Immigration and Nationality Department and Ali was granted exceptional leave to remain.

Example: Asylum, discretion, art 8, care order, residence order

Danielle was a two-year-old Senegalese national. Her father, Christopher, was also from Senegal and was a failed asylum-seeker who had gone underground for fear of arrest. He was married to Danielle's mother, Marie, but they separated just before she was born. Marie was also from Senegal and had also applied for asylum and been refused. Marie and Christopher had been in the UK since 1994. Christopher saw Danielle every couple of weeks or so from when she was born until she was about 12 months old.

When Danielle was 12 months old she was placed on the 'at risk' register as a result of bruising. When she was 14 months old she was admitted to hospital with severe injuries including fractured skull, leg, arm and severe bruising. Care proceedings were issued. Marie was charged with attempted murder and remanded in custody pending hearing. She was convicted, when Danielle was 19 months old, of grievous bodily harm and other offences. She was sentenced to imprisonment, the sentence commencing during the care proceedings.

Danielle was placed with foster parents. The guardian ad litem argued that Christopher should have contact only. Christopher argued for care and control. After much expert evidence a residence order was made in favour of Christopher for Danielle with occasional supervised contact to Marie while she remained in prison. (Marie had a history of violence towards supervising social workers during contact visits prior to the criminal hearing, on one occasion throwing the child's dinner at the social worker.)

An application was made for Danielle and Christopher to be granted indefinite leave to remain. After a lengthy battle, this was won.

Two years later, when Danielle was four years old, Marie, having been released from prison, was awaiting removal from the UK as a failed asylum-seeker. She applied for a residence order for the child, or alternatively a contact order. This was refused. An application for leave to remain on her part failed. A combination of her behaviour and the lack of contact with Danielle after her release from prison meant that she could not sustain her claim that there was family life worthy of protection.

Rights has recognised that a family relationship may arise between a child and either parent on conception.[55] It has also accepted that family life continues even if different members of the family are not cohabiting.[56] In the same case, the court recognised that where a young child is concerned, the contact needed to sustain a family relationship will need to be direct and that it would be difficult for such a child to maintain any meaningful relationship with a parent if the only contact was by letter or telephone.

4.52 Article 8 does not provide an absolute right to family and private life and the court will consider whether there are any wider public interest factors, such as national security, public safety, the economic well-being of the country, the need to prevent disorder or crime, the protection of health or morals or the protection of the rights and freedoms of others, which would justify a breach. It will be for the decision-maker to decide whether, in the light of these wider factors, there is actually a need to breach the individual's rights. He or she will then have to decide whether the harm caused to the individual will be proportionate.

4.53 A court or tribunal considering whether breach of ECHR art 8 would occur should consider each of these separate requirements of ECHR art 8 before reaching its decision.[57] It has also been held that the question of the proportionality of the decision is a matter of law for an appellate court to decide and that it is not sufficient just to consider whether a decision was *Wednesbury* reasonable.[58]

4.54 In determining whether a breach of ECHR art 8 has occurred, the interests of the child will clearly be central. The Court of Appeal has confirmed that in private law matters, there is no conflict between the need to respect the ECHR art 8 rights of a child and the principle that the interests of the child are paramount.[59] However, the courts have, in the past, been unwilling to accept that a child's rights are paramount when they compete with the public interest in immigration control.[60]

4.55 Article 8 does not provide an individual with the right to choose where he or she wishes to exercise his/her right to enjoy a family or private life.[61] If both the child in question and his/her other family

---

55 *Keegan v Ireland* [1994] 3 FCR 165. See also *Ciliz v Netherlands* [2000] 2 FLR 469.
56 *Berrehab v Netherlands* (1989) 11 EHRR 322.
57 *Nhundu and Chiwera*, 01/TH/613.
58 *B v Home Secretary* [2000] INLR 361, CA. See also *Nuruwa*, 00/TH/2345.
59 *Payne v Payne* [2001] 1 FCR 424.
60 *R v Home Secretary ex p Begum* [1996] Imm AR 582.
61 *Abdulaziz v UK* (1985) 7 EHRR 471.

members share the same nationality or would be able to live together in another country and all do not have the right to remain in the UK, a breach of ECHR art 8 will not occur if they are all removed together to that country. Although *Sorabjee*[62] (an admissibility decision by the European Commission), held that this was the case even if the child in question was a British citizen, there is still an arguable challenge depending on the length of time the child has lived in the UK.

4.56 The Court of Appeal has also held that where a couple marry in the knowledge that one partner has no entitlement to vary his/her leave, while they were still in the UK, no breach of ECHR art 8 would occur if they were obliged to leave the country in order to apply for entry clearance.[63] This case sets out the approach to be taken in determining the potential conflict between the enforcement of immigration control and the ECHR.

- A state has a right under international law to control the entry of non-nationals into its territory, subject always to its treaty obligations.
- Article 8 does not impose on a state any general obligation to respect the choice of residence of a married couple.
- Removal or exclusion of one family member from a state where other members of the family are lawfully resident will not necessarily infringe ECHR art 8 provided that there are no insurmountable obstacles to the family living together in the country of origin of the family member excluded, even where this involves a degree of hardship for some or all members of the family.
- Article 8 is likely to be violated by the expulsion of a member of a family that has been long established in a state if the circumstances are such that it is not reasonable to expect the other members of the family to follow the member expelled.
- Knowledge on the part of one spouse at the time of the marriage that the rights of residence of the other were precarious militates against a finding that an order excluding the latter spouse violates ECHR art 8.
- Whether interference with family rights is justified in the interests of controlling immigration will depend on:
  – The facts of the particular case; and
  – The circumstances prevailing in the state whose actions are impugned.

---

62 *Sorabjee* App 239938/93 (1995) unreported.
63 *R (on the application of) Mahmood v Home Secretary* [2001] INLR 1.

> **Example: Right to private life/home of unaccompanied minor**
>
> Tina, a Colombian, was brought up abroad by her grandmother. She was sent to the UK when she was 13, to join her mother who had applied for asylum here. Her mother was refused asylum and removed and was murdered on her return to Colombia. On arrival in the UK, Tina went to live with her maternal aunt and uncle. Her uncle sexually assaulted her and Tina went into voluntary care. Tina's grandmother rejected her for making the allegations against her uncle. She was accommodated by the local authority. Tina made an application for asylum in her own right.
>
> It was not until Tina had just turned 18 years old that her asylum application was refused. An extensive statement of additional grounds was submitted, stressing among other points, that the UK was Tina's only home and, given her age, and the particularly difficult circumstances of her past, was of particular significance to her. In addition, although Tina had no family in the UK, she had been given extensive support by social services since she had left care, and she had formed strong friendships during her teenage years in the UK. These were sufficient to demonstrate a private life worthy of respect under ECHR art 8.

4.57 The European Court of Human Rights has so far limited the definition of family to exclude same-sex partners, but accepts that they have a right to enjoy a private life which is protected by ECHR art 8.[64] Article 8 also protects the right to physical and psychological integrity and imposes a much lower threshold for physical ill-treatment than ECHR art 3.[65] This aspect of ECHR art 8 could be used to protect children against sexual abuse[66] or excessive corporal punishment.[67]

4.58 The right to respect for private life and home may also be relevant to unaccompanied minors. They will usually have been accommodated by a local social services department with a foster carer. They will often have been with that carer for a number of years before their immigration status is resolved. They may have developed close ties with these carers, with fellow students at school and in the local community. Their home in the UK will be the only home they know.

---

64 *Lustig Prean v UK* (2000) 29 EHRR 548. The UK courts have been more progressive in this respect, see *Fitzpatrick v Sterling Housing Association Limited* [2001] 1 AC 27.
65 *Raninen v Finland* (1998) 26 EHRR 563.
66 *X and Y v Netherlands* (1986) 8 EHRR 235.
67 *Costello-Roberts v UK* (1995) 19 EHRR 112.

> **Example: Right to private life**
>
> Juanita, a South African born in 1983, arrived in the UK in 1992 as an unaccompanied minor after her extended family had been massacred. On arrival, she was placed in a children's home in Sussex and has remained there ever since. She has no relatives in this country and has had very little contact with any South Africans since she came here. She attended a local secondary school and sang in the church choir twice a week. She also helped at the local riding stables on Saturday and Sunday, in return for free tuition and hoped to study to be a riding instructor in the future.
>
> She was very popular at school and around the village, where she had made many good friends. However, the local authority neglected to apply for her immigration status to be regularised and, therefore, when she became 18, the Home Secretary made removal directions for her to be returned to South Africa.
>
> She appealed against this decision on the basis that removal would breach her right to enjoy a private life under ECHR art 8. At her appeal hearing, the proprietor of the riding school, the local vicar, a number of social workers and students from her school, the village postmistress and many parents of her friends gave evidence on her behalf and the adjudicator held that it would be disproportionate for her to be removed to South Africa in the light of the social relationships she had developed here and the fact that, if she were removed, she would have no social or family networks to support her.

In contrast, they may have very little, if any, family to return to abroad. This may be because their families have been killed in a civil war or have had to flee persecution. It may also be that there are doubts about the family's ability to care for and protect the child in any event. In such cases, it can be argued that to remove them would be a disproportionate response. Recently, under domestic law, an elderly woman, who had lived in a residential home for a number of years and believed that she would be able to spend the remainder of her life there, successfully argued that it would be a breach of ECHR art 8 to move her to another residential home against her wishes.[68] The European Court of Human Rights has also held that respect for private life must also comprise to a certain degree the right to establish and develop relationships with other human beings.[69]

---

68 *R v North and East Devon Health Authority ex p Coughlan* (1999) 2 CCLR 284.
69 *Niemietz v Germany* (1993) 16 EHRR 97.

Article 14

4.59 Article 14 prohibits discrimination on a large number of grounds. Age is not specifically mentioned but there is a reference to 'other status' at the end of the definition and age could come within this category.[70] There is a current European Commission proposal for a common definition of a refugee that includes reference to age as being the basis for an application as a member of a particular social group.[71]

4.60 This article is not freestanding and has to be linked to an alleged breach of another article of the ECHR, but it is not necessary for that breach to be proved before discrimination can be found to have occurred.[72]

4.61 Discrimination can be said to have taken place if there has been inequality of treatment, which has no objective or rational basis.[73] It is necessary, therefore, to consider the aim and the effect of any proposed measure and consider whether the means employed are proportionate to the proposed aim. Indirect as well as direct discrimination is prohibited.[74]

4.62 However, the exclusion of children of unmarried British fathers from an automatic right to British citizenship has been held not to be a breach of ECHR art 14.[75]

Protocol 1, article 2

4.63 This article provides a right to education in certain circumstances. It is not an absolute right. It provides a right of access to such educational establishments as may exist[76] and a right to official recognition of academic qualifications. Since all member states had a system of elementary education in place when the protocol was opened for signature, the court has limited this right to a right of access to primary education to about the age of 12. It also provides a right to effective, but not necessarily the *most* effective education. It does not give rise to

---

70 See Karon Monaghan, 'Limitations and Opportunities: A review of the Likely Domestic Impact of Article 14 ECHR' [2001] EHRLR 167.
71 Proposal for a Council Directive on Minimum Standards on Procedures in Member States for Granting and Withdrawing Refugee Status 500PCO578.
72 *Belgian Linguistic Case (No 2)* (1979–80) 1 EHRR 252.
73 Ibid.
74 *Thlimmenos v Greece* (2001) 31 EHRR 15.
75 *R on the application of Mario Montano v Home Secretary* [2001] INLR 148.
76 *Belgian Linguistic Case (No 2)* (1979–80) 1 EHRR 252.

a right to be educated in any particular country. The Court of Appeal recently held that returning a Polish child to Poland and, therefore, causing her to suffer some educational detriment was not a breach of the protocol.[77]

> **Example: The right to education**
>
> At one of the new IND detention centres, a fully-equipped schoolroom has been provided for children aged between five and 16, who are detained with their parents. Two teachers have also been employed. No resources have been allocated to engage interpreters, nor have any of the educational materials been translated into the languages likely to be spoken by the children.
>
> Rafiq, who is eight years old, alleges that his rights under ECHR protocol 1, art 2 have been breached, as he is being denied access to education. He has been in the centre for six months, as his father, who is an asylum-seeker, has a history of failures to comply with reporting restrictions imposed by the IND. He is advised to challenge this lack of provision in the Administrative Court and that his application is likely to be successful.

---

77 *Holub & Holub v Home Secretary* [2001] INLR 219.

CHAPTER 5
Family aspects of asylum

5.1	Introduction
5.2	**The family**
5.3	**Divorce**
5.5	Where the family has limited leave
5.7	Where the family is settled
5.8	**Domestic violence**
5.9	**Unaccompanied children**
5.10	Returnability of children
5.15	Disputed age
5.16	Trafficked children
5.17	Where child is a refugee or has exceptional leave to remain
5.19	Where a child's immigration status is unknown
5.23	**Where sponsor is an asylum-seeker**
5.25	**Mixed applications**
5.27	**Where sponsor is a refugee**
5.27	Dependants in the UK
5.35	Dependants outside the UK
5.38	**Where sponsor has exceptional leave**
5.39	Dependants in the UK
5.43	Dependants outside the UK

continued

5.44	Where a person is recognised as a refugee in another country
5.45	Unmarried partners
5.46	Divorce and separation
5.47	Failed asylum-seekers and exceptional leave to remain or enter
5.50	Family aspects of immigration
5.52	Marriage and divorce

Introduction

5.1 This chapter looks at family issues relating to asylum. Immigration Rules (IR)[1] paras 327–352F deal with asylum applications, while paras 349 and 352A–352F deal specifically with family reunion of refugees. The Asylum Policy Instructions (API)[1a] and the Immigration Directorate's Instructions (IDI) also give guidance to case-workers on family reunion, and children and families of those recognised as refugees or who have exceptional leave to enter or remain. General instructions are issued to entry clearance officers (ECOs) on entry clearance applications.[2] Detailed texts such as *Macdonald's Immigration Law and Practice*[3] provide critiques and guidance on applications that appear on the face of it to comply with the rules and reference should be made to these if an application is to be made.

The family[4]

5.2 In a letter[5] the Deputy Representative of the United Nations High Commission for Refugees (UNHCR) stated that:

> ... the integrity of the refugee's family is a paramount protection concern. That families take diverse forms and are created in a variety of ways only serves to highlight the need to ensure protection for the refugee's family in as wide a variety of circumstances as possible. UNHCR's view, as reflected in the UNHCR handbook, is that the proper application of the family unity principle[6] requires a generous and human approach in keeping with the principle's humanitarian underpinnings. Paragraph 352A(ii) [of the IR as amended] ... appears to diverge from the generous and human spirit required to address matters of family unity. This is because it purports to exclude from the benefits of the family unity principle refugees whose marriages took place after departure from the country of habitual residence. This is unduly restrictive, as, in the UNHCR's view, refugee families bona fide formed after departure from country of origin should no less be entitled to international protection.

1 HC 395 as amended.
1a The API in this chapter are as at March 2002.
2 See Appendix B.
3 5th edn, Butterworths, 2001.
4 See chapter 1.
5 13 March 2001.
6 See Appendix to the Convention Relating to the Status of Refugees, Final Act of the 1951 UN Conference B and *UNHCR Handbook* p43.

Divorce

5.3 Where a decision on an outstanding application is awaited, there is a duty on applicants to inform the Home Office of any material change in circumstances pending determination of any application.[7] Separation or divorce constitute a material change of circumstance.

5.4 By letter dated 8 December 1998 from Kathy Casey of the Home Office to the Refugee Council, it was stated in relation to the measures announced for dealing with the backlog of undecided asylum cases that they:

> ... would take a sympathetic view where the break-up of a marriage had forced a dependant who would have otherwise qualified for consideration under the backlog measures, to make an application in their own right after 31 December 1995.

In practice this appears to mean that such dependants will benefit from the backlog policy in the same way as the principal applicant. However, it is important not to make assumptions. Consideration should be given to the submission of an application for asylum by the former dependant. There may also be financial problems, which will need to be resolved.

Where the family has limited leave

5.5 If divorce is contemplated before both parties and their children are settled or have been granted leave to enter the UK, careful consideration must be given to the effect of divorce or separation on the couple and/or the family. If one of the couple or members of the family have returned to the country of origin, this could, in the event of separate applications being submitted, result in the person who returned being refused further leave to remain on the basis that the criteria that led to the grant of exceptional leave no longer apply. Unless an individual has indefinite leave to remain in the UK it is not advisable to travel to the country of origin, in case there is, in the future, a relationship breakdown.

5.6 If a couple has divorced, separate applications for further leave to remain have to be submitted. If there are children of a family that separates and there is continuing contact between the parents and children then the fact of separation will not normally affect the right to settlement. However there may be problems if there are no

---

7 This is stressed on the application forms.

children or if the children are now adults.[8] If there are children, the European Convention on Human Rights (ECHR) art 8 can be used to argue in favour of the separated parent remaining in the UK to enable family life to continue.[9]

Where the family is settled

5.7 Once a family has indefinite leave to remain the fact of divorce or separation will not affect any returning family members' residence status other than in accordance with the IR.

Domestic violence

5.8 The Home Office has issued policies that refer to domestic violence. These policies should be examined carefully in relation to the evidence required and the extent to which the policy is applicable.[10]

Unaccompanied children

5.9 An unaccompanied child is a person who at the time of making the application is under the age of 18,[11] is applying for asylum in his/her own right and is without family members or guardians to turn to in the UK. If an unaccompanied child becomes 18 years old before a decision is reached or while waiting for an appeal, he or she will continue to be treated as a minor[12] in accordance with IR paras 350–352. However, if a decision is taken to remove him/her from the UK, appropriate reception arrangements do not have to be in place.[13] The API state that it will 'rarely be acceptable to hold an application from an unaccompanied child without any action being taken on it for longer than 6 months'.[14]

---

8 See chapter 8.
9 See chapter 4.
10 See para 6.56.
11 HC 395 as amended para 349.
12 API Ch 2, s5, para 3.6; HC 395 as amended paras 349–352.
13 API Ch 2, s5, para 3.6.
14 API Ch 2, s5, para 3.3.

Returnability of children

5.10 No unaccompanied child under the age of 18 will be removed unless the Home Office is satisfied that adequate reception arrangements have been made in the country to which the child is to be removed.[15] Inquiries by the Home Office about potential returnability frequently commence before finalising the decision about leave to enter or remain. The reason given for this is to ensure that a decision can be taken on leave at the same time as on asylum and if a child is not returnable then no time will be wasted. In order to show that adequate reception arrangements can be made the Home Office case-worker must identify, on the file, 'that a potential carer has been identified and that there is a realistic prospect of setting up suitable arrangements for the child's return. This, in effect, means that a parent, guardian or some other person who can be trusted to care for the child's welfare will be able to meet the child at the port of arrival.' Case-workers will make inquiries by contacting the relevant British diplomatic post but the 'entry clearance officer (ECO) should be reminded not to disclose during the enquiries that the applicant is an asylum seeker'. The API point out that reception arrangements can vary from case to case and country to country. The API also state that '[m]aking acceptable reception arrangements will usually involve locating the child's parents or other close relatives who will be able to look after the child. Alternatively, the social services or equivalent in the child's home country may be able to provide for the child. This will depend very much on the quality of care provision available.'

5.11 There is no reference in the API to the welfare principle or to the UN Convention on the Rights of the Child 1989. There is no reference to the standard of care, education, etc, that would be provided in the event of the child's return to his/her country of origin and how that should be balanced against the need to maintain immigration control. There is no guidance to the case-worker on whether to take into account, and if so to what extent, the experiences of the child in the UK, the effect on the child of having been sent away from his/her parents or carers or the effect of removal from the UK on the child. These are therefore issues which should be raised in representations or used to form the basis of a human rights application.

5.12 The guidelines state that if the asylum application is to be refused and it is impossible to make satisfactory reception arrangements for

---

15 API Ch 2, s5, para 3.5.

> **Example: Minor/adult children and asylum**
>
> Sally is 19 years old and her sister Amy is 16. They came to the UK eight years ago. They were accommodated by the local authority (without a formal decision having been taken by them under CA 1989 s20) four years ago. They were originally dependants of their mother's asylum application and then when their father came to the UK they became dependent on his application as well. The family relationship broke down. Neither has contact with either their mother or father and they do not know whether a decision has been taken on either application. Neither has a substantive claim for asylum in her own right.
>
> Amy, who is still a minor and has been in the UK for more than seven years, will be able to rely on the Home Office concession, irrespective of the status of her mother or father.
>
> Sally is now an adult. If one or other of her parents has been granted leave to remain, she, as a dependant, may well have been granted leave in line. If she has not, consideration should be given to arguing that because she was a minor at the time a decision was taken on her mother's or father's application she should have been granted leave at the same time.
>
> If her parents have been refused it is essential to separate Sally from their claims and submit an application to remain in her own right. Refer to ECHR art 8 (her sibling, no other home, private life), length of time in the UK (more than seven years, the majority as a minor), failure of social services to act responsibly in making an application when she was looked after, the continuing responsibility of social services, the requirements that would have to be complied with were she simply being removed from social services care and sent abroad, full details of her current life and what would happen to her if she were sent to her country of nationality. There is no guarantee that the application will be successful, given her age.
>
> This illustrates the potential problems that arise where an application is not submitted while an individual is under 18 years old.

an applicant who is still under the age of 18, then the presumption should generally be to grant exceptional leave to enter or remain.[16]

5.13 If the child has reached the age of 18 by the time of the asylum decision, the Home Office no longer considers it necessary to ensure

---

16 API Ch 2, s5, para 3.5.

> **Example: Asylum-seeker initially a minor, but adult at decision time**
>
> Admira is a 17-year-old from Kosovo and will shortly be 18. There is no decision on her asylum claim which was submitted when she arrived in the UK three years ago and she has been accommodated for that length of time. She has no relatives in the UK. She has discovered that two of her (older) brothers are alive and are in Greece. Despite attempts through the Red Cross she has been unable to find any trace of her parents or other siblings. When she fled there was heavy fighting in her home village and it is presumed that they are dead.
>
> This is a difficult situation: should an application for judicial review be made to force the Home Office into making a decision before Admira becomes 18 years old? Current Home Office policy is that Kosovan children who are refused asylum are granted exceptional leave to remain only until their 18th birthday. The advantage would be that at least Admira will have a period of leave to remain, which could assist her in accessing education and, when she reaches the age of 18, obtaining financial support. She would also be able to apply for a variation of her leave when she reaches 18. Making a decision about an application for judicial review would depend on the detailed facts of the case.

there are adequate reception and care arrangements. However, inquiries, if started, may continue because the Home Office is of the view that they may lead to information useful to the asylum claim.

5.14 In some cases a child will be given exceptional leave to enter or remain until he or she reaches the age of 18. It has been the policy to give such leave to Kosovan minors since October 2000.[17] This policy is being extended.[17a]

Disputed age

5.15 Home Office instructions state that a minor child 'is a person under eighteen years of age or who, in the absence of documentary evidence appears to be under that age'. Where there is a dispute as to age the

---

17 Telephone call between Immigration Law Practitioners Association and Nick Swift at Country Information and Policy Unit, Kosovar desk, on 13 September 2001.
17a SBSH para 4.57.

> **Example: Disputed age**
>
> Ahmed is 17 years old. He travelled to the UK on a false passport which gave his age as 22. Although he gave his correct age on arrival when he claimed asylum, he was disbelieved and put in detention. While in detention he claims that one of the guards came in while he was having a shower and touched him inappropriately.
>
> This case illustrates potential problems of children being held in adult prisons, where no checks are made about the suitability of guards in charge of children. It also raises the problem of obtaining other evidence available to establish a child's age. Ahmed should be referred to the Refugee Council's Unaccompanied Minor Asylum Seeker Panel. Consideration should be given to a criminal prosecution of the guard.

burden is on the applicant to demonstrate that he or she is a minor. The Home Office comment that adjudicators 'tend to give the applicant the benefit of the doubt'.[18] In all cases where an applicant claims to be a minor a reference must be made to the Refugee Council's children panel.[18a] The Royal College of Paediatrics and Child Health has produced a report[19] that, among other issues, gives guidance to paediatricians on the assessment of age. In particular it takes the view that it is not possible to give an accurate assessment within five years either way. The British Medical Association (BMA) states 'that it is extremely difficult to accurately assess the age of a child and almost impossible when the child is between the ages of 15 to 18'.[20] If a disputed age child is detained he or she will be detained with adults. Consideration should be given to the issue of proceedings (in addition to a bail application) to move the child to accommodation suitable for a child where, for example, the necessary child protection checks have been undertaken. Questions to the detaining authorities as to what checks have been undertaken should be considered. The protection of a child is essential and it is imperative that a child is moved from a potentially abusive situation immediately.

18 API Ch 2, s5, para 3.7.
18a *Firmer, fairer, faster* White Paper, para 12.6.
19 Roz Levenson and Anna Sharma, *The Health of Refugee Children. Guidelines for Paediatricians* (Royal College of Paediatrics and Child Health, November 1999).
20 Letter from BMA to Association of Visitors to Immigration Detainees, 28 May 1998. See also para 4.44.

Trafficked children

5.16   These vulnerable children are not referred to in the various Home Office policies relating to refugee and asylum-seeking children.[21] Little specific work has been done for them to date apart from some pioneering work by West Sussex Social Services Department. However, *Secure Borders, Safe Haven* does recognise that many children are being trafficked to the UK each year for sexual exploitation or domestic 'slavery'.[21a]

Where child is a refugee or has exceptional leave to remain

5.17   There is nothing in the IR or the API that refers to family reunion for adult family members where a child is recognised as a refugee or has exceptional leave. However, a letter from Home Office Minister Barbara Roche[22] appears to indicate that minors who are recognised as refugees can apply to have parents join them in the UK.[23] The Entry Clearance General Instructions[24] require ECOs to advise applicants that they may not be successful, but in the event of the application being proceeded with an interview should be 'conducted to establish the background and circumstances to the application with a view to determining whether there are compelling compassionate circumstances involved'. Particular problems arise when parents have fled from the home country and are in an irregular position in a third country. In these circumstances ECOs can be reluctant to accept applications for entry clearance. Consideration needs to be given to judicial review.

5.18   Where parents arrive in the UK, even where it is stated on arrival that they are arriving as part of a family reunion application, they will be treated as fresh asylum applications and have to go through the asylum determination process.

Where a child's immigration status is unknown

5.19   Where a family has broken up and children are accommodated or subject to a care order, the child's immigration status is frequently

---

21   See paras 4.37–41.
21a SBSH para 4.40.
22   To Lord Archer of Sandwell dated 30 June 2000. See Appendix K.
23   See Appendix K.
24   Vol 1, para 16.5. See Appendix B.

> **Example: Refugee minor and family reunion**
>
> Habibi has been in the UK since she was 12 years old. She is recognised as a refugee and is now 22 years old, married and has a daughter aged three. While she was still a minor an application was made for her grandmother, mother and siblings to be granted entry clearance to the UK. The application was refused on the grounds that she had not been part of the family unit seeking entry clearance. The Immigration Appeal Tribunal remitted it back to the Home Office for further consideration within the facts found by the adjudicator that Habibi was part of the family unit. After considerable delay and still no decision on the remittal, a further application for entry clearance was made on the same facts, which was refused and appealed. Detailed representations were submitted referring to the Barbara Roche letter and ECHR art 8 together with a threat of judicial review proceedings if a decision on the remittal was not made and a hearing date not given for the second appeal. Entry clearance was granted.

unknown. The child may not have any documents identifying his/her status either in his/her own right or as a dependant. If there is doubt as to the child's status seek clarification from the Immigration and Nationality Department (IND). If no clarification is forthcoming or the IND is unable to trace the child, it may be advisable to submit an application for the child to be granted leave to remain. Issues such as length of residence and the child's personal circumstances must be considered at that time. If they are not considered, such an application may jeopardise the child's continued stay in the UK. In some circumstances consideration should be given to trying to establish as much information as possible before submitting an application.

5.20 If an application is submitted for a child it is important to be aware that there may be a conflict between the child and the child's carer or former carers' best interests. For example, if it is argued that a child has been abandoned by his/her carers this may lead to the child being granted leave to remain but place the former carers at risk of removal.

5.21 If a child arrives in the UK as, for example, a visitor, and joins parents who are settled in the UK or have exceptional leave to remain, it is frequently thought that the child will automatically be treated as having the same status as the parents on whom he or she is dependent. This is not so. An application must be submitted for the child to be granted leave in line with the responsible parent.

5.22 If a child or other family members have been granted leave to enter or remain in false names it will be important, particularly in relation to the children's education and so on, for the correct identities to be established and leave granted in the correct names. Proof of identity will normally be required by the Home Office, for example, correct original birth certificates. In the event of proof not being forthcoming statutory declarations signed by those who have had close dealings with the children and/or their family will be required or a statutory declaration of change of name can be made on behalf of the child.

Where sponsor is an asylum-seeker

5.23 Dependants will usually have been identified on the statement of evidence form or during the course of the initial or substantive interview.[24a] UK-born dependants who are not British citizens may be included as dependants and their inclusion constitutes an application for leave to remain. Family members who arrive in the UK before the main applicant's asylum claim has been determined can be added as dependants but should also be advised on the merits of a claim in their own right.[25] Refusal as a dependant does not carry an independent separate right of appeal.[26] If the sponsor is subsequently refused asylum and the dependant has previously been refused asylum in his/her own right and exhausted his/her appeal rights, IR para 349 permits removal of the dependant even if the sponsor has not exhausted his/her appeal rights. The rules do not permit the removal of a dependant who has not had his/her own claim for asylum finally determined. Whilst an application for asylum is pending there are no family reunion rights.

5.24 If a family breaks up prior to a decision being taken on the principal applicant's asylum claim, submission of an application for asylum by the dependant in his/her own right should be considered. Such an application may raise issues around family unity, contact, and ECHR art 8 as well as issues of asylum. Children may have their own claim in connection with ECHR art 8 even if they have no separate asylum application. If no application is submitted, the dependant has no pending application and thus no right to stay in the UK

24a The recently introduced screening pro forma has a biodata section. It is important to complete this with full family details, making relationships clear, eg, step, adopted, de facto adoption, caring or otherwise.
25 Heaven Crawley, *Refugees and Gender: Law and Process* (Jordans, 2001).
26 API Ch 6, s1, para 8.3.

pending a decision. There will be no entitlement to National Asylum Support Service aid or other benefits.[27]

Mixed applications

5.25 There is currently no prohibition on applying for leave to enter or remain in the UK on more than one basis. For example, an asylum-seeker who marries a person settled in the UK can apply for leave to enter the UK as a spouse. That application will be considered and a decision taken. The Home Office and the Immigration Service frequently assert that it is not possible to have more than one application pending at the same time. The guidance in force until about December 2001[28] stated that where an in-country asylum applicant also had an application for leave to remain under another category, the non-asylum application should usually be considered before the asylum application.

5.26 An application for leave to enter or remain on a basis other than asylum is unlikely to carry with it rights of appeal under the IR. However, consideration should be given to whether there is an appeal under Immigration and Asylum Act (IAA) 1999 s65.

Where sponsor is a refugee

Dependants in the UK

5.27 In order to be granted leave as a dependant the applicant must be related as claimed[29] to the sponsor, be wholly dependent on the sponsor and have formed part of the pre-existing family unit abroad. Family members, defined in the API as spouse or minor children, will usually be considered as dependants. Unmarried partners should be treated in the same way as spouses. Where a minor child reaches the age of 18 prior to determination of the sponsor's claim, he or she will continue to be treated as a minor for the purposes of the application. Relatives other than a spouse or child may be recognised as dependants in exceptional circumstances, for example, an aged dependent parent, a very young child with older sister or brother.

27 See paras 3.20–3.24.
28 API Ch 2, s7, 'currently being revised'. See Appendix C for previously available API. the recently introduced screening pro forma makes it clear that dual applications are possible.
29 See paras 6.38 onwards.

> **Example: Mixed applications**
>
> Mr Tahir arrived in the UK in January 1997 and applied for asylum on arrival. He submitted his statement and was interviewed in September 1997. In July 1998 he met Ms Williams, a British citizen. They started a relationship and in January 1999 they started living together. They were married in October 2000 and in November 2000 they had a little girl. In December 2000 the Home Office and the port were notified of the marriage and the birth of the baby and a formal application using Form FLR (M) was submitted to the Home Office and copied to the port with documentation showing length of relationship, birth of baby, details of relatives, finance and referring to the circumstances of the relationship and ECHR art 8. The Immigration Service, at the port, interviewed the couple in April 2001.
>
> On the day of the interview Mr Tahir was refused leave to enter the UK as a spouse on the grounds that he had not arrived in the UK with the requisite entry clearance. He was told that he had no right of appeal exercisable in the UK. Further detailed representations were submitted reiterating the points already made, asserting that Mr Tahir wished to exercise his right of appeal which he had under IAA 1999 s65 and enclosing grounds of appeal arguing, inter alia, that the Immigration Officer had failed to comply with the obligations under the IAA 1999 to consider whether his/her action would constitute a breach of the ECHR and that to remove him would be a breach of ECHR art 8. Although acknowledged, no further action was taken by the Home Office in connection with this appeal. Notification of the refusal of the asylum application was given in October 2001 together with an Annex B letter (notification to state any further non-asylum grounds within seven days). Further reference was made to the ECHR art 8 application and appeal. The asylum application was refused in October 2001.
>
> It is important to appeal every decision, and ensure that earlier applications and appeals are cross-referenced. This will become very important if the proposals in the White Paper *Secure Borders, Safe Haven* come into effect. It is proposed that only a prescribed group of decisions will be susceptible to appeal under IAA 1999 s65.

5.28 'Wholly dependent' is not defined. There is no requirement for financial or emotional dependency to be proved.[30]

30 API Ch 6, s1, para 3.1.

Family aspects of asylum

5.29   The concession on unmarried partners announced on 10 October 1997 enabled an overseas national to be granted leave to enter or remain as the unmarried partner of a person who has been granted asylum. That concession is referred to in the API.[31] The concession (amended to reduce the time the couple are to have lived together) has now been incorporated into the IR[32] but there is no reference to unmarried partners of refugees in the rules. The API have not been amended to take account of the incorporation of the concession. The IR so far as asylum is concerned refer to husband or wife but not unmarried partner.[33]

5.30   Dependants will usually have been identified in the statement of evidence form or during the course of the initial interview on arrival. Dependants who followed the sponsor at a later date will be treated in the same way.

5.31   Dependants who are in the UK will normally be recognised as refugees and granted leave in line with the sponsor, ie, indefinite leave.[34] Adult dependants will be issued with their own letter of recognition; children will usually be included on the mother's. The issue of recognition letters can be problematic where the child, although a minor, is no longer living with the sponsor or spouse. Leave to enter or remain will usually still be granted but it can be important for the child to be able to prove status in the future. In many cases it is simpler and quicker to apply for a travel document rather than spend many months trying to obtain a separate recognition letter from the Home Office.

5.32   If a dependant does not wish to be recognised as a refugee or does not fall within the Refugee Convention (for example, if he or she is a national of a third country), he or she will still be granted leave in line but not issued with a recognition letter. Leave will be endorsed on the dependant's passport.

5.33   UK-born children who are not British citizens and who have been added to the sponsor's asylum claim will, if the sponsor is granted asylum or exceptional leave to enter or remain, be granted leave in line. If the child was not added and the sponsor is granted asylum or exceptional leave to enter or remain, the child will remain without leave unless and until an application is made for leave in line.[35]

---

31 API Ch 6, s1, para 3.
32 HC 395 as amended rr295A–295I.
33 HC 395 as amended r349.
34 HC 395 as amended r349.
35 A UK-born child of a person granted indefinite leave to enter or remain (as refugees are on recognition), is entitled to register as British under British Nationality Act 1981 s1(3).

5.34   If the sponsor married a non-British citizen or a non-EU citizen in the UK, the application for leave to remain is considered in accordance with the Immigration Rules. Case-workers are enjoined to 'be flexible about the application of the maintenance and accommodation requirements. This is because it might be unreasonable to expect someone who has fled persecution to be able to be self-sufficient immediately.'[37] Where the marriage took place after the sponsor entered the UK, 12 months leave to remain will usually be granted to the spouse in the first instance and a similar period given to any children.

Dependants outside the UK

5.35   'Only pre-existing families are eligible for family reunion, ie, the spouse and minor children who formed part of the family unit prior to the time the sponsor fled to seek asylum.' Other family members such as elderly parents may be 'allowed' to come to the UK if there are 'compelling, compassionate reasons'.[38]

5.36   Even if the family members are not the same nationality or do not wish to be recognised as refugees they would still be admitted to join the sponsor. The sponsoring refugee does not have to meet the maintenance and accommodation requirements of the IR.[39] They will usually be granted indefinite leave in line with the sponsor.

5.37   If the marriage took place after the sponsor fled from his/her home country, case-workers are enjoined to 'be flexible about the application of the maintenance and accommodation requirements. This is because it might be unreasonable to expect someone who has fled persecution to be able to be self-sufficient immediately'.[40]

Where sponsor has exceptional leave

5.38   There is no entitlement for dependants to be granted leave to enter or remain. Although the right to respect to family life is embodied in ECHR art 8, there is no element of choice as to where family life can be enjoyed. Clearly, where the sponsor has exceptional leave to enter or remain because he or she has been granted protection under the ECHR it is simply not possible to enjoy family life in his/her home

37 API Ch 6, s3, para 3.
38 API Ch 6, s2, para 2.
39 API Ch 6, s2, para 3.1.
40 API Ch 6, s3, para 3.

country. It may also be possible to argue that the level of protection offered in a third country is insufficient. The Home Office, in deciding whether to exercise discretion to permit dependants to remain in the UK, will consider whether it is in fact disproportionate to cause the family unit to make its home in the country of origin. One of the factors that would be taken into account would be how safe it would be for the sponsor to return to his/her country of origin. If time has been spent in the country of origin since grant of initial leave this is obviously a factor that would be taken into account.

Dependants in the UK

5.39 If the pre-existing family is already in the UK permission to remain will usually be granted on a discretionary basis in line with the sponsor.[41] The API do not refer to unmarried partners being granted leave to remain, although it should be possible to draw an analogy with the position of refugee sponsors.[42]

5.40 If the marriage took place after the sponsor entered the UK and the sponsor has not completed four years, leave may be granted to the spouse on a discretionary basis.[43] There is no specific indication in the API on what basis that discretion will be exercised, although caseworkers are reminded that the Human Rights Act 1998 incorporates the ECHR and attention is drawn to ECHR art 8.

5.41 Maintenance and accommodation requirements should be met where the sponsor has not completed four years although leave would 'never be refused solely on those grounds'.[44]

5.42 Where the spouse arrives in the UK without entry clearance and the sponsor has completed less than four years, consideration should be given to an asylum application in his/her own right. An application for leave to enter as a spouse should also be made. Reference should be made and analogy drawn to API Ch 6, s3, para 3. If leave to enter is refused, appeal rights under IAA 1999 s65 should be invoked. Changes of circumstances, for example birth of children, should be reported to the port and to the Home Office with a request for reconsideration given the further time that has elapsed and the considerable change in circumstances.

---

41 API Ch 6, s2, para 3.2.
42 See para 5.27.
43 API Ch 6, s3, para 3.
44 API Ch 6, s3, para 3.

Dependants outside the UK

5.43 Entry clearance will usually only be granted where the sponsor has completed four years and is able to meet the maintenance and accommodation requirements. Applications before the four years will be granted where there are 'compelling, compassionate circumstances'[45] or in a subsequent section of the policy where there are 'truly exceptionally compelling compassionate circumstances'.[46] The Entry Clearance General Instructions refer to 'compelling compassionate circumstances'.[47] This area is ripe for challenge under ECHR art 8.

Where a person is recognised as a refugee in another country

5.44 Applications will be considered in accordance with the IR and policy depending whether the sponsor is a refugee or has exceptional leave to enter or remain, as above. The marriage application will be dealt with first and then it may be appropriate to consider an application for transfer of refugee status.[48]

Unmarried partners

5.45 Unmarried partners including same-sex partners have now been brought within the IR,[49] but they do not refer to leave to remain as the unmarried partners of a refugee or person with exceptional leave. The API make no specific reference to unmarried partners of people with exceptional leave.

Divorce and separation

5.46 If a marriage breaks up and the dependent spouse would otherwise be considered under the White Paper backlog measures, then the Home Office policy is to 'take a sympathetic view' and treat a post-

---

45 API Ch 6, s2, para 3.2.
46 API Ch 6, s3, para 3.
47 Vol 1, para 16.5. See Appendix B.
48 API Ch 6, s3, para 2.
49 HC 395 as amended paras 295A–M.

31 December 1995 application for asylum as if it had been made at the same time as the original application for asylum by the former spouse.[50] There is no mention of unmarried partners.

Failed asylum-seekers and exceptional leave to remain or enter

5.47 The Home Office policy for the grant of exceptional leave to enter or remain for failed asylum-seekers was set out in the Asylum Policy Instructions.[51] In the past exceptional leave was granted in a number of circumstances. The policy (until December 2001) stated that:

> Where the 1951 UN Convention requirements are not met in the individual case but return to the country of origin would result in the applicant being subjected to torture or other cruel, inhuman or degrading treatment, or where the removal would result in an unjustifiable break up of family life.
>
> Where there is *credible* medical evidence that return, due to the medical facilities in the country concerned, would reduce the applicant's life expectancy and subject him to acute physical and mental suffering, in circumstances where the UK can be regarded as having assumed responsibility for his care. In cases of doubt, a second opinion should be sought from a credible source.
>
> Where the applicant does not satisfy the 1951 UN Convention criteria for refugee status but there are compassionate or humanitarian reasons which merit not requiring the person to return to their country of origin or habitual residence.

5.48 This was a change from the previous policy which stated where there was '*credible* medical evidence that return would result in substantial damage to the physical or psychological health of the applicant *or his dependants*' (emphasis supplied). The change meant that a dependant who fell within the policy would need to make an independent application for leave to remain on an exceptional basis with the original asylum applicant as a dependant.

5.49 An applicant can rely on breaches of articles 3 or 8 of the ECHR to assert a right of appeal under IAA 1999 s65. In cases involving a medical condition he or she will now have to fall within the current AIDS, HIV and serious illness policy.[52]

---

50 Letter from Home Office to Refugee Council, 8 December 1998. See also para 5.4.
51 API Ch 5, s1 has been withdrawn and is 'currently being revised'.
52 See paras 6.61–6.72.

Family aspects of immigration[53]

5.50 The IR set out the requirements to be met for applicants seeking to join a spouse or cohabitee who is in the UK on either a temporary or permanent basis; for children to be granted leave to enter or remain as family members; and for applicants to be given leave to enter for the purpose of exercising rights of access.[54] If the applicant complies with the requirements of the IR he or she should be given leave to enter or remain in accordance with the application made. When taking instructions, care should be taken to ensure that full details are taken not only of the applicant's circumstances but potential citizenship. For example, a South American may have an entitlement to Spanish citizenship in which case consideration should be given to an application on the basis of exercise of Treaty of Rome rights rather than dependent spouse; a national of the Central and Eastern European countries that have entered into an Association Agreement with the EU may be able to apply to set up in business if there are no compelling compassionate circumstances that enable a successful application in accordance with the API.

5.51 A number of independent policies exist, which are not referred to in the IR but can lead to the grant of leave to enter or remain. Details of these are given in chapter 6.

Marriage and divorce

5.52 The IAA 1999 gave considerable powers to marriage registrars to investigate and report 'suspicious' marriages.[55] Applicants who are considering marriage should be warned of the possibility of referral to the IND for investigation and the potential for detention.

5.53 Marriage in many countries does not result in a certificate. The lack of a certificate does not necessarily mean that the marriage is not valid under UK law. Consideration should be given to whether a divorce is required prior to remarriage taking place.[56] In those circumstances it may be appropriate for an application to be made in accordance with the 'unmarried partners' rules rather than delay until the divorce and remarriage has been finalised.

---

53 *Macdonald's Immigration Law and Practice* (5th edn, Butterworths 2001).
54 HC 395 as amended para 246.
55 See para 1.9 and Appendix L.
56 IDI Ch 8, Annex D, paras 1–4 provide a reasonable summary of marriage provisions.

5.54 If a spouse originally obtained indefinite leave on the basis of his/her first marriage and subsequently seeks to sponsor a second spouse, it is advisable to check that the grounds of divorce did not inadvertently provide evidence that the couple were not cohabiting at the time that indefinite leave to remain was obtained. This could lead to difficulties for the sponsor in any application for a new partner.

5.55 Divorce obtained outside the UK or not from a UK civil court may not be valid in the UK.[56]

---

57 See para 1.13. IDI Ch 8, Annex D, para 5 provides a reasonable summary of divorce provisions.

CHAPTER 6

Applications outside the rules: Home Office practice and general principles

6.1	Introduction
6.4	Sources of policies
6.9	Legal position of Home Office policies and concessions
6.12	Home Office policies outside the rules regarding children
6.13	Under-12 concession
6.18	Children 'looked after' by local authority
6.22	Children who reach 18 before their applications are decided
6.24	Children without parents in the UK
6.37	'Over-age' children and DNA testing
6.48	Marriage concession relating to the 'one year' rule and domestic violence and widowed partners
6.55	The domestic violence concession and EU law
6.56	Separated spouses and EU law
6.60	AIDS, HIV infection and other serious illnesses
6.71	EEA nationals
6.72	Psychiatric illness

continued

6.76	**Long residence concessions**
6.77	The ten-year lawful residence concession
6.86	14-year long residence concession
6.91	**Administrative removal and deportation**
6.98	Cases involving children or marriage
	Marriage • Marriages that post-date enforcement action
6.109	Children and Home Office deportation and removal policies
	Children and marriage – policy DP 3/96 • Children with long residence in the UK – policy DP 069/99 (formerly DP 5/96) • Deportation of children whose parent(s) are subject to deportation action – policies DP 4/95 and DP 4/96 • Children with parents in the UK – policy DP 4/96 • Unaccompanied children – policy DP 4/96
6.132	Families with children who have lived in the UK for seven years or more
6.135	Removal of family units
6.136	**Citizenship issues**
6.136	Registration of minors as British citizens
6.144	Sibling groups split by nationality
6.146	Illegitimate children

Introduction

6.1 The published Immigration Rules (IR)[1] set out the criteria for admission and stay in the UK. However, the IR do not provide a complete or accurate picture of how immigration controls are operated in practice.

6.2 The Home Office operates a number of policies and concessions which in some cases enable people who are within the policies to qualify for admission or to remain in the UK when they would not do so if the strict IR were applied. The Home Office may make statements on how the rules will be interpreted in practice by officials – which may be more generous than that suggested by the courts. A recent amendment to the rules[2] incorporated some long-standing concessions and the Home Office has announced a review of the current rules which may include more of the concessions.

6.3 There are also many areas of immigration practice about which the rules are wholly silent and Home Office practice can only be understood from statements of practice and policy or sometimes gleaned from practical experience of cases and decisions. Concessions can be introduced, amended or withdrawn. The mailings of the Immigration Law Practitioners Association (ILPA) and the Refugee Legal Group, and *Legal Action* quarterly immigration updates are the most effective way of keeping up-to-date.

Sources of policies

6.4 Evidence of Home Office policy and practice can be found in a number of sources ranging from the Home Office's internal Immigration Directorate's Instructions (IDI)[3] letters to professional associations such as the Law Society and ILPA, letters to practitioners, answers to parliamentary questions and ministerial announcements.

6.5 Since 1998, the disclosable version of internal instructions to Home Office staff have been made available either through the internet or in hard copies placed in certain libraries. The publicly-available instructions do not contain anything like a comprehensive account of all concessions and in some respects are out-of-date. It is possible to

---

1 Currently, HC 395 as amended.
2 Cm 4851, September 2000.
3 IDI, NI and API are available on www.homeoffice.gov.uk/ind/idi. In this chapter the IDI are as at January 2001.

register electronically with the Home Office to receive automatic updates of the IDI, the Nationality Instructions (NI) and the Asylum Policy Instructions (API), although, in practice, this is not yet working effectively. Apart from being out-of-date and incomplete, the layout of the IDI is not particularly easy to use.

6.6 Instructions relating to children are found in chapter 8 of the IDI:
- s3 relates to children generally;
- s4 relates to children born in the UK who are not British citizens;
- s5 relates to adopted children.

6.7 In addition, guidance is found in the Annexes:
- Annex M contains guidance on interpreting the rules in children's cases generally;
- Annex N contains guidance on DNA testing and over-age children;
- Annex O contains guidance on the children of fiancées;
- Annex P contains guidance on children born in the UK who are not British citizens;
- Annexes Q to T contain guidance on adopted children;
- Annex U contains refusal formulae.

6.8 Chapter 13 of the IDI deals with deportation and administrative removal. Chapter 20 deals with illegal entrants. The NI are more clearly laid out. Chapter 9 of the NI deals with the use of discretion in the registration of minors.

Legal position of Home Office policies and concessions

6.9 The Home Office cannot operate a policy that is stricter than the IR. However, there is no bar to the Home Office operating a policy or practice that is more generous than the rules or indeed a policy to cover a situation not dealt with by the rules. Where it can be established that the Home Office has acted inconsistently with a policy the decision may be amenable to judicial review.[4] Where the Home Office has represented to a person that it will deal with his/her case according to certain criteria, a failure to do so can found judicial review on the basis of breach of a legitimate expectation.[5] However, a policy is merely that and not a rule, and the Home Office need not

---

4 See *R v Home Secretary ex p Amankwah* [1994] Imm AR 240.
5 *Khan (Asif Mahmood) v IAT* [1984] Imm AR 68.

follow it rigidly provided that adequate reasons are given for deviating from the policy.[6] The Home Office interpretation of its own policies can be challenged on grounds of irrationality, that is, if it has failed to take the policies into account or has interpreted them incorrectly.[7]

6.10 Where there is a right of appeal to an adjudicator against a Home Office decision the adjudicator is not entitled to decide whether the Home Office should have departed from the IR. However, the adjudicator can decide whether the decision is 'in accordance with the law'.[8] This will include a factual consideration of whether the appellant has been wrongly denied the benefit of a Home Office policy.[9] If he or she was, then the application can be remitted to the Home Secretary for reconsideration.

6.11 Following the introduction of the Immigration and Asylum Act (IAA) 1999, awareness of concessions is even more important as reference to a particular concession can be made in the statement of additional grounds. Moreover, many of the concessions relating to families will give rise to issues under European Convention on Human Rights (ECHR) art 8.

Home Office policies outside the rules regarding children

6.12 There are numerous concessions and policies outside the rules relating to children. Many of these are set out in the IDI, but these are not complete and can be contradictory, illustrating the tension between immigration policy and more child-oriented social policy. This section will deal with the main concessions relating to children, in relation to entry clearance, country applications and citizenship applications.

Under-12 concession

6.13 Where a child seeks entry clearance to join one parent who is settled in the UK, the other parent being elsewhere, the IR require proof of 'sole responsibility' by the sponsoring parent, that is that the

---

6 *Home Secretary v Hastrup* [1996] Imm AR 616, CA.
7 *R v Home Secretary ex p Gangadeen* [1998] INLR 206, CA.
8 IA 1971 s19.
9 See *Abdi v Home Secretary* [1996] Imm AR 148.

sponsoring parent has been exclusively responsible for the child, or that the exclusion of the child would be 'undesirable'.[10]

6.14 There is a long-standing Home Office concession[11] that exclusion will be assumed to be undesirable where the child is under 12 years of age, provided that there is adequate accommodation. Earlier versions of the IDI on the concession included a requirement that where the UK parent is the father, there is a female relative in the household willing and able to care for the child. A 'female relative' appeared to include a woman cohabiting with the father but not married to him. This requirement has now been deleted from the guidance in the IDI but the other requirements of the rules relating to sponsoring dependent children must be complied with, although there is no requirement to maintain without recourse to public funds.

6.15 The concession is often overlooked by entry clearance officers (ECOs), and its existence and terms should be drawn to their attention. The IDI make it clear that admission under the concession is not automatic and situations may arise where the decision-maker would be justified in denying admission. For example, admission should be refused where the UK-based parent is not capable of caring for the child due to physical or mental incapacity or where there are siblings applying who are aged 12 or over, particularly if the older siblings are near work age. The Home Office policy is not to split sibling groups,[12] and if the group is established in a home abroad, 'and it would cause no hardship to them to be excluded from the UK, the right course might be not to admit any of them, including those under 12'.[13] In reaching a decision, the ECO will look at:

> ... the numbers of children on either side of the dividing line (it would not be right, for example, to allow a number of children of working age, or approaching it, to gain admission because one child under 12 is seeking admission; on the other hand, it might cause hardship to a single older child if the admission of a group of siblings under 12 were to leave him alone in his own country);
> whether or not the children have been living together as a group; and the adequacy of accommodation available in this country and the arrangements for caring for the children.

---

10 See HC 395 as amended para 297(e) and (f).
11 IDI Ch 8, Annex M, para 12.
12 'The principle underlying any decision should be to preserve the unity of families and for this reason, the children of a family should be considered as a group.' IDI Ch 8, Annex M, para 12, 2.1.2.
13 IDI Ch 8, Annex M, para 12, 2.1.2.

6.16 Thus, in certain circumstances, it would be appropriate to admit a child older than 12 years, to avoid splitting a family.

6.17 In addition, if the mother of the child is polygamously married to the father and she does not herself qualify for admission, then the concession should not be applied.[14]

Children 'looked after' by local authority

6.18 Chapter 1 above contains a description of the various types of order relating to children who are 'looked after' by the local authority, whether provided with accommodation or subject to a care order. The IDI contain instructions about various policies[15] relating to children looked after by the local authority but they are not always consistent and are occasionally contradictory. The IDI state that the 'future of children in the care of the local authority should be left primarily in the hands of their social services department as they will be best placed to act in the child's best interests'.[16] This statement, which appears to acknowledge the importance of accepting professional opinion about the welfare of a child, is contradicted elsewhere in the IDI. In the preceding section relating to abandoned children (who are frequently placed in local authority care) the instruction is that although social services' views can be 'valuable in assessing the welfare considerations of a case'[17] and should be taken into account, '[i]t will not always be right to act on their recommendation, particularly if there is independent evidence to justify proceeding with refusal and removal'.[18] Nevertheless, there is a clear statement in the IDI that where parental rights and duties have been vested solely in the local authority then the child should be granted settlement.[19]

6.19 Many local authorities are unaware of this policy, and indeed may not consider a child's immigration position until he or she is about to leave care. This can be disastrous as the IDI state that where a child is approaching 18 years, then limited leave only should be granted.

6.20 The IDI contain a further proviso, that the conferring of parental

---

14 For a discussion on the position of polygamous wives and their children within the IR, see *Macdonald's Immigration Law and Practice* (5th edn, Butterworths, 2001) pp418–425.
15 IDI Ch 8, Annex M, para 8 .
16 IDI Ch 8, Annex M, para 8.
17 IDI Ch 8, Annex M, para 6.1.
18 IDI Ch 8, Annex M, para 7.1. There is nothing to state what this 'independent evidence' should consist of.
19 IDI Ch 8, Annex P, para 8.

> **Example: Very young abandoned child**
>
> Abdullah has serious physical disabilities. His parents (who were living in a refugee camp) feared he had cancer. There was no possibility of Abdullah receiving appropriate treatment in the refugee camp. The parents made the difficult decision to send Abdullah to the UK when he was two years old, hoping that he would receive treatment here. He travelled with an acquaintance who abandoned him on the airport concourse. The Immigration Service treated Abdullah as having made an application for asylum, which was rapidly refused, but he was granted exceptional leave to enter. In the meantime, Abdullah was looked after by the local authority and placed with foster parents. The local authority was reluctant to apply for indefinite leave for Abdullah as he had parents whom it considered should make this decision. Eventually, contact was made with Abdullah's parents who authorised the application which was granted. If it had not been possible to make contact, then an application to the court to appoint CAFCASS[19a] would have been considered. This would have enabled the application for indefinite leave to remain to be made, in order to secure Abdullah's position in the UK.

responsibility on the local authority must be 'long term or permanent'. If not, for example, if there is a possibility of the child being returned to his/her parents, limited leave only should be granted.

6.21 If a care order under Children Act (CA) 1989 s31[20] in favour of a local authority is made, then an application for settlement should be made as soon as possible.[21] A report from the local authority social services department, detailing the child's history and why it was necessary for the child to go into local authority care, should be submitted with the application. The report should give a recommendation as to why, in the social services' view, it is in the child's interests to be granted settlement. This is particularly important for children who are approaching 18 years. If a court judgment has been given, this can be very useful, but it will be necessary to obtain the court's

---

19a Children and Family Court Advisory and Support Service.
20 See chapter 1 for more information about care orders.
21 Unless a child is nearing 18 years, when consideration should be given to seeing if the child could benefit from any status likely to be granted to his/her parents. This is because Home Office policy is to grant limited leave only to a child who is nearing his/her 18th birthday. See paras 6.20–6.23.

permission to disclose a judgment to the Home Office. Given that the Home Office may refuse an application when a child is nearing 18 years, and that it sometimes takes time for a local authority to produce the type of report that is necessary, it is often advisable to submit a basic application immediately, with an indication that further documentary evidence in support will follow. Frequently, the Home Office has granted indefinite leave on the production of a care order alone, without it being necessary to provide supporting evidence, but this probably depends on factors such as the age of the child and the length of time he or she has been in care.

Children who reach 18 before their applications are decided

6.22 The usual rule is that applications for entry clearance, leave to enter and after-entry variation (apart from asylum decisions) are decided in the light of circumstances at the date of the decision. However, provided the application was lodged before the child reached 18 years old, applications will be treated as if the child were still under 18. This also applies to children who have been granted entry clearance for settlement and who reach 18 before arrival. Usually, this would be a change in circumstances that would lead an immigration officer to refuse entry. If the fact of reaching 18 years old is the only change in circumstance, then entry should be permitted.[22]

6.23 Similarly, if a child is given leave to enter or remain with a view to settlement as the child of a parent given limited leave with a view to settlement,[23] then the fact that the child has reached 18 is not a reason for refusing settlement. This concession does not apply to children who are admitted in a temporary capacity, other than under IR para 302, and who are aged 18 or over at the time of the application for settlement. Even in these circumstances, refusal is not mandatory and a discretionary application can be made. It should be noted that although this is the usual position, the Home Office has stated that the concession for families where there are children who have lived in the UK for seven years or more does not apply if a child reaches 18 before the application is considered by the Home Office.[24]

---

22 IDI Ch 8, Annex M, para 2.
23 HC 395 as amended para 302.
24 See para 6.132.

Children without parents in the UK[25]

6.24 Children from abroad can be separated from their parents in a number of ways. They can be abandoned here, placed into private foster care which fails, taken into local authority care[25a] or sent here from abroad by desperate parents seeking safety, medical treatment or a better life for their child. The IDI contain guidance for children who are in effect abandoned in the UK. The guidance does not relate to adopted children, children living with a relative other than their parents or who are the subject of residence orders made by a UK court.

6.25 The general aim of the Home Office is to return the child to his/her parents and/or country of origin. Potentially, this could conflict with the basic welfare principle in childcare law, as set out in CA 1989 s1, of the welfare of the child being paramount. Although the Home Office accepts that the welfare of the child is a relevant consideration, it is not the 'paramount' consideration although this may take 'precedence over the immigration implications of allowing a child to remain in the UK'.[26] The Home Office considers that the welfare of the child carries more weight in relation to younger children and, as a result, if a child is abandoned, then an application should be made to the Home Office promptly. The Home Office accepts that a child is not always responsible for his/her parents trying to evade immigration control by bringing him/her to this country and abandoning him/her here: 'Where a child's parents abuse the control by leaving a child here, the child cannot always be held responsible for their predicament'.[27]

6.26 Having accepted that the welfare of the child is a significant factor when dealing with abandoned children, the IDI continues that the fact that a child may be 'better off' remaining in the UK is not a factor that on its own would permit a child to remain here. The vagueness of the phrase 'better off' is unhelpful.

6.27 Even if a child would be 'better off' in the UK, if a parent or relative is 'able to care for him in his own country or the relevant authorities in his own country have agreed to make any necessary welfare arrangements for him, and the care would not be substantially below that usually expected in the country concerned, refusal (and eventual removal) should be considered'.

25   IDI Ch 8, Annex M, para 6.
25a See chapter 1.
26   IDI Ch 8, Annex M, para 6.1.
27   IDI Ch 8, Annex M, para 6.1.

6.28　The IDI enjoins case-workers to act 'swiftly' when dealing with children's applications. This is not so that a child is left in immigration limbo for as short a time as possible, but because 'the longer a child remains in the UK the more upsetting it is likely to be if he is required to leave'. In reality, the Home Office frequently does not act quickly when dealing with children's applications, and numerous reminders may have to be sent, quoting this internal instruction.[28]

6.29　The IDI makes no reference to the fact that children's circumstances can change. A child may be accompanied when he or she came to the UK, but by the time removal is a reality, he or she may have no family to whom he or she could turn to in his/her home country. The case of Sujon Miah concerned an 11-year-old Bangladeshi child who arrived here unaccompanied and travelling on a fake passport. He was refused leave to enter, but his parents rejected him and were not willing to accept him back. The court quashed as irrational directions for his removal as if he were to be returned, he would literally have had to live on the streets.[29]

6.30　The Home Office accepts that expert opinion from a local authority social services department can be 'valuable' in assessing the welfare considerations of a particular case, and if they are not already involved the Home Office case-worker should notify them. Although social services' views are to be sought, their views are not necessarily definitive if, for example, there is 'independent evidence' to justify refusal and removal. 'Independent evidence' is not defined by the Home Office.

6.31　Home Office case-workers are told to look at the following considerations:[30]

- How did the child come to be in the UK?
- Who looks after the child here; what arrangements have been made with the child's family; how long do they expect the arrangement to continue?
- Where do(es) the child's parent(s) or guardian(s) live and what is their occupation?
- What are the child's parents'/guardian's long-term plans for the child? Is it intended that the child should return to his family abroad? If so, when? It not, why not and what would happen if the child had to leave the UK?

28　See chapter 5.
29　CO/3391/1994, 6 December 1994, unreported, but quoted in *Macdonald's Immigration Law and Practice*.
30　IDI Ch 8, Annex M, para 7.

- What is the family's income; what sort of accommodation do they occupy; how many children do they have; who looked after the child before he or she came to be without them in the UK; who looks after his/her siblings (if applicable) now and where are they?
- If the child is old enough (usually aged seven or older) to express an opinion, what does he or she feel about the situation and where does he or she consider his/her future lies?

6.32 Clearly, when making representations these factors should be taken into account. However, taking into account the views of a child aged seven or over is questionable. The family courts will usually take into account the views of children aged 12 or 13 years. Furthermore, how are children's views to be ascertained? Any suggestion that a child should be interviewed by the immigration service should be resisted strenuously.[31] One way of ascertaining a child's views could be through obtaining a professional view from an independent social worker or child psychologist.

6.33 The IDI details the factors to be taken into account when considering an abandoned child. These are:

- The age of the child. The younger the child the more difficult it is for him/her to be removed. However, the Home Office considers that children aged 15 and above may have been abandoned in the UK for immigration reasons and that this is a reason for taking deportation action.
- The length of the child's stay in the UK. The longer a child has been in the UK, the more settled in he or she will be and thus the 'more disturbing' for him/her to be removed, particularly if he or she is 'young and/or has spent most of his formative years here'. This links with the concession for families who have children who have spent seven years or more in the UK.[32]
- The type of care the child has in the UK. By this, the Home Office means the child's domestic circumstances. The Home Office states that a child is more likely to have settled down if he or she is member of a family in the UK. Children in local authority or foster care may also be settled.
- The circumstances abroad. If the care a child would receive abroad

---

31 Obviously, the adviser should try to ascertain the child's own views; see chapter 7. The White Paper *Secure Borders, Safe Haven* refers to an intention to interview children over 14 years old, see SBSH para 4.58. Already, children are interviewed at the asylum screening interview, sometimes quite aggressively.
32 See para 6.130.

would be 'substantially below that usually expected' in that country, this should also be taken into account.
- The child's own feelings. If the child is old enough to express an opinion then this should be taken into account. The Home Office considers that a child of seven and older is able to give an opinion.[33]

6.34 The IDI stresses that these points are guidelines only and that each case must be considered on its individual merit in the light of all the available information. When making representations to the Home Office about an abandoned child, it is important to address these points but also to point out where there are other, overriding factors such as a serious illness or a mental or physical handicap.

6.35 If the Home Office rejects an application then the child will be expected to leave voluntarily. If he or she does not, enforcement action will be taken. If it is not possible to remove a child the IDI state that consideration should be given to granting leave to remain. If there is a realistic chance of reuniting the child with his/her parents abroad in the future, then the child will be given 12 months' leave to remain only. If there is no such chance, the IDI state that the child should be given leave to remain for four years. In both cases settlement can be granted after four years' limited leave, if there is no prospect of removal.[34]

6.36 Notwithstanding the IDI, if a care order has been made in respect of a child, of whatever age, even if there is a realistic prospect of reuniting the child with his/her family, advisers should argue vigorously for indefinite leave. A family court has ruled that it is in the best interests of the child for a care order to be made. It is therefore inappropriate for the Home Office to substitute its own views. If settlement is refused but limited leave granted, appeal, but at the same time consideration should be given to resubmitting a settlement application as often this will be dealt with more quickly than waiting for an appeal to be processed.

'Over-age' children and DNA testing

6.37 Children aged 18 or over must usually qualify for admission in their own right or show that they are dependent and living alone in the most exceptional compassionate circumstances.[35]

---

33 See chapter 7.
34 IDI Ch 8, Annex M, para 7.3.
35 See HC 395 as amended para 317.

6.38 Problems have arisen in the past where children previously refused entry clearance on the ground that they are not related as claimed have, since attaining the age of 18, been able to prove the relationship by way of DNA testing. In such cases the Home Office will grant entry clearance provided the child continues to be financially dependent on the parents and there are strong compassionate circumstances.[36] Few applicants have benefited from this concession and most cases to which the concession applies are likely by now to have been processed.

6.39 A government scheme has been in operation since 1991 which enables ECOs to offer to arrange DNA testing where there is a question over whether a child is related as claimed to his/her UK sponsor. The IDI state that the arrangements apply where a child is applying for the first time for settlement or refugee family reunion. They do not apply to family reunion applications for those on exceptional leave nor to repeat applications.[37] The IDI has extensive guidance on DNA testing and its use in immigration cases and it is marked for its sensitivity in how to approach information that may be revealed by DNA testing.

6.40 It is becoming increasingly common for ECOs to demand DNA proof that children are related as claimed by the sponsor, although the value is questionable. If a decision has been taken that a child is a child of the family, then it is surely irrelevant to know if the child is biologically related. As disputing this as a point of principle may cause delay, most families are prepared to take the tests. A further problem is that many ECOs state that the sponsor should pay for the DNA tests even when these are being taken at the request of the ECO. Again, disputing this can cause delay, and many families do pay.

6.41 The ECO arranges for a blood sample to be taken from the applicant and this is sent to one of the DNA testing laboratories. The sponsor in the UK also gives a supervised blood sample and the samples are then compared. DNA tests can be made by Cellmark Diagnostics, Forensic Science Service and University Diagnostics Limited.[38] When commissioning a report from one of the DNA testing laboratories, it should be made clear to whom the reports should be sent. The laboratories have been known to send the report direct to the applicants, rather than to the commissioning advisers. When the

---

36 Ministerial statement, 14 June 1989; IDI Ch 8, s3, Annex N.
37 IDI Ch 8, Annex N, para 1.1. ECOs may not be aware of the policy contained in the IDI and may ask for DNA tests in these circumstances.
38 See Appendix M for contact details.

reports have been negative, this can cause great difficulties in families and it can be better to have this information filtered through an adviser.

6.42 The IDI gives instructions on how to assess DNA reports. If the DNA report concludes that the probability of a relationship is at least three times greater than any other relationship this should be accepted as proof of the relationship without any further inquiry. If the conclusion is that the probability of a relationship is only twice as likely or less than any other relationship then the case should be reviewed, while bearing in mind that even this low probability is 'substantial evidence and should be accepted unless there is strong evidence to the contrary'.[39]

6.43 If the relationship was the sole ground for refusal, and the DNA result is positive, then Home Office case workers are instructed to concede appeals. If there were other grounds for refusal, then it may be appropriate to concede the relationship, but still maintain the refusal.

6.44 Even if the DNA test is negative, there may still be grounds to concede the application. The IDI first considers a child who is not related to the sponsoring 'parents' or only distantly related. In such a case the application should be considered as a de facto adoption and in the light of the concession for de facto adoptions.[40]

6.45 If the child is related to one of the 'parents' then consideration should be given to whether the child qualifies for admission under the rules relating to dependants of a relative other than a parent.

6.46 If the child is revealed to be the child of the father but not the mother, then an explanation is to be sought from the family. The IDI warn that the child may have been born to another wife of the sponsor. Case-workers are told to establish who has brought up the child and in particular whether the child lives with the birth mother or the alleged mother. If the birth mother is not seeking entry or does not qualify for admission the sponsor would usually need to demonstrate that he or she has had sole responsibility for the child. If a previously undisclosed earlier marriage is revealed, then this may result in queries over polygamy and legitimacy. If the sponsor cannot give a satisfactory explanation, then the application should be refused.

6.47 The position is different if a child is revealed to be the child of the mother but not the alleged father. Here, the IDI shows great delicacy

---

39 IDI Ch 8, Annex N, para 2.3.
40 See chapter 2. The IDI on adoption only partly take into account the latest legislation on adoptions.

> **Example: DNA**
>
> Samuel is Kenyan. He has been in the UK for ten years, following an initial grant of exceptional leave to remain, on the refusal of an asylum claim. Once he obtained indefinite leave to remain, Samuel, who by this time had started working, applied for his 13-year-old daughter, Jenny, to come to join him in the UK. Jenny had been living with her mother, who was not married to Samuel, and she had died recently. Samuel satisfied all the requirements of the IR to sponsor his daughter. The ECO ordered that DNA tests be taken. Samuel considered objecting to this, but decided that this would cause too great a delay. He went ahead with the DNA test.
>
> To his complete shock, Samuel discovered that he was not Jenny's biological father. The entry clearance application was rejected on the basis that Jenny was not related to Samuel as claimed. An appeal was lodged arguing that as Samuel (and the rest of his family) had always treated Jenny as Samuel's child, a de facto adoption had occurred. Reference was made to the Home Office's IDI guidance on DNA results in these circumstances. On consideration of the grounds, the ECO reversed the original decision, and Jenny was granted entry clearance.

about the effect on a family of the revelations of DNA testing concerning parentage. The IDI notes that a child may therefore be illegitimate, and the sponsoring father may be unaware of this. The impact of a disclosure of adultery (particularly in cultures where marital dignity is of great importance) could be disastrous for women. The IDI suggests that Home Office case-workers should make inquiries about the family's background and circumstances from their representatives. If an illegitimate child has been 'brought up as (the) child of the family it will usually be appropriate to admit the child'.[41]

Marriage concession relating to the 'one year' rule and domestic violence and widowed partners

6.48 The position of women who have come to the UK as spouses, but whose marriage has broken down in the first 12 months as a result of domestic violence, has been a source of concern for many years. Many women would find it difficult, if not impossible, to return to

---

41 IDI Ch 8, Annex N, para 2.9.

their home countries as rejected wives. As a result of consistent campaigning by, among others, Southall Black Sisters, a concession[41a] was initially announced in a parliamentary answer on 16 June 1999 and this has now been incorporated, with conditions, into the IDI. It is not an Immigration Rule.

6.49 The concession relates to a person who has limited leave to remain in the UK as a spouse or unmarried partner of a person who is present and settled in the UK and whose relationship breaks down during the probationary period as a result of domestic violence. In these circumstances indefinite leave to remain can be granted, exceptionally, outside the rules provided that the domestic violence occurred during the probationary period and this can be proved by one of the following:

- an injunction, non-molestation order or other protection order against the sponsor (other than an ex parte or interim order); or
- a relevant court conviction against the sponsor (ie, the husband); or
- full details of relevant police caution issued against the sponsor.

6.50 The application of the concession within the Home Office appears to be variable. The evidential requirement has been imposed in some cases, but not in others. In many cases the evidence required and outlined under the concession will be unavailable. As the Home Office has a varied response to the lack of documentary evidence, the reasons for this being the case should be explained in detail.

6.51 If the applicant did not take the matter forward to the police an explanation must be provided and be detailed. Similarly, an explanation should be given if he or she sought help from the police, but did not press for charges to be brought against the abuser. It is essential to explain an applicant's state of mind as events unfolded while explaining the reasons why he or she made certain choices (for example, not to take a matter further or to the police).

6.52 Where an applicant obtained protection and safety in a refuge, then a letter or report from the refuge detailing the circumstances leading to the agreement to provide sanctuary should be obtained.

6.53 If the applicant obtained the protection of other relatives or friends, then letters of support must explain the circumstances leading to the friend or relative providing assistance and also detail the extent and depth of the ties between the client and the friend. In all cases, the ties a client has established in the UK should be explained.

41a This concession is currently under review by the Home Office.

6.54   In many cases, a woman may fear return to her country of origin because of the treatment she will receive from her family or her husband's family. In such cases, consideration should be given to making an application under ECHR art 3 or an application for asylum.[42]

The domestic violence concession and EU law

6.55   The domestic violence concession does not apply to third country national spouses of those admitted under EU law. This is because it only applies to the spouses of those who are present and settled in the UK. If the EEA national is not settled, then the third country national spouse cannot benefit from the concession. The reasoning behind this apparent discrimination is that the concession is beneficial to the EEA worker's spouse, not the EEA national him or herself. Thus, the spouse is not covered by the non-discrimination clause.[43]

Separated spouses and EU law

6.56   The right of a spouse to live with his/her husband or wife in a member state stems from European Council Regulation 1612/68, art 10(1); Directive 68/360, art 1; and Directive 73/1148, art 1(1). The Regulation and the Directives refer simply to 'spouse'. Community law does not permit an examination into how the couple met or why they married. However, the issue of whether a marriage of convenience is a marriage acceptable under Community law has not been authoritatively determined. The Home Office view is that such a marriage is outside the protection of Community law and does not give rise to any right. The Immigration Appeal Tribunal has taken the same line. Nevertheless, it is clear that Community law does not require a couple to live under the same roof and a genuine relationship as husband and wife can exist irrespective of cohabitation.

6.57   This point arose in the case of Mrs Diatto[44] who married a French national living and working in Berlin. She had been working continuously in Berlin since February 1978. After living with her husband for some time she left him in August 1978 with the intention of

---

42 See Heaven Crawley, *Refugees and Gender: law and process* (Jordans, 2001) Ch 6.
43 Reg 1612/68 art 7(2).
44 *Diatto v Land Berlin* [1986] 2 CMLR 164, ECJ.

obtaining a divorce and had since then had been living separately. The European Court held that members of the family of a migrant worker had the right to install themselves with the worker but it did not require the member of the family concerned to live there permanently. The court also held that marital relationships cannot be regarded as dissolved unless they have been terminated by a competent authority. The implication is that a spouse is protected until he or she is divorced.

6.58 In a later case in the Court of Appeal,[45] the couple separated and the applicant's wife had returned to her home country in Germany. The court held that the applicant could no longer claim the protection of European law as his wife was no longer exercising Treaty of Rome rights in the UK.

6.59 Under IR para 255 an EEA national who has exercised Treaty of Rome rights[46] and who has been issued with a residence permit is entitled to apply for settlement provided that he or she continues to exercise Treaty of Rome rights in the UK. His/her dependants can be included in the application. The Home Office has confirmed[47] that a separated spouse is entitled to apply for indefinite leave to remain when his/her partner applies. There is no requirement that the couple are living together, provided the EEA national remains working in the UK.

AIDS, HIV infection and other serious illnesses

6.60 Until 19 December 2000, the Home Office had a separate policy for people who suffer from AIDS or are HIV positive. The policy was not generous. It stressed that the fact that a person had AIDS or was HIV positive was not in itself a ground to justify the exercise of discretion by the Home Office. When considering an application outside the IR the Home Office took into account the following factors:

- the availability of treatment in the person's own country;
- the fact that medical facilities abroad are less advanced does not, of itself, constitute a ground for allowing the person to remain;

---

45 *R v Home Secretary ex p Sandhu* [1983] 3 CMLR 131.
46 For instance, as a worker or self-employed person only. The IR state that those in the UK as students are not entitled to benefit from this paragraph, but this is of dubious legality. Certainly, the Home Office has conceded a grant of indefinite leave to an applicant who had spent some of the four years in the UK as a student when sent a letter before action preceding judicial review.
47 Letter from Home Office to Waltham Forest Citizens Advice Bureau Legal Service, 6 June 2001.

- if there are no facilities for treatment, and there is evidence to show that this will shorten the person's life expectancy then leave to remain is usually given.

6.61 A separate policy relating to enforcement action (known as DP/3/95) was issued in January 1995.[48] This stated that enforcement action could be taken against those with 'full blown AIDS or who are HIV positive' unless there was medical evidence that the person was not fit to travel and/or 'their life expectancy would be substantially shortened' if they were to be forced to leave the UK. The policy went on to repeat that the fact that medical facilities abroad would be 'substantially less advanced than those available in the UK', although a factor to be considered, was not, in itself, a ground for permitting a person to stay in this country. Reflecting the case of *D v UK*,[49] the policy noted that in the case of a terminally-ill person, 'where there are *no* facilities for treatment',[50] removal might be inappropriate.

6.62 Following developments in the treatment of AIDS and HIV infection, this policy changed on 19 December 2000. Applications made before that date are dealt with under the old policy. Applications for further leave to remain when leave had been granted in the past under the old policy will continue to be dealt with under the old policy.[51] The current policy[52] relates not only to those suffering from AIDS or HIV infection, but also to those suffering from other serious illnesses. By this, the Home Office means seriously debilitating, terminal or life-threatening medical conditions. The current policy is much stricter than the old policy although it repeats that the fact that a person has AIDS, is HIV positive or is suffering from some other serious illness is not in itself a ground to justify the exercise of discretion by the Home Office. The current test is threefold:

- the UK must have assumed responsibility for the person's care; and
- there must be credible medical evidence that return, due to a complete absence of medical treatment in the country concerned, would significantly reduce the applicant's life expectancy; and
- return would also subject the person to acute physical and mental suffering.

---

48 Since 19 December 2000 this policy has not been operated.
49 (1997) 24 EHRR 423.
50 Emphasis in the original.
51 Letter from Home Office to Bindman & Partners, 23 July 2001.
52 IDI Ch 1, s8, para 3.3.

Applications outside the rules 119

The second and third points are expressed in similar terms to the previous exceptional leave policy for failed asylum-seekers.[53]

6.63 The Home Office considers this policy to be 'article 3 proof' and its view has been reiterated in a letter to Wandsworth and Merton Law Centre.[54] The IDI point out that recent domestic and Strasbourg case-law has been unhelpful to applicants suffering from serious illnesses. While in *D*[55] the European Court of Human Rights prevented the expulsion of a convicted man terminally ill with AIDS to a country where he would be likely to receive no or very little treatment and where he would be without the carers with whom he had formed a bond, on the basis that he would be subjected to acute physical and mental suffering, later case-law has distinguished this case. *SSC v Sweden*[56] (an admissibility case) held that a person is not entitled to remain merely in order to continue to benefit from medical, social or other forms of assistance provided by the expelling state. Similarly, in *ex p K*,[57] a renewal of an application for permission in the Court of Appeal held that where treatment would not be available to a person due to its cost, this alone did not amount to inhuman and degrading treatment.[58] Nor was it found unreasonable to return a man with schizophrenia to Algeria where there were conflicting reports on the accessibility of treatment.[59] More positively, in the Dianne Pretty assisted suicide case, there is dicta from Lord Bingham which suggests that there is a positive obligation on a state to ameliorate pain.[60]

6.64 The IDI stress that the fact that an applicant has AIDS, HIV or another serious illness is not in itself a ground for refusing an applicant who otherwise qualifies under the rules. Despite this, applications for entry clearance from those who disclose that they are suffering from such a condition will not be dealt with by the ECO but will be referred back to the Home Office via the Joint Entry Clearance Unit. Evidence of the person's ability to fund any treatment that may

---

53 This policy has been deleted from the API and is currently being rewritten.
54 11 July 2001.
55 *D v UK* (1997) 24 EHHR 423.
56 App 46553/99 (2000) 29 EHRR CD245.
57 *R v Home Secretary ex p K* [2001] Imm AR 11. There is an anonymity order in this case, which the Home Office has not respected in the IDI.
58 See chapter 4 for further discussion of the Human Rights Act 1998.
59 *Bensaid v Home Secretary* [2001] INLR 325.
60 *R v DPP ex p Dianne Pretty and Home Secretary* (2002) 1 All ER 1. At para 14 Lord Bingham states that the position of the applicant in *D* might be analogous to that of Mrs Pretty, if a public official refused to provide her with pain-killing or palliative drugs.

be needed during his/her stay in the UK will be demanded. The referral to the Home Office seems unnecessary and suggests that the Home Office suspects all such people of wishing to remain in the UK and take advantage of the NHS.

6.65 Once a person makes an application for leave to remain on compassionate grounds on the basis of suffering from a serious illness, provided an express claim is made that removal would be a breach of the person's rights under ECHR art 3, access to support by the National Asylum Support Service is activated.[61]

6.66 The application to the Home Office should include a letter from a doctor addressing the following points:

- the nature of the specific medical condition;
- the treatment the person has been receiving, its duration and the consequences of stopping the treatment once commenced;
- the person's life expectancy;
- the person's fitness to travel if required to leave the country.

6.67 The impact of stopping medication once a person has started to receive treatment can be particularly significant for those with AIDS. Stopping combination anti-retroviral therapy once started can reduce life expectancy. In any event, the drugs used in combination therapy have to be administered and monitored carefully. Frequently, a strict diet regime has to be observed. Advisers should make inquiries to find out if the medical infrastructure is in place in the country to which it is proposed to remove an individual to monitor any medication prescribed. This is a significant factor particularly for those with AIDS and for those prescribed anti-psychotic medication.

6.68 Obtaining evidence of the medical services available in other countries is not easy. The IDI refer Home Office case-workers to the Country Information and Policy Unit reports, but these are often too general to be helpful. It is not usually sufficient to obtain an opinion from the patient's consultant in the UK (unless he or she has specialist knowledge of the country concerned). Many embassies do not give accurate information of the realities of medical care in their countries, but information can be found from non-governmental organisations such as Medicins Sans Frontières or Save the Children.[62]

---

61 This is because an application that claims that removal would be a breach of the UK's obligations under the ECHR is defined as a 'claim for asylum' under IAA 1999 s94 (1).
62 See Appendix M for contact details.

6.69 Occasionally, the Home Office asks for authority to investigate the person's health records. For this it seeks advice from the Department of Health.

6.70 Removals should not take place if the person is terminally ill and has 'only a few months to live'.[63] In such cases, leave to remain on compassionate grounds should be given. In these circumstances, advisers should press for the grant of leave to remain. It may ease the applicant's mind to know he or she has been granted permission to stay, but will also facilitate entry clearance applications by relatives who wish to visit. The general policy on removal is that removal should be effected unless the person is not fit to travel. Somewhat heartlessly, the IDI interprets this as an instruction to undertake removal action as soon as possible in case the person becomes more ill.[64]

EEA nationals

6.71 The current policy applies to EEA nationals and their family members. Although one of the three grounds for refusing entry to an EEA national is public health,[65] those with AIDS or who are HIV positive do not fall within this category. An EEA national or his/her dependent family members who are coming to the UK specifically for NHS treatment cannot be refused on that ground alone. However, they would be expected to have obtained a certificate from their national authorities confirming that that state will bear the costs of treatment.

Psychiatric illness

6.72 The Home Secretary has the power to remove an individual who has leave to remain in the UK, but does not have the right of abode and is receiving in-patient treatment for psychiatric illness.[66] The IDI make it clear that 'the initiative for seeking the removal of a psychiatric patient lies with the hospital concerned under the direction of the case doctor. The Home Office should not take steps to repatriate a

---

63 IDI Ch 1, s8, para 3.3 and see chapter 3 for a discussion about access to health care.
64 IDI Ch 1, s8, para 3.7.
65 Directive 64/221, art 4.
66 Mental Health Act 1983 s86 and Mental Health (Scotland) Act 1960 s82, as amended by IA 1971 s30.

psychiatric patient unless first approached by the patient's medical adviser.'[67] The Home Office has to obtain a warrant for the removal of the individual and has to obtain the approval of the Mental Health Review Tribunal (MHRT). The criteria to be met to obtain a warrant for the removal of a psychiatric patient are set out in the Mental Health Acts. These are:

- the patient must be an in-patient;
- specific arrangements must have been made for the care and treatment in the patient's own country;
- the doctor in charge of the case must consider it in the interests of the patient to remove him/her;
- the patient must be fit to travel;
- a medical escort must be provided to accompany the patient to his/her destination;
- the patient must have a valid passport and any necessary transit visas.

6.73 The fact that a patient has been removed does not stop him/her returning, even if the costs of his/her removal have been paid by the government. Obviously, if the patient is not an in-patient, then there is nothing to stop him/her leaving the UK without reference to the Home Office.

6.74 Despite the IDI, the court in the case of *X v Secretary of State for the Home Department*[67a] held that the Home Secretary can choose whether to use his powers under the Immigration Act 1971 or under Mental Health Act 1983 s86.

6.75 The position of psychiatric patients who are not in-patients is different and there are few protections in place. The Home Office does not have to go through the process of obtaining the approval of the MHRT and the only judicial overview is through an appeal on Human Rights Act grounds. Thus, the issues for psychiatric patients are the same as for those suffering other serious illnesses.

Long residence concessions

6.76 There are two very well-known concessions which, in certain circumstances, permit people to remain in the UK. The concessions are set out in the IDI Ch 18 and relate to those who have lived lawfully in this country for ten years or more, and those who have lived unlawfully, or

---

67 IDI Ch 1, s8, para 4.2.
67a [2001] INLR 205.

who have a mixture of lawful and unlawful stay, for 14 years or more. The reason for the concession is to enable the UK to comply with the European Convention on Establishment art 3(3).[68] This provides that nationals of any contracting party who have been lawfully residing for more than ten years in the territory of another party may only be expelled for reasons of national security or for particularly serious reasons relating to public order, public health or morality. The Home Office practice has been to extend this provision in three respects:

- to include all foreign nationals, not just those of countries who are signatories to the Convention;
- to grant indefinite leave (rather than simply refrain from removing such a person); and
- to allow those who are in the UK illegally to benefit.

Ten-year lawful residence concession

6.77 Those who remain in the UK lawfully for more than ten years will usually be allowed to stay here permanently. If the person has completed this period of residence, then the Home Office will usually grant indefinite leave without making any further inquiries, although a serious criminal record will be taken into account.[69]

6.78 The concession does not mean that the person cannot leave the UK at all. Short periods of absence from the UK, up to six months, will not break the period of continuous residence, provided the trips are not frequent. In addition, time spent while waiting for the Home Office to make a decision about an application also counts towards the ten years.

6.79 The Home Office treats the ten-year period and the legality of residence strictly. Thus, if a person has overstayed this will not count towards the ten-year lawful residence. However, there are certain circumstances when time spent in the UK without permission will count towards the ten years. These are:

- time spent waiting for an appeal against a Home Office refusal will count towards the ten-year period if the appeal was subsequently successful;
- if an appeal is unsuccessful, but leave is subsequently granted, then the time spent may be treated as lawful if:
  – the leave was granted on the recommendation of the Adjudicator; or

---

68 Ratified by the UK on 14 October 1969.
69 Minor, non-custodial offences will be ignored. See IDI Ch 18, para 2.

> **Example: Child of person exempt from control**
>
> Zoe was brought to the UK as the dependent of her mother who was exempt from control, as she worked for an Embassy. Her mother remarried, and Zoe did not get on with her stepfather. The family relationship broke down and Zoe left home. She was looked after by the local authority for a couple of years. At the age of 17, the local authority realised that Zoe needed to sort out her immigration position. A successful application was submitted to the Home Office to bring Zoe into immigration control and for indefinite leave as a looked-after child. Zoe's sister had also left home due to family problems. She was aged over 18 but had completed 10 years residence in the UK. A successful application for indefinite leave under the concession was made.

- the leave was granted in any capacity during the period before the determination; or
- where a further successful application in any capacity was submitted shortly after the determination.

6.80 Short delays in submitting an application for further leave to remain may be treated as lawful residence, if the application for leave is subsequently granted.

6.81 The concession is often used by those who have studied in the UK. It also applies to students (and their dependants) who are sponsored by their national governments or an international organisation.

6.82 Time spent exempt from control can count towards the ten-year period, but in order to apply, the person has to bring him/herself within control. For example, a person who has worked for a diplomatic mission, or one of the designated international organisations, and his/her dependants are exempt from control. In the past, all employees of embassies were exempted from control but this is now limited to more senior members of foreign missions. If an exempted person wishes to apply under the concession, he or she must stop employment with the relevant organisation (or be a dependant). He or she is then deemed to have been given leave to remain in the UK for 90 days, without a prohibition on employment, and thus an application under the concession can then be made.[70]

6.83 Frequently, local authorities do not recognise that a child has an immigration problem until the child is nearly 18 years and about to

70 IDI Ch 14, s1, Annex C, para 1.

leave care. This can be problematic for young people with criminal records, particularly those who have not got lengthy residence in the UK.

6.84 Applications from people who have not completed ten years' continuous lawful residence will be refused, unless there are very strong compelling circumstances. Thus, if an individual is short of the ten years' residence necessary, an application under the concession should not be made. The IDI stresses that '[t]he strength of ties with the UK, the continued ties with the home country, the total length of the continuous period and the proportion of it which is lawful are the primary determining factors when deciding to grant or withhold indefinite leave to remain'.

6.85 When making the application it is helpful to set out the circumstances of the person's residence in the UK and to stress any close connections with this country, as well as employment prospects.

14-year long residence concession

6.86 Although it does not appear in the IR, the Home Office has stated that if people remain in the UK, whether lawfully or unlawfully, for over 14 years, then they will usually be allowed to stay permanently, provided that there are no strong countervailing factors such as a criminal record or 'a deliberate and blatant attempt to evade or circumvent (immigration) control'.[71]

6.87 Criminal offences which are spent under the Rehabilitation of Offenders Act 1974 and behaviour which happened five years or more ago should not usually be sufficient to outweigh positive ties with the UK. Where the continuous residence is in excess of 14 years unless the countervailing factors are exceptionally serious, indefinite leave should usually be granted.

6.88 An application can be made where a person has completed between ten and 14 years' continuous residence (not all of it lawful), but there is no presumption that he or she will be granted indefinite leave. Although each case should be considered on its merits, the Home Office takes into account:
- the quality of the residence;
- the length of the period of continuous residence;
- the proportion of it which is lawful;
- the strength of the ties to the UK (particularly family ties).

71 IDI Ch 18, para 2.

6.89 If an applicant has children living with him/her, then the seven-year concession should be considered, if appropriate. In any event, the applicant's rights under the ECHR should be raised, particularly ECHR art 8, the right to respect for private and family life.

6.90 If, after application, it transpires that a deportation order was made against an individual, but he or she did not know of it, this does not stop the clock for calculating the years of residence.[72]

Administrative removal and deportation

6.91 The power to deport is contained in the Immigration Act (IA) 1971 s5. Deportation is a very serious matter as it means that there is a permanent prohibition on an individual re-entering the UK. Furthermore, a deportation order, once made, will not usually be revoked unless the individual has been out of the UK for a minimum of three years.

6.92 On 2 October 2000, IAA 1999 s10 replaced deportation of those in breach of their conditions of stay with administrative removal, a process that is identical to the removal of illegal entrants.[73] The deportation process remains for those whose presence is held not to be conducive to the public good,[74] their family members[75] and those recommended by a court following conviction for an offence punishable by a sentence of imprisonment.[76] Home Office policies set out in the IDI and elsewhere should now be read as referring to removal as well as deportation.

6.93 The IR governing the exercise of discretion in deportation and removal cases are set out in HC 395 Pt 13. A balancing process is carried out, weighing the public interest (generally, but including that involved in maintaining an effective immigration control) against the compassionate circumstances of the case and taking into account various factors. These factors are:

---

72 This can occur, for example, if the order was sent to an address but not received by the applicant and returned to the Home Office or if, under the Home Office practice in the 1980s where, if a deportee's whereabouts were not known, the deportation order was served 'on the file'. See *Macdonald's Immigration Law and Practice* (5th edn, Butterworths, 2001) p721.
73 See HC 395 as amended para 395A. The exception is those that applied under the short-lived 'regularisation scheme for overstayers' between 8 February 2000 and 1 October 2000 can still benefit from an appeal against deportation under IA 1971.
74 IA 1971 s3(5)(a) as amended by IAA 1999 Sch 14, para 44(2).
75 Ibid s3(5)(b).
76 Ibid s3(6).

Applications outside the rules 127

> **Example: Care orders, discretion, deportation orders, illegal entry**
>
> Mrs Brown has indefinite leave to remain. She has severe mental health problems and has periodically been sectioned under the Mental Health Act 1983. She has two children, one aged eight and one aged 12 who both have indefinite leave to remain. As a result of her treatment of the two children they are subject to a care order and were placed with Mr and Mrs Harris in 1998 where they continue to live. Mrs Harris is the sister of Mrs Brown. Mr and Mrs Harris have two children of their own who are under 14. Mr and Mrs Harris and their two children are subject to deportation orders signed in 1999 following an unsuccessful appeal before an adjudicator. Removal has not been enforced. Submissions made in late 1999 that Mrs and Mrs Harris should be permitted to remain in the UK given their length of residence (eight years by then) and their responsibilities towards the children of Mrs Brown were rejected.
>
> Mr Brown then arrived in the UK having been given leave to enter as a visitor. It is likely that he is an illegal entrant as he failed to disclose on entry that he was married or that he had children resident in the UK. He commenced living with his wife who became pregnant. He worked without paying tax or national insurance.
>
> Shortly after the birth of Mrs Brown's child, an application was made for Mr Brown to be granted leave to remain on the basis of his marriage, the baby and the two children who were subject to the care order. He was granted leave to remain for one year and subsequently indefinite leave to remain.
>
> A successful application was submitted for Mr and Mrs Harris to be granted leave to remain, this time relying on the incorporation of the ECHR as well as the previous arguments raised.

- age;
- length of residence in the UK;
- strength of connections with the UK;
- personal history, including character, conduct and employment record;
- domestic circumstances;
- previous criminal record and, if relevant, the nature of the offence of which the person has been convicted;
- compassionate circumstances;
- any representations received.[77]

77 HC 395 as amended para 395b.

6.94 Immigration Act 1971 s3(5)(c) (as amended) permits the deportation of family members of the principal deportee. When considering deporting or administratively removing family members the factors listed in IR paras 365–368 are taken into account. These state that the wife of a deportee will not usually be deported if:

- she has qualified for settlement in her own right; or
- she has been living apart from the deportee.

6.95 Examples of when deportation action is taken against spouses on the ground that the principal family member is being deported are given in a letter dated 13 July 1998 to the Greater Manchester Immigration Aid Unit. These are:

- the spouse is an overstayer or breaches the conditions attached to the grant of leave but he or she has limited leave;
- the spouse is recommended for deportation by the court;[78]
- the spouse is convicted of a serious offence and the Home Secretary decides that his/her presence is not conducive to the public good;[79]
- the spouse has obtained leave by deception.[80]

6.96 The same letter makes it clear that family member deportation would not be used against a spouse who had overstayed as well: that person would be deported in his/her own right under IA 1971 s3(5)(a).[81]

6.97 The rules state that in the exercise of the power to deport the Home Secretary will act in a manner that is 'consistent and fair as between one person and another, although one case will rarely be identical with another in all material respects'.[82] This means that an individual is entitled to rely on policy pronouncements concerning deportation, whether published or unpublished.[83]

Cases involving children or marriage

Marriage

6.98 The Home Office has issued a number of policies to be taken into account when considering the deportation or administrative removal of an individual in cases involving a marriage or children. These are

---

78 IA 1971 s3(6).
79 Ibid s3(5)(b).
80 Ibid s3(5)(aa).
81 See below for Home Office policies on the deportation or removal of children.
82 HC 395 as amended para 364.
83 However, a policy is not a rule, and need not be followed rigidly provided adequate reasons are given for deviating from the policy. See para 6.9.

contained in documents DP 3/96, DP 4/96 and DP 5/96 (now known as DP 069/99).[84] These replace and restrict the previous guidelines contained in DP 2/93. Although the guidelines are not part of the IR a failure to follow them by the Home Office may give rise to a successful challenge by way of judicial review. DP 2/93 was designed to be compatible with ECHR art 8, and was held to be such.[85] However, decisions made in accordance with the policies should always be examined in the light of the ECHR and human rights considerations.[86]

6.99 There is no automatic right to remain in the UK merely by virtue of marrying a British citizen or a person settled in this country. The situation for those who marry EEA nationals exercising Treaty of Rome rights in the UK is entirely different. Irrespective of the person's immigration history, he or she will usually be given leave to remain in line with the EEA spouse.[87]

6.100 The IR set out the requirements for sponsoring a spouse for entry clearance or for leave to remain.[88] The rules are the starting point when advising a person who is in the UK in an irregular position and who has married a person settled in this country. Obviously, it is helpful if the couple can satisfy the rules relating to maintenance and accommodation. The requirements relating to lawful presence in the UK or entry clearance appear to prevent any applicant who is in the UK in an irregular position from making an application on the basis of marriage to a person settled here. This is not the case. In addition to the rules, there are the guidelines which apply to all cases in which the marriage comes to the attention of the immigration authorities after 13 March 1996, irrespective of the date on which the marriage took place.[89]

84 See Appendix D.
85 See *R v Home Secretary ex p Gangadeen* [1998] INLR 206, CA.
86 See *B v Home Secretary* [2000] INLR 361; [2000] Imm AR 478, and chapter 4.
87 See para 6.56 for a discussion on EU nationals, marriage, and separated spouses.
88 HC 395 as amended paras 277–289 require that: (a) the foreign party to the marriage is married to a person present and settled in the UK, or who is on the same occasion being admitted for settlement; (b) the parties to the marriage have met; (c) the couple each intend to live permanently with each other as husband and wife and the marriage is subsisting; (d) adequate accommodation for the parties will be available without recourse to public funds in accommodation which the parties own or occupy exclusively; (e) the parties will be able to maintain themselves and any dependants adequately without recourse to public funds; (f) the applicant has limited leave to remain in the UK; and (g) the applicant has not remained in breach of the immigration laws.
89 Copies of the guidelines are to be found in Appendix L.

6.101　The current policy came into effect on 14 March 1996 and is more restrictive than the previous policy. It states that if the marriage has taken place before enforcement action has taken effect then the foreign spouse will be permitted to remain in the UK provided that:
- the marriage is genuine and subsisting; and
- the marriage has lasted for at least two years before the commencement of enforcement action; and
- it is unreasonable to expect the settled spouse to accompany his/her spouse on removal.

6.102　When considering whether it is unreasonable or not to expect the settled spouse to leave the UK, the following factors concerning the settled spouse have to be taken into account:
- if he or she has very strong and close family ties in the UK, such as older children from a previous relationship that form part of the family unit; or
- whether he or she has been settled and living in the UK for at least the preceding ten years; or
- if he or she suffers from ill health and medical evidence conclusively shows that his/her life would be significantly impaired or endangered if he or she were to accompany his/her spouse on removal.

6.103　The reference to 'commencement of enforcement action' is also clarified in the policy and it depends on the immigration status of the person concerned. It is either a letter from the Home Office ordering the person to leave with a warning of liability to deportation (or removal) if he or she fails to do so, or service of the notice of intention to deport, or service of illegal entry papers, and includes service of papers previously on an individual when he or she has returned to the UK in breach of a deportation order, or a recommendation for deportation by a criminal court as part of a criminal sentence.

6.104　The commencement of enforcement action effectively 'stops the clock' in terms of the two-year qualifying period for which a marriage must have subsisted. No further time can then be accrued to meet this criterion.

Marriages that post-date enforcement action

6.105　Where a person marries after the commencement of enforcement action it is 'only in the most *exceptional circumstances* that removal action should be stopped and the person allowed to stay'.[90] The policy

90　Emphasis in the original.

makes it clear that 'marriage cannot ... in itself be considered a sufficiently compassionate factor to militate against removal'. Given this, in such cases detailed inquiries to ascertain whether the marriage is genuine and subsisting will not usually be undertaken by the Home Office and the onus is on the applicant to put forward reasons and evidence both as to the genuineness of the relationship and the compassionate reasons why enforcement action should not be taken.

6.106 The guidelines make it clear that they operate as a general rule and that fulfilment of the criteria is not conclusive in a person's favour. In addition, a poor immigration history may justify enforcement action even where the normal criteria indicate that deportation/removal should not as a general rule be enforced.

6.107 If a foreign spouse who would usually benefit from the policy has committed a criminal offence, the 'severity of the offence' is balanced against the strength of the family ties. Thus, serious offences which can be punished by a prison sentence or conviction for a series of lesser offences 'which show a propensity to re-offend' would usually outweigh family ties.

6.108 Despite the guidelines, deportation or removal has to be justified as proportionate if it is to satisfy the public policy considerations of ECHR art 8.[91]

Children and Home Office deportation and removal policies

6.109 The three policies include specific reference to people facing deportation who have children. These policies make no mention of the 14-year residence policy and predate the introduction of the seven-year policy, and thus should be read with these policies in mind.

Children and marriage – policy DP 3/96[91a]

6.110 This policy relates to those who are married to a person settled in the UK and who are liable to deportation and removal. No reference is made to those who are not married, but who are cohabiting, but given that long-term cohabiting relationships have been recognised within the IR it is arguable that the policy should be applied to cohabitees.[92]

---

91 See *B v Home Secretary* [2000] INLR 361; [2000] Imm AR 478.
91a See para 6.92 above.
92 In the cases that dealt with DP 2/93 the courts chose to construe the married relationship strictly, but these cases predated the rule change which recognised long-term cohabiting partnerships.

The policy includes reference to marriages where there are children of the relationship and accepts that the existence of a child with the right of abode is a 'factor to be taken into account'.[93] However, it is not automatic for families with children to be permitted to remain in the UK. The policy makes reference to the concept of 'adaptable age', that is the age when it is acceptable for a child to be expected to be able to adapt to life abroad. The policy continues:

> In cases involving children who have the right of abode the crucial question is whether it is reasonable for the child to accompany his/her parents abroad. Factors to be considered include:
>
> *the age of the child* (in most cases a child of ten or younger could reasonably be expected to adapt to life abroad);
>
> *serious ill-health* for which treatment is not available in the country to which the family is going.[94]

6.111 The health test is onerous and makes no reference to the ability of a family to pay for appropriate health care if the family is being removed to a country where there is limited or no free health care.[95]

6.112 The policy has a note explaining that not all children born in the UK have the right of abode. It does not explain that children who are born in the UK and have lived in this country for ten years are entitled to register as British under British Nationality Act (BNA) 1981 s1(4). The note stresses that fathers cannot pass on their British citizenship to illegitimate children. However, no reference is made to the Home Office policy that permits such children (whether born in the UK or abroad) to be registered as British on application.[96]

Children with long residence in the UK – policy DP 069/99 (formerly DP 5/96)[96a]

6.113 This policy relates to deportation and removal cases where there are children with long residence in the UK. The original policy DP 5/96 pre-dated the seven-year concession[97] and made no reference to the 14 year residence concession. Instead, it dealt with the position of children who had spent ten years or more in the UK:

---

93 DP 3/96 para 7.
94 Emphasis supplied.
95 See para 6.60 for the policy relating to those with serious illnesses and para 5.47 for the exceptional leave to remain policy.
96 See para 6.146.
96a See para 6.92 above.
97 See para 6.132.

The purpose of this instruction is to define more clearly the criteria to be applied when considering whether enforcement action should proceed or be initiated against parents who have children who were either born here and are aged ten or over or where, having come to the UK at an early age, they have accumulated ten years or more continuous residence.

6.114 Once again, no mention is made of the rights of children born in the UK who have lived here for ten years to register as British citizens under BNA 1981 s1(4). The policy repeats the general rule that 'each individual case must be taken on its merits' but sets out the following factors:

- the length of the parents' residence without leave;
- whether removal has been delayed through protracted (and often repetitive) representations or by the parents going to ground;
- the age of the children;
- whether the children were conceived at a time when either parent had leave to remain;
- whether return to the parents' country of origin would cause *serious hardship* for the children or put their health seriously at risk'.[98]

6.115 The age of the child is presumably a reference to the concept of the 'adaptable age' under which a child is presumed to be able to adapt to life abroad. It is hard to understand the relevance of when a child has been conceived. Possibly this could be a similar notion to the fact that under the marriage policy, a marriage entered into after enforcement action can be discounted. However, the idea that a child should be somehow to blame for being conceived while his/her parents were in the UK unlawfully is curious to say the least, and is at odds with other statements of policy.[99] It reflects the generally held view within the Home Office that parents use children as a tool to get round the IR.

Deportation of children whose parent(s) are subject to deportation action – policies DP 4/95 and DP 4/96[99a]

6.116 The power to deport family members of a principal deportee is contained in IA 1971[100] s3(5)(b). This includes the principal deportee's

---

98 Emphasis supplied.
99 See para 6.25 and, in particular, IDI Ch 8, Annex M, para 6.1, and para 6.120 below.
99a See para 6.92 above.
100 As amended by IAA 1999 Sch 14, para 46.

children under 18 years of age including adopted children and, if the principal deportee is a man, his wife's children. An illegitimate child is considered to be the child of the mother.[101] Unlike most deportation orders which last indefinitely unless revoked, a deportation order made against a person on the basis of belonging to the family of another person ceases to have effect if the person ceases to belong to the family of the other person. A child ceases to belong to the family on reaching the age of 18.[102] In addition, if the deportation order made against the principal deportee is revoked, then those against family members are also revoked.[103]

6.117 IR paras 366–367 have additional criteria (over and above the usual factors set out in para 364)[104] to be taken into account when considering deporting a child aged under 18. A child will not usually be deported if he or she:

- and his/her mother are living apart from the principal deportee; or
- has spent 'some years' in the UK and is nearing the age of 18; or
- has left home and has established him/herself independently; or
- has married before deportation came into prospect.[105]

6.118 In addition, the Home Secretary must take into account:

- the effect of removal on a child of school age; and
- the practicability of any plans for a child's care and maintenance in the UK if one or both of his/her parents were deported.[106]

6.119 Policy DP 4/95 provides guidance on the operation of IA 1971 s3(5)(c).[107] It introduced internal procedures for the Home Office to take steps to include the deportation of children at the outset when initial action is taken to deport the parents 'rather than waiting to see whether or not the parents are willing to take their children with them when they are deported'. Nevertheless, there have been cases since 1995 where deportation action has been taken against the parents but not the children.

6.120 The policy in the past has been for parents to be served with deportation proceedings on the assumption that their children would accompany them. Where parents refuse to take their children with

---

101 IA 1971 s5(4).
102 Ibid s5(3) and IAA 1999 s10(5).
103 Ibid s5(3).
104 See para 6.93.
105 HC 395 as amended para 366.
106 HC 395 as amended para 367.
107 As amended by IAA 1999 Sch 14, para 46.

them they have either been removed from the UK with the children placed into care or they have been allowed to stay with their children while steps are taken towards deporting the children. Home Office policy in the past has been not to taint a child with the stigma of deportation when obtaining leave to enter or remain is usually outside a child's control. This position is reflected in a letter to the Greater Manchester Immigration Aid Unit,[108] which states:

> We consider that children under the age of 16 are the responsibility of the parents. It would be difficult for the child to seek to abide by his/her conditions of stay. This would mean that he or she would need to either seek leave in his/her own right or leave the country alone.

Despite this, as deportation action against a child under the family member provisions ceases if the child reaches the age of 18, the Home Office consider it appropriate to commence deportation action under IA 1971 s3(5)(b) even if the child is aged under 16 in order to be sure that they can finish the process in time.

6.121 For children over 16, the policy is clear: if the child is overstaying, then deportation action should be considered. Policy DP 4/95 states that, '[w]here a child is 16 or over and *is liable to deportation as an overstayer* consideration should be given to taking action against him/her...'.[109] Since 2 October 2000, administrative removal is more likely to be used by the Home Office. DP 4/95 notes the following exception (also contained in IA 1971 s 5(3)):

> ... a deportation order cannot be made against a dependant if more than 8 weeks have elapsed since the parent has left the UK after the making of a deportation order against him.[110]

6.122 The policy does not apply to children who are born in the UK, who have never left, but who have never been granted leave to remain. These children are not overstayers, nor in breach of any conditions of stay, nor are they illegal entrants. Prior to the IAA 1999 children born in the UK while their parents were without leave were not themselves removable as there were no provisions for this purpose.[111] However,

---

108 Letter from the Home Office to the Greater Manchester Immigration Aid Unit, 13 July 1998.
109 DP 4/95 para 3, emphasis in the original. The letter predates the amendments to IA 1971 contained in IAA 1999 and thus refers to IA 1971 s3(5)c throughout.
110 Ibid para 8. This excludes any period while an appeal is pending.
111 IAA 1999 makes it possible to enforce the administrative removal of a child (as a family member of a person against whom removal directions have been made) under IAA 1999 s10(1)(c).

in line with DP 4/95, IAA 1999 s10(3) only allows for removal directions to be issued where written notice of the intention to remove the family member has been provided in writing 'not more that eight weeks after the other person left the UK in accordance with the first directions'.

6.123 Clearly, if a child has lived in the UK for 14 or 7 years continuously, he or she falls to be considered under the 14-year residence concession or the seven-year concession respectively.[112] The policy requires that parents must be notified in writing that a child is still able to leave voluntarily as required by IR para 368.

6.124 Unusually for these policies, DP 4/95 mentions a child's right to register as British under BNA 1981 s1(4) and stresses that deportation action should not be taken against a British citizen.

Children with parents in the UK – policy DP 4/96[112a]

6.125 A year later, a further policy (DP 4/96) was introduced, covering the position of people who are liable to removal from the UK and who are either children themselves, or are parents who have children present in the UK. The policy is supplemental to and to be read in conjunction with the previous policies DP 3/96 (concerning marriage cases where there are children), DP 5/96 (concerning children who have lived in the UK for ten years or more – now modified by the seven-year concession) and DP 4/96 on the deportation of family members of a principal deportee.

6.126 The tone of the policy is made clear in the first sentence of the policy which stresses that 'there is no bar to taking deportation/illegal entry action against children of any age who are liable to such action'. When dealing with children who are with their parents in the UK, the policy acknowledges that the children's presence is a significant factor although not an overriding one:

> Where deportation/removal action is being considered against a parent or parents the existence of children in the UK is a factor that must be taken into account when assessing the merits of such action. The weight to be attached to children as a compassionate factor will vary from case to case and has to be balanced against or along with other factors.[113]

---

112 See para 6.76 for the long residence concession, and para 6.132 for the seven-year concession.
112a See para 6.92 above.
113 DP 4/96 para 4.

The policy continues:

> In all cases *the longer the child has been here the greater will be the weight to be attached to this as a factor*; but the general *presumption* will be that a child who has spent less than ten years in the UK will be able to adapt to life abroad.[114]

6.127 The time factor is open to challenge. Since the introduction of the policy, the Home Office itself has acknowledged that the length of time demanded is too high, and has introduced the seven-year concession, which reduces the time a child has to spend in the UK to seven years.[115]

Unaccompanied children – policy DP 4/96[115a]

6.128 The policy also looks at the position of children who are on their own in the UK. It repeats that children who are on their own in the UK should only be deported if a voluntary departure cannot be arranged. Nor should a child on his/her own be removed from the UK unless 'the child will be met on arrival in his/her home country and care arrangements are in place thereafter'.[116] This sentiment is presumably behind the current Home Office policy of granting young Kosovan asylum-seekers[117] who have been refused asylum leave to remain until their 18th birthday. Thereafter, there will be no requirement that the young people be appropriately looked after on their return to Kosovo, and thus it will be easier to remove them. However, issues may arise under the local authorities' duties to young people under the Children (Leaving Care) Act 2000.[117a]

6.129 Ensuring that a child will be met on arrival in his/her country and that appropriate care arrangements are in place is not easy. When dealing with prospective deportees under 18 years, Home Office caseworkers are enjoined to contact the welfare section of the appropriate Embassy or High Commission as well as the local social services department. Home Office escorts can get over part of the problem. But otherwise, only if there is 'evidence, not just a suspicion, that the care arrangements are seriously below the standard usually provided in the country concerned or that they are so inadequate that the child would face a serious risk of harm if returned' should the case-worker

---

114 Ibid para 5. Emphasis supplied.
115 See para 6.132.
115a See para 6.92 above.
116 DP 4/96 para 2.
117 Race Relations (Amendment) Act 2000 makes discrimination on grounds of nationality lawful.
117a See para 1.100 above.

consider abandoning enforcement action. This is a high test, and is clearly not in accordance with the usual welfare principle in childcare law. It suggests that there is one welfare test for children who are looked after by a local authority,[117b] and another, much less onerous test for other children who are in an irregular position in this country.

6.130 Although the Home Office is obliged to make its own inquiries about the care arrangements available abroad, it is always best for legal representatives to make their own inquiries. These will also be made through the relevant Embassy or High Commission and social services in the country concerned, but they could also include other sources of information such as International Social Services. It should be remembered that not all countries have functioning or effective social services departments, and inquiries made through International Social Services will be carried out by the local social services department. If the local social services department is not effective, one option could be to send a social worker from the UK to investigate the position. Difficulties may arise with getting the authorities to co-operate. In addition, the authorities representing a country at an Embassy in the UK may state that adequate provision is available in the home country, while the authorities in the home country itself may be of the opposite opinion. Non-governmental organisations may also be able to help with obtaining home reports.[118]

6.131 To ensure that all the authorities concerned have considered all the factors relating to a particular case, it is important to ensure they are informed of any special needs or other factors relating to a child's welfare that will need to be taken into account before they can confirm there are appropriate reception facilities in the country of origin. Thus social and medical reports are of primary importance even if the Home Office has refused to accept such reports as providing adequate reason for a child to be allowed to remain in the UK.

Families with children who have lived in the UK for seven years or more

6.132 Where children have lived in the UK for seven years or more, the Home Office will not usually enforce removal or deportation.[119] There is no requirement for the child to have been born in the UK.[120] Excep-

---

117b See para 1.103 above.
118 See Appendix M for contact details.
119 See HC Written Answer, 24 February 1999, pp309–310 and IDI Ch 8, Annex M, para 7.
120 See letter from Immigration Service headquarters to UKCOSA, 14 May 1999.

Applications outside the rules 139

> **Example: Home Office discretionary policy**
>
> Washington is 15 years old and is from Nigeria. He has been in the UK since he was about seven and is accommodated. He lives in a children's home. He wants to travel to France with his school. The social worker applied for a passport but was told by the Passport Office that he was not entitled to one. The social worker intends to authorise the school to put him on a joint passport for the school trip.
>
> If the social worker does this, on return to the UK, Washington will be an illegal entrant. The child's immigration status needs to be regularised by making an application to the Home Office.

tions to the concession include where there has been a 'flagrant abuse of the immigration law or where the parent has been convicted of a serious criminal offence which outweighs the compassionate circumstances of the case, including the length of residence of the child'.[121]

6.133 The Home Office has argued that the concession only applies to deportees and illegal entrants[122] and does not apply to those being refused leave to enter. The Home Office backed down at application stage in a judicial review in the High Court on this point. Indeed, it is hard to see how, from the child's point of view, living in the UK under temporary admission following an application for leave to enter at the port differs from living in this country as an illegal entrant or an overstayer. The Home Office has suggested that it is not possible to make an application under the concession.[123] However, there is nothing to prevent an application being made to regularise a family's position quoting the concession. Certainly, reference to it should be made when relevant in a statement of additional grounds made under IAA 1999 ss74 and 75.

6.134 There is no cut-off point to the application. The significant factor is not the parent's immigration status, but the fact of a child having lived in the UK for seven years. The concession applies even if a deportation order has been signed.[124] However, contrary to the general policy in relation to applications made by children, the policy is only

---

121 See letter from Immigration and Nationality Department to Immigration Law Practitioners Association, 1 September 1999.
122 See letter from Immigration Service headquarters to Afrifa & Partners, 19 April 1999.
123 See letter from Immigration Service headquarters to UKCOSA, 14 May 1999.
124 See letter from Immigration Service headquarters to Afrifa & Partners, 19 April 1999.

> **Example: Less than seven years' residence, child born UK**
>
> Esther came to the UK seven years ago as a visitor. She was trading but ran into financial problems and did not leave at the end of her visa. She borrowed a friend's national insurance number and has been working since then save for a short period after she gave birth to her daughter four years ago. She has no contact with the father of the child who makes no contribution either financially or emotionally. Esther's health is deteriorating. She suffers from progressive degenerative problems with her spine which cause her great pain, particularly since her job – cleaning – involves quite heavy lifting. She has applied for housing benefit and been refused.
>
> Esther has not been in the UK for sufficient time to enable her to benefit from the long residence concessions. Her daughter has not been in the UK long enough to benefit from the seven-year concession and nor can she be registered as a British citizen. Esther's deteriorating health renders it likely that she will be reliant on public funds if she is granted leave to remain.
>
> Evidence of the availability of medical treatment and other support for Esther and her daughter in Esther's country of origin will be required. The likely effect on the child of removal will need to be examined, in particular in relation to standard of living in comparison to other children of her age, and access to education. The closeness of ties in the UK will have to be explored, as will the potential for future contact with the child's father. The failed application for housing benefit may have been drawn to the attention of the Home Office.
>
> A decision will have to be taken whether to apply for leave to remain now (relying on ECHR art 8 – private life, family life, no other home, moral and physical integrity; ECHR art 3 – inhuman and degrading treatment, severe lack of medical and social care, education protocol) or whether to wait until the Home Office makes inquiries or the child completes seven years' residence. There is a risk that during the waiting period the Home Office will in any event make inquiries and thus an explanation of the delay in applying will have to be given. There will also be increasing financial problems.
>
> A successful application to remain in this case does not look very likely at this stage.

applied when there is a child aged under 18 at the time the case is considered by the Home Office.[125] As this is contradicted by policy elsewhere in the IDI[126] this may be open to challenge.

Removal of family units

6.135 If a person from abroad is to be removed, and he or she wishes his/her family to accompany him/her, then the Immigration Service will usually pay the family members' travel costs. The Immigration Service has confirmed that if the person intends to apply for entry clearance to return to the UK, then it will not pay the family's travel expenses. The Operational Enforcement Manual (which is not in the public domain) states at para 36.3:

> In all cases the spouse should be given the opportunity to accompany the subject (at public expense if the family intend making their home abroad). If it is clear that the illegal entrant proposes to apply from abroad for entry clearance to return to the UK, he may be removed alone.[127]

Citizenship issues

Registration of minors as British citizens

6.136 Since 1 January 1983 (the coming into force of the British Nationality Act (BNA) 1981) not all children born in the UK are born with British citizenship. The child's citizenship depends on the citizenship and immigration status of the parents. If a child is born in the UK and his/her mother or father (if married to the mother) is a British citizen[128] or has settled status then the child will be born a British citizen.[129] He or she may also have other citizenships through his/her parents, depending on their nationality, and the nationality laws of that country.

6.137 If the mother or father (if married to the mother) is not British or settled then the child will not be born British, but in certain

---

125 See letter from Immigration Service headquarters to Powell & Co, 21 July 1999.
126 See para 6.22 above and IDI Ch 8, s3, Annex M, para 2.
127 Faxed letter to Sue Shutter, (office of Fiona Mactaggart MP) from Andy Smith, Office of the Deputy Director, Immigration Service, 22 August 2001. On occasion, the Immigration Service has stated that entry clearance cannot be applied for unless six months has elapsed from departure. This is not correct.
128 Other sorts of British citizenship do not confer full British citizenship solely by birth of a child in the UK.
129 BNA 1981 s1(1).

> **Example: Registration of a child living abroad**
>
> John, a British citizen, had lived in another EU member state for many years. He had no intention of marrying or of returning to live in the UK for the foreseeable future. He was not married to his partner, who was a national of a third country. His daughter was born in the EU member state. There was no question over the parentage of the child: John acknowledged her as his daughter, and his name appeared on her birth certificate as her father. An application to register the child as British under BNA 1981 s3(1) was successful.

> **Example: Registration of an illegitimate child, mother in irregular position in UK**
>
> David, a British citizen, had lived with his partner, from Cambodia, for some time. They had a child together, abroad, and the mother and the child came to the UK, initially to live with David. The relationship failed, although the couple remained on reasonable terms. The mother's application for leave to remain on an exceptional basis was unsuccessful and was appealed. In the meantime, a successful application to register the child as British was made.

circumstances he or she can be registered as British. If one of the child's parents becomes settled, then a child born in the UK has a right to register as British.[130] If the child is born in the UK and lives in the country for ten years (with absences of 90 days per year permitted) then, under BNA 1981 s1(4), he or she has a right to register as British. This right is not restricted to minors.[130a] If the child was born outside the UK then the child will usually have to wait until one or other of his/her parents applies to naturalise themselves.

6.138 Under BNA 1981 s3(1) the Home Secretary has an overriding discretion to register any child as British if he or she thinks fit. On the face of it this is a very broad discretion, but the Home Office policy is to restrict its application to certain circumstances. The child can be in the UK or abroad, but the Home Office policy is not to register a child living abroad 'unless his/her future can be seen clearly to lie in the UK and at least one of his parents is a British citizen'.[131]

---

130 Ibid s1(3).
130a See Laurie Fransman *British Nationality Law* (2nd edn, Butterworths, 1998) p296, para 12.2.2.
131 Letter of 13 June 1997 from Home Office to Bindman & Partners quoted in Laurie Fransman *British Nationality Law* (2nd edn, Butterworths, 1998) p343.

6.139 Home Office policy on nationality matters is available through the Nationality Instructions (NI). The main point that the Home Office considers is where the future of the child is likely to lie.[132] The Home Office look at the family's past behaviour as an indicator of whether a life in the UK has been established and, if there are no contrary indicators, the Home Office should 'accept at face value that the child intends to live here'.[133] Factors that might alert the Home Office to the possibility that the child's future is outside the UK include:

- the child, or one or both parents, has recently left the country for a period of more than six months;
- the child is about to leave the UK;
- one or both parents is resident abroad.[134]

6.140 The NI set out the criteria for the registration of a child living in the UK, but born abroad. The first point examined is the citizenship and/or immigration status of the child's parents. If the child's application is part of his/her parent's application for British citizenship, both parents should have settled status and the success of the child's application will be dependent on that of the parent's. If the application for the child is made independently, the NI state:

> We should usually expect:
> - at least one parent to be a British citizen; and
> - both parents to be settled here; or
> - if the parents have been divorced or separated for a long time, that the parent having the day-to-day responsibility for the child is a British citizen; or
> - if the responsible parent is settled here but not a British citizen, that there are good reasons why registration would not be appropriate.[135]

6.141 A child who is applying for discretionary registration as British should usually have settled status. This requirement may be waived, if one or both of the child's parents are British citizens or have come to live in the UK permanently and the child otherwise meets the criteria for registration.[136] If a non-settled child applies to register, the Home Office will consider internally if the conditions attached to the child's stay would be removed and settlement likely to be granted, if applied for, and if so, treat the child as if he or she were settled.[137]

132 NI Ch 9, s15.2.
133 NI Ch 9, s15.2.
134 NI Ch 9, s15.3.
135 NI Ch 9, s15.11.
136 NI Ch 9, s15.27.
137 NI Ch 9, s15.28.

6.142 The policy requires a child aged 13 or over to have completed two years' residence in the UK, although this requirement is less important for children aged under 13.[138] An application can be made if the child has been in this country for less than two years, if there are compassionate factors. Examples listed in the NI[139] include:

- where a child will reach the age of majority before the expiry of the last two months of the two-year period and thus could not re-apply under BNA 1981 s3(1), but could not have come to the UK earlier due to circumstances outside the family's control;
- where there are compelling compassionate reasons or refusal would cause severe hardship, for example, a minor with severe learning difficulties who would not be able to swear an oath of allegiance as an adult;
- where the minor would be the only family member who would not become a British citizen;
- where the minor's residence has been broken by trips abroad, but could be aggregated;
- a further example confirmed in a letter from the Home Office policy section is if a child goes abroad on a school trip and has to return through one immigration channel, while the rest of the school returns through the EU channel, and thus is made to stand out.[140]

6.143 In summary, the factors that the Home Secretary takes into account include:

- where the child's future is likely to lie;
- the child's connections with the UK;
- the views of the parents, if appropriate;
- the nationality of the parents – one parent is expected to be a British citizen or applying for citizenship and settled in the UK;
- whether the child has settled status;
- the length of time the child has lived in the UK;
- whether the child is of good character.

These last two points will only be considered in the case of older children, over 16 years of age.[141] If a care order has been made in respect of a child, then the Home Secretary will also take into account the view of the social services department.[142]

138 NI Ch 9, ss15.19.
139 NI Ch 9, s15.22.
140 Letter dated 26 November 2001 from Tony Dalton of IND Liverpool to Bindman & Partners.
141 NI Ch 9, ss15, 29–32.
142 NI Ch 9, s22.

Sibling groups split by nationality

6.144 A further useful point is that the Home Office policy is not to split sibling groups by nationality. The policy has been set out in a letter as:

> There have been a couple of cases recently where the eldest child in the family, the one who has lived in the UK the longest, has been the only one not to be British, and we have registered two children (different families) where the parents were unable or unwilling to apply for British citizenship. We are still developing our policy in this area but the above presents the position as it is today.[143]

6.145 The policy relating to sibling groups split by nationality appears to be developing: a recent application on behalf of a child of recognised refugees whose sibling was entitled to register under BNA 1981 s1(3) was rejected on the basis that the child had only lived in the UK for three years and his parents intended to apply for citizenship once they were eligible to do so. The refusal letter comments that the policy:

> Typically ... may involve a child who has lived here for many years, and whose parents, for whatever reason, were not considering applying for British citizenship in the foreseeable future.[144]

This appears to be in contradiction to the philosophy behind the previous policy and may represent a retraction of the more liberal approach taken earlier.

Illegitimate children

6.146 Under the BNA 1981 a child cannot automatically acquire British citizenship through his/her father unless the father was married to the mother.[145] Subsequent marriage will legitimise the child from the date of the marriage, and mean that the child can take the father's citizenship.[146] However, under BNA 1981 s3(1) the Home Office will usually register as British the illegitimate child of a British citizen father if there are no obvious doubts as to paternity, no reasonable objections from either parent or those with parental responsibility and there are no good character objections, bearing in mind the age of the child.[147]

---

143 Letter of 13 June 1997 from Home Office to Bindman & Partners quoted in Laurie Fransman *British Nationality Law* (2nd edn, Butterworths, 1998) p343.
144 Letter to Bindman & Partners, 23 October 2001.
145 BNA 1981 s50(9).
146 Ibid s47.
147 NI Ch 9, s9.

6.147 An illegitimate child of a dead father, even a child who was born after the father's death, can also benefit from this policy.[148] Until recently, the Home Office policy was to require the child to be living in the UK, but this has been dropped. The mother's immigration status should not be a relevant factor, as the policy makes no reference to it, although caution should be exercised if the mother has an irregular immigration position, as the application form requires the mother to give her current address.

148 Letter to Bindman & Partners, 31 March 2000.

CHAPTER 7

Interviewing and preparation

7.1	Introduction
7.4	**Taking instructions**
7.6	Instructions from a child
7.22	Instructions from parents/carers
7.24	Where a child is subject to a care order
7.25	**Issues that may have to be addressed by experts**
7.25	Assessment of child's future in UK
7.26	Benefits for child if allowed to remain in UK
7.27	Assessment if child's parents are in UK
7.28	Effect on child if forced to return to country of origin
7.29	Developmental years in UK
7.30	**Obtaining reports in support of the application**

Introduction

7.1 This chapter looks at how to take instructions from a child, other vulnerable individuals and family members in general and how to instruct those who might be able to assist by preparing a report.

7.2 Representations to support an application to remain in the UK or to prevent removal of individuals or families with children or other dependent family members require a detailed analysis of the extent to which the particular circumstances of the child and/or family can comply with the Immigration Rules (IR)[1] or policy. An assessment of the length of time an application will take to be considered by the Home Office will be relevant, given that circumstances may change during that time thus enabling a further, different application relying on different policy considerations to be made.

7.3 Detailed instructions will be required, not only in terms of the strict immigration status and requirements but in terms of the factors that actually affect the child and his/her family. Judith Timms[2] divided the factors affecting decision-making in care proceedings into both general and specific factors. General factors include 'the legislative framework, local authority childcare, structures and policies, society's expectations'. Specific factors include the 'wishes and feelings of the child, parents and carers, the child's physical, emotional and educational needs, the characteristics of the child, secure attachments, identity and passage of time'. She comments:

> Among all these other interests and imperatives the voice of the child can be a still small voice that often goes unheard and the best interests of the child can, all too easily, become subsumed within the vested interests of other parties to the proceedings.

This warning is also relevant to the manner in which information is obtained and representations formulated to ensure that the Home Secretary is aware of the potential short and long-term consequences of any decision he or she may take in relation to a child's right to remain in the UK.

---

1   HC 395, as amended.
2   Former Chief Executive of the National Youth Advisory Service in her address to the National Association of Guardians ad Litem and Reporting Officers conference on 19 March 2001, *Best Interests and Best Practice; Improving Outcomes for Children*.

> **Example: Discretion, minor/adult**
>
> Josephine came to the UK when she was 13 years old and claimed asylum, claiming that she had come to look for her father and that she had paid for her passage by way of sex. She claimed that she had previously been looked after by a woman who initially claimed to be her mother but whom she subsequently discovered was unrelated. This woman had violently abused her. Her application for asylum was rejected when she was 16 years old but there was a strong recommendation from the Immigration Appeal Tribunal that she should not be removed to Ghana until proper arrangements were made for her reception. Nothing further has been heard from the Home Office.
>
> She is now 18 and has a child who is two and a baby who is three months old. She is due to return to work when the baby is six months old. The father of the children does not live with her but with his mother. He provides some financial support. He has an application for leave to remain outstanding at the Home Office. His mother is a British citizen.
>
> If an application is made to regularise her stay, given the limited time spent in the UK and the insecure nature of the father's position, it is highly unlikely that the application will be successful.

Taking instructions

7.4 Instructions should be obtained from all those who have an interest. It may well emerge that some members of a family have alternative views as to what should happen and what application should be made. Teenage children may have very differing views as to how long they wish to remain in the UK and what they wish to do compared to younger children or a parent. Initial instructions may identify a conflict, which will necessitate separate representation for the child from his/her parents.

7.5 Set out below are extensive details on taking instructions from a child. The same principles apply to taking instructions from vulnerable adults. Great care needs to be exercised to identify potential conflict and to ensure that the mere taking of instructions does not inflict additional problems. Consideration should be given in all cases as to whether the practitioner is the correct person to be seeking the information or whether others should obtain the instructions after detailed briefing from the practitioner as to the information required.

> **Example: Refugee who left before getting indefinite leave to remain, impact on children**
>
> Sarah was from a southern African country. She had been recognised as a refugee and granted four years' leave to remain. Her three children (two of whom were born in the UK) were granted the same leave. Sarah made an application for indefinite leave, but became increasingly distressed at the long delay in dealing with the application. It is possible she had some mental health problems, but she appeared able to look after her children adequately. She returned to her home country. By this time, her eldest child had lived in the UK for over ten years. She did not wish to return to Africa. A separate, successful application was made on her behalf for indefinite leave. Sarah was advised about the possibility of the younger children making an application under British Nationality Act (BNA) 1981 s1(4) (which could have continued after the children had left the UK). She chose not to do so. The eldest daughter could have applied for a residence order, but she did not wish to intervene in her mother's decision. The mother and the two youngest children returned to Africa but faced great difficulties. The eldest child had sporadic contact with the family but has now lost contact with her siblings.
>
> Although Sarah did not appear to be acting in the children's best interests, the adviser could not approach social services to intervene on the children's behalf, as this would have meant a breach of client confidentiality.

Instructions from a child

7.6 The UK family courts vigorously maintain the concept of the best interest of the child. The procedures for dealing with children have this concept as the underlying principle. Practice and procedure is geared to ensuring that the primary concern of those involved in the upbringing and continued welfare of children is their best interest.

7.7 Establishing best interest requires not only an assertion to that effect but full and proper training of all the professionals involved in the child's life, proper monitoring and the taking into account of the child's wishes and desires for the future. This latter is particularly so where a child is considered to be old enough to be able to express a reasoned view and to be able to understand his/her situation. Such a view would generally be considered the case for children aged 14 and above.[3]

7.8 In each and every case, an assessment has to be done as to whether and to what extent a child is able or capable of expressing a view. The circumstances in which those views are taken or acted upon are then determined by that assessment. Children who have been traumatised or have suffered bereavement may well not be at a sufficient level of maturity at an age when similar aged children are considered to be capable of giving instructions. Practice and procedure is then, in non-immigration areas of law, modified accordingly.

7.9 The basis on which children in conflict situations are interviewed or have their circumstances explored is and has to be one of trust and understanding. The child is always to be made aware that the purpose of any investigation or exploratory interview or examination is to ensure that the child's best interests are properly identified and then acted upon. The process can only be carried out where the purpose has been accurately and properly explained to the child.

7.10 The development of a young person's trust is time-consuming and lengthy. The combination of, for example, the reasons why a child has had to flee, the loss of family, the possible lack of knowledge of the whereabouts of family, the lack of responsible and caring adults, the major life changes in terms of schooling, housing and general living, and the loss of friends are all seen by children in stark terms. The potential undischarged anger at adults who have failed to protect the child and the underlying need and requirement to start to build up trust in the adult community again can be overwhelming.

7.11 In areas other than immigration where children come into contact with the law, not only are interviewing processes geared to children but the whole judicial procedure is adapted to their special needs. Assessment is done at an early stage to ascertain whether the child can in fact give evidence and, if he or she can, whether there is a need for special adaptations to be made to normal procedures. Non-immigration courtrooms are increasingly specifically designed to ensure lack of intimidation. Solicitors on the Law Society's specialist Child Care Panel[4] undertake not to pass on the handling of the case to others. Continuous training has to be undertaken to ensure that professionals remain up-to-date with childcare practice.

---

3   See IDI Ch 8, Annex M, para 7, which relates to children aged 7 and above. See also para 6.31 above.
4   Only those solicitors on the panel qualify for a Legal Services Commission contract.

7.12 Immigration law and practice make no concessions where children are concerned. For example, there is no consideration given to the wording of refusal letters to ensure that a child can understand why he or she has been rejected. There is no consideration given to the effect a refusal can and does have on a child who may have already lost everything that was of any stability in his/her life. Immigration court proceedings are not geared to children. No arrangements are in place for special hearing rooms or centres. No arrangements are made for children to be able to give evidence in an informal but structured way. No attempts are made to enable, for example, for video evidence to be given.

7.13 The interviewing of children requires great skill and is very time-consuming. A child may well not disclose information for all sorts of reasons. He or she may be afraid or may have been told by an adult in his/her country of origin not to disclose any or sometimes specific information. Anxiety or trauma may cause a child to 'blank out' memories of the persecution. The child may not wish to enter into any discussion about the past because of the memories that such conversations provoke. There is no one set pattern.

7.14 An interview with a child cannot be scheduled for a couple of hours, during which the child is expected to 'tell all'. The circumstances of the journey to the interview, whether something special at school has been missed, whether the child has had an argument with a friend, can all have an immediate impact on the ability or willingness of the child to talk about those particular matters on a particular day, to that particular person through that particular interpreter. Interviews are frequently fixed with representatives and have to be postponed simply because the child is non-communicative. Such matters have to be factored in when acting for children

7.15 Although children very quickly learn new languages, when they first arrive in the UK communication has to be through interpreters. The quality and control of interpreters used on a self-employed basis cannot be governed save in terms of language ability. Yet a child will frequently feel that he or she is talking to an interpreter, not the interviewing officer. This must be considered during the course of any interviews.

7.16 Explanations to children who are being interviewed must be honest and truthful. If the evidence is being tested a child must be told that in words that can be understood by the child taking into account the child's age, background, knowledge and level of understanding. A failure to do so would be dishonest and undermining. On the other hand, if it is a testing and potentially confrontational interview, this

> **Example**
>
> Hanna, aged 14, was sent from Latin America to the UK by her grandmother with whom she had lived for many years. Her mother was already in this country as an asylum-seeker, but by the time Hanna arrived, she had been refused and was in detention. Hanna was told by her grandmother to tell the Immigration Service that she had come to join another relative, and aunt and uncle, who had also made an application for asylum. Hanna did as she was told, and went to live with her aunt and uncle. The uncle sexually assaulted Hanna and six months after her arrival she was accommodated by social services. By this time, her mother had been removed from the UK and her grandmother disowned her for making the allegations against her uncle.
>
> Hanna was called to an interview by the Immigration Service in order to clarify her intentions. Hanna was accompanied by her solicitor and a representative of the Refugee Council's panel for unaccompanied minor asylum-seekers, who acted as the 'responsible adult'. The interview took place in the airport's secondary examination area in a windowless room. There was a considerable wait before the interview took place in a waiting area with other, adult interviewees. Even though the Immigration Service made an effort to treat Hanna gently, using a Spanish speaking female immigration officer and asking first if she was hungry or thirsty, still Hanna found the experience intimidating and frightening. In addition, if the solicitor present had not intervened, the immigration officer would have asked questions about the basis of the child's claim to asylum, contrary to the Immigration Rules.

could have serious consequences for the child's psychological well-being.

7.17   Very young children and those who have been seriously disturbed should not usually be interviewed to obtain anything other than very basic outline information. Detailed information should be obtained through other professionals, for example, a child psychologist.

7.18   The place in which interviews take place has to be very carefully considered. Grey walls and chairs screwed to the floor do not engender a sense of trust. But then neither, necessarily, do children's homes. Travelling long distances for an interview, waiting with many other people, being shunted around by officious doormen, will all contribute to a complete sense of overwhelming fear on the part of a child. It may well be worth considering having an initial interview at a local café or in the park.

7.19 At the very least, an attempt should be made to try and ensure that children are given an opportunity to state their views in as many areas of the case as possible:

- To help children remember the past, try and take instructions in a chronological order. Places where they have lived or moved to are usually easier to recall than dates.
- Take children through their childhood abroad. Ask about friends and, in particular, their names; ask about school and family life at that time. Ask children to recall what their main memories are of life in the country of origin. If they speak about any traumatic events, try to find out what they recall and how they feel about those memories today.
- Try to learn about why and how they travelled to the UK. How did they feel when told they were going to the UK?
- Find out how they initially settled into life in the UK and what difficulties they encountered, for example, language, new school and unfamiliar environment.
- Find out how they overcame these problems. Did they make many friends? Do they have a best friend? Have they been able to speak to their friend(s) about any problems? This could include uncertain immigration status or any traumatic events that may have happened in the past either in the home country or in the UK (such as being taken into care).
- Find out what relatives they have in the UK and the extent to which they provide a network of support.
- Find out about all the places they have lived in, the people they have lived with and the quality of the accommodation.
- Try to find out how they have developed over the years by comparing their situation today with the past. Have they gained in confidence? Do they have any idea of what to do in the future and any plans to follow this up?
- Find out what they do in their social time, who they go out with and what they do. Find out what they like about the UK; what music they like; what sports they play and what they do generally.
- Ask what their best language is and whether they speak the language of the country of origin fluently.
- Find out how they think of themselves culturally. Do they consider themselves to be British?
- Ask how they feel when told they may have to leave the UK.

- Find out what they know about the country that they may be sent back to.
- Try to discover whether they think they will cope after having been away for several years. Will they be able to continue their education and pursue their career aspirations?
- Where will they live and how will they support themselves if they are forced to return to their country of origin? Will their relatives help them. If not, why not?
- Ask what they would want to say to the Immigration Minister if they had an opportunity to speak to him.
- Suggest that they may also wish to write a letter addressed to the Minister. (It is a good idea to send this letter with your representations and consider asking the Minister to respond directly to the child and copy his/her letter to you. If the child presents a letter, without prompting, inform the Home Office of this fact.)

7.20 Both older and younger children may voluntarily draw pictures depicting their previous life, fears or experiences in the UK. These can be as powerful as words in expressing a child's view of his/her predicament.

7.21 Despite the manifest difficulties obtaining information from children, the Government is proposing in *Secure Borders, Safe Haven* to interview children.

Instructions from parents/carers

7.22 Information from parents/carers will mirror much of the instructions obtained from the child but the descriptions/perceptions and explanations given may be different. Discrepancies and conflict will have to be resolved to ensure that the application put before the Home Office is consistent. Many apparent discrepancies will in fact be differences of perception. Apparent conflicts should be explained.

7.23 The information to be obtained should include detailed instructions:
- the basis upon which the child/family entered the UK;
- if the child/family entered illegally, the manner of entry, the reason for such entry having been necessary, the extent to which the child was aware of the reasons or the purpose of their being brought to the UK;
- if accompanied to the UK, who accompanied, what is their relationship to the child, is there any continuing contact and if so to what extent;

- if the child was abandoned in the UK, the circumstances leading up to the abandonment, the age of the child on arrival, when taken into care, and at the time of application.

Where a child is subject to a care order

7.24 The information that is available to the court by way of reports, local authority care plans and medical reports will usually be sufficient to enable a detailed application to be made for a child to be granted indefinite leave to remain.[5] It will rarely be necessary to go through all the history again and cause potential trauma to a child. Additional evidence may be required if an argument is being put for adult members of the family to remain for contact purposes, but the local authority care plan should give sufficient information to argue this. If documents that were before the court in the care proceedings are to be relied upon then leave of the court will be required to enable disclosure.[6]

Issues that may have to be addressed by experts[7]

Assessment of child's future in UK

7.25 This assessment should cover the child's education and employment prospects, and the extent to which the child will require continuing support.

Benefits for child if allowed to remain in UK

7.26 The benefits to be assessed include the psychological and emotional benefits, the educational benefits, and the continuation (and development) of community ties.

Assessment if child's parents are in UK

7.27 If the child's parent(s) are in the UK, an assessment should look at:
- on what basis are they living in the UK (British citizens, indefinite leave to remain, students, facing removal, etc);

---

5 See paras 6.18–6.21 above.
6 See para 1.40.
7 Although Civil Procedure Rules Pt 35 does not apply directly to immigration matters, it does give guidance on the duties owed by experts to the court and this can be relevant in immigration appeals. See Expert Witness Institute at www.ewi.org.uk.

- the extent of contact between the child and the parent(s) (how regular, how long for on each occasion, how consistent has the contact been, the benefits of the contact for the child);
- whether the same (or similar) level of contact can be maintained if the child is removed from the UK;
- why the child cannot depend on any parents abroad, and the disadvantages for the child of being supported or cared for by any parents abroad;
- whether or not there are any other relatives abroad who can provide the child with care. Note that the older the child is, the more likely relatives abroad will be seen as providing support for the child to be able to integrate to life abroad. Other factors to be taken into account include how close the relatives are to the applicant, to what extent they can reasonably be assumed to be willing to take up responsibility for the applicant's care or support, the relatives' circumstances and ability to provide care and support;
- whether the parents are to benefit if the child is allowed to remain in the UK (by also being allowed to remain for the purpose of caring for the child or continuing contact with the child);
- the extent to which the parents' actions since arriving in the UK, and following any care or contact arrangements, have been aimed at securing their own status in this country;
- the extent to which the child has been aware of these intentions of the parent(s) and to what extent the child may have been complicit in furthering these intentions;
- to what extent the child has been helpless in relation to any of the parents' actions aimed at keeping the child in the UK.

Effect on child if forced to return to country of origin

7.28 An expert should assess the likely effect on the child if forced to return to the country of origin in terms of psychological and emotional effects, education and employment, and ability to support him/herself.

Developmental years in UK

7.29 The extent to which the child has spent his/her developmental years in the UK, and other reasons why it would be unreasonable for the child to be removed, should be considered. Examples of factors to be taken into account include:

- the extent to which the child is culturally dependent on life in the UK;

- the extent to which the child is familiar with the culture of the country of origin and life in the country of origin;
- whether the child speaks the language of the country of origin;
- the extent to which the child will be able to begin a new life in the country of origin;
- if the child will be an adult when removed from the UK, or if the child will be expected to live independently if removed from the UK, the extent to which this will be possible in the country of origin (taking into account all the disadvantages the child/deportee will have to face and overcome).

Obtaining reports in support of the application

7.30 Reports in support of an application fall into two categories: (a) those provided by individuals, whether professional or friends who have had some form of continuing contact with the child and his/her family, and (b) those which can be categorised as expert reports, commissioned to deal with specific issues from the knowledge and expertise of the provider, whether it be in terms of knowledge of, for example, provision of particular forms of health care in the proposed country of return or the condition and availability of education or childcare.

7.31 Consideration should be given, in the light of the nature of the case, as to what reports will be required. For example, reports from social workers, teachers, doctors and child psychologists as to the effect on the child of any removal from the UK or potential separation not only from parents and relatives but also friends may well be helpful. These reports should consider the effect generally of removal, but should also address the impact of removal on the specific child.

7.32 The letter requesting a report or letter in support should specify exactly why the report is required and the nature of the report requested, the issues to be covered and the timescale within which it is required.[8] The tone of the letter would obviously vary according to

---

8 Detailed guidance in drafting letters of instruction is given in children's proceedings by the Expert Witness Group. In brief the letter of instruction should include: (1) the current immigration status of the child or young person; (2) the issues that it is intended should be placed before the Home Office; (3) an indication of the wishes of the child or young person to remain in the UK; (4) a chronology; (5) relevant immigration or other documents, eg, medical reports, court orders; (6) the specific questions/issues you wish the professional to address; (7) timescale for production of report; (8) confirmation that you wish the professional to restrict him/herself to a professional opinion (not provide

whom it was addressed and the nature of the support sought, but it should be remembered that many individuals will want guidance on the issues that they should address. The purpose of the letter or report must be identified, failing which the report received will be unlikely to be relevant.

7.33 Reports frequently used in support of asylum applications may also be of relevance. For example, the US State Department Reports[9] have substantial detail as to the economic situation in particular countries as well as the provision of education and social welfare support. Human Rights Watch reports carry similar information. These are of relevance in determining the balance to be struck when comparing a child's physical, educational and emotional needs, how these are met in the UK and how they will be met in the country to which it is proposed a child and his or her family should be sent.

7.34 It will be important, before commissioning any report, to have obtained an outline of the background information and the likely basis of the representations to be made in support of the application.

7.35 If the reports are not available at the time that the application is being submitted, consideration should be given whether to refer to the future production of the report or whether to wait until the report is received before referring to it. It is important that, if reference is made to the forthcoming production of a report, that report is later produced. If it becomes apparent on receipt of the report that it should not be disclosed then an explanation as to why it has not been produced may be sought from the Immigration and Nationality Department (IND). It may also trigger the IND to produce a report of its own.

---

opinions that he or she would not be able to sustain under cross-examination) and to comply with the Expert Witness Protocol; (9) a request that the professional qualifications be included as an annex to the report; (10) confirmation of estimate/payment of fees.

9   See www.state.gov/g/drl/rls/hmpt/2002/.

CHAPTER 8

Making the application

8.1	Introduction
8.4	Assessing the claim
8.12	When to approach the Home Office
8.17	Use of family court orders
8.23	Section 8 orders
8.26	Care proceedings
8.28	Use of the European Convention on Human Rights
8.29	Use of other international conventions
8.30	How to make the application
8.33	Preparing an application
8.40	Appeal rights

Introduction

8.1 This chapter looks at the factors to be taken into account in determining what sort of application should be made if it does not fall within the policies set out in the Immigration Directorate's Instructions (IDI)[1] or the family aspects of asylum, when it should be made and the structure of the application to be made. It is important that in considering the following aspects the detailed issues referred to in chapters 4, 5 and 6 are borne in mind.

8.2 The IDI refer to the need to take quick decisions in connection with children. They state that it will be rare for an application involving children to take more than six months. This has to be taken into account in the timing of the lodging of the application and in deciding whether the Home Office should be urged to make a decision and whether proceedings should be issued to force a quick decision. Factors to be taken into account are not simply the circumstances of the particular child but the effect of the application on the whole of the family.

8.3 The Asylum Policy Instructions (API)[2] refer to family issues where there is an asylum aspect.

Assessing the claim

8.4 Reasonably detailed instructions about the current status of the child and his/her parents or carers will have to be taken initially. This need not, at this stage, include the detailed background information but should include sufficient information to identify the following factors:
- removability of the applicant;
- removability of other family members either now or in the near future;
- applicability of one or more of the established published concessions or IDI;
- non-British children in the family born in the UK;
- whether the child or other family member is (or could be) a refugee or has been granted exceptional leave;
- any issues for any member of the family around health (mental

---

1 See chapter 6.
2 See chapter 5.

and physical, short and/or long-term), support for elderly or needy relatives, special needs;
- whether the adults are married, cohabiting or in polygamous relationships;
- whether there are any 'step' children for whom one or other or both of the family members are responsible or have contact (access) with;
- the length of time each person who is threatened with removal has spent in the UK;
- any adverse indications, for example, illegal entry, working with false documents, criminal convictions or previous failed applications.

8.5 This information will enable a decision to be taken about the nature of the application to be made. If the case falls fully within the IDI, API or announced concessions, the application should be drafted to ensure that each and every requirement of the relevant policy or concession is addressed and supported where possible with documentary evidence.[3] Where the applicant is unable to produce the necessary information or is unable to comply fully with the requirements, detailed consideration must be given about whether, when and what type of application should be submitted.

8.6 The following additional information will be required to enable full representations to be made in support:
- length of time that each family member, who is resident in the UK and forms part of the family unit but is not threatened with removal, has spent in the UK;
- length of time spent in the UK by any other person with whom the person under threat has a relationship, for example, carer, step-parent, foster carer;
- documentary evidence to prove relationships and amount of contact with or care given to needy or dependent relatives (for example, a written agreement, attendance allowance or utility bill);
- financial position of the parent or carer including work history;
- details of the education being received by the children of the family and whether there are any specific reasons for this;
- complexity of the family/relationship tree in terms of contact, caring, and lawful residence of the various members in the UK;
- any charitable or voluntary work.

---

3 See chapters 5 and 6.

8.7 Information will be required about conditions in the country to which the Home Office could remove or propose to remove the applicant:
- relatives abroad, their age, the nature of contact that has taken place (if any), their financial situation and state of health;
- facilities available to meet identified special needs, for example, health (physical and psychological), care for the elderly, accommodation (specifically what would the cost be and would those being removed be able to pay for it?);
- any safeguards in place to meet identified needs of children (see, for example, the requirements placed on local authorities if they wish to remove a child from the jurisdiction)[4] or the elderly;
- consider what the Home Office asserts would be the standard of care in the 'home' country and how that compares with the standards that would have to be met in Children Act proceedings;
- any disclosures to or by the entry clearance officer (ECO), for example, disclosure to official bodies in the 'home' country that a member of the family is a failed asylum-seeker;
- social circumstances of the country that it is proposed to send the child/family to, for example, conditions arising from war/famine/natural disaster that would make return unduly harsh;
- quality of care available to the child from relatives other than parents, and details of why the parents sent the children away (is this indicative of lack of care, lack of desire or an inability to look after the children?);
- any possible issues around trafficking of children;[5]
- details of any contact between child and putative carer.

8.8 Issues should be identified that would arise in the UK in the event of the Home Office removing a family:
- additional costs, for example, in providing home help, placing elderly people in a home, children being placed in children's homes;
- failure to comply with community care policies;[6]
- continuity and supervision of medical and nursing care;
- breaches of family court orders.[7]

---

4 See para 1.103.
5 See para 4.37.
6 *R v Home Secretary ex p Zakrocki* [1996] COD 304.
7 See chapter 1.

8.9 Potential problem areas should be identified to enable such issues to be addressed in the application or to be taken into account in determining if and when an application should be submitted or whether the Home Office should be pressed for a quick decision, for example:

- the sponsor was divorced at the time that he or she applied for and subsequently obtained indefinite leave to remain;
- the dates of birth of the children from the current relationship indicate that the relationship was on-going during the previous relationship which led to the grant of indefinite leave to remain;
- the children, although British citizens, have no contact at all with the applicant;
- criminal convictions that are not yet spent or are very serious, for example, the applicant has spent some considerable time in prison;
- the settled spouse and or family members have not spent much time in the UK and could arguably resettle elsewhere;
- there is a considerable history of untruths being told to the Home Office, for example, marriage applications that were held to be 'for convenience';
- there are numerous children by different partners, possibly with various levels of involvement by the local authority;
- the applicant is approaching 18 years old;
- the eldest child is over 18 years and no longer dependent, having, for example, moved out of the family home to live with his/her partner.

8.10 Clients should be reminded that the Home Office keeps very detailed records dating back years and that they should be completely frank about their immigration history and circumstances.

8.11 Some difficult issues may need to be considered:

- Should a separate application be made for a minor who has previously been treated as a dependant but is no longer part of the family unit? Or should a minor remain as a dependant?
- Should an application be made to delay removal as opposed to requesting settlement? Are there factors which would indicate that this would be more likely to succeed?
- If there is a non-removable child should care proceedings be considered, or a supervision or a residence order be sought?

When to approach the Home Office

8.12   Where a child was originally part of the parent's application, for example, as a dependant of an asylum applicant or a student, the Home Office will not have a separate record of the child. It requires considerable tenacity to persuade the Home Office to open a separate file and to take a decision on the status of the child in his/her own right. If a separate file is not opened and the parent is refused, the child will also be refused despite having a separate claim.

8.13   If the application is part of a family application, it is usually better to wait until all relevant documentation has been collated. However, there will inevitably be exceptions to this where, for example, an existing time limit is due to expire or where removal directions are pending.

8.14   If Home Office policy is clear then submit an application without delay even if full supporting documentation is not immediately available. The decision-making process within the Home Office, even for cases involving vulnerable children, is distressingly slow and the sooner that the process is commenced the sooner a decision can be achieved. For example, if a child is subject to a care order or the subject of care proceedings and it is anticipated that a full care order will be made, the Home Office should be notified of the proceedings and formal application made for indefinite leave to remain, even though there may well be little more documentation than a letter from social services confirming that the proceedings are pending. Once the care order is made it should be sent to the Home Office. There should be no delay following this. Delay is counter-productive for the development of the child. Consideration should be given to the issue of judicial review proceedings for a mandatory order, if no decision has been forthcoming within six months of the making of the care order.[7a]

8.15   The delay in obtaining a response from the Home Office can not only be frustrating but can be severely disruptive in terms of children's education, training and employment. The applicant's local Member of Parliament[8] can be asked to intervene to request a quick decision. Full details of the applicant's name and address should be given and full details of the background to the case and the attempts

---

7a   See also para 5.9 above.
8   The MP's name can be obtained from www.parliament.uk/commons/lib/alcmad.htm or telephone 020 7219 4272 and quote the constitutent's post code or contact House of Commons Information on 020 7219 3000.

made to obtain a response from the Home Office. If the MP does not obtain a satisfactory response (or any response) consideration should be given to complaining to the Parliamentary Ombudsman.[9] This has to be done through the MP, or if the MP is unwilling to do this, then through a Member of the House of Lords.

8.16 There will be many cases where, on close examination of the facts of the case, it will be apparent that there is little chance of success. There may be insufficient compassionate circumstances to bring the family within the various policy statements of the Home Office, they may not have been in the UK for a sufficiently long period of time, or the children may be too young to argue that it would be disruptive to remove them to their country of origin. In those instances it is extremely important that the full consequences of either notifying the Home Office or not notifying the Home Office are explained to the applicant. Financial destitution may lead the applicant to approach social services for assistance.[10] This may have the consequence of the local authority contacting the Home Office in order to confirm his/her immigration status. The client should be told this. It is critical that advisers should on no account deceive the Home Office; to do so is a criminal offence.

Use of family court orders

8.17 If there are outstanding applications before the family court, the Home Secretary will usually be willing to defer removal pending the outcome of the applications. He is more likely to do so if the application is one that had already been commenced and not one that appears to have been embarked upon when the adult has exhausted all his/her immigration appeals.

8.18 The family court determines what order should be made by an analysis of what is in the best interests of the child, taking all the circumstances of his/her case into account. The potential conflict between the need to maintain immigration control for reasons of public policy and the best interests of the child can be exploited in representations to the Home Office.

8.19 In *Re F*[11] it was held that a special adjudicator should have before him/her all the material that was properly available and that,

---

9 Forms are available from www.ombudsman.org.uk.
10 See chapter 3.
11 *Re F (Child Case: Disclosure of Documents)* [1995] 1 FCR 589.

therefore, statements and transcripts from a family case could be made available, if that appeared to be in the interests of the child or children involved. In that case, which involved an application for asylum, the statements made by the parents for the family court went to their credibility. It should however be remembered that documents and statements, whether favourable or not, obtained in the course of Children Act (CA) 1989 proceedings have to be disclosed to all the parties involved in the family proceedings.[12] Therefore, for example, medical or other expert reports will be disclosed in the family proceedings, even if not supportive in terms of the arguments being put forward in the immigration case. Applications for full disclosure to the Immigration Appellate Authority may result in some unhelpful documents being presented.

8.20 Arguments put forward in a family case may also apply to appeals against removal or decisions to refuse to grant exceptional leave to remain on human rights grounds and can have a powerful effect on immigration status decision-makers. Copies of judgments can be particularly helpful if they reveal the reasoning leading to the grant of, for instance, a residence or contact order. This is especially so when the judge in the family court has rehearsed the evidence in support of such an order and shown that he or she has taken into account the fact that the adult or child, as the case may be, does not have settled status in the UK and may be removed. Yet an order has been made on the grounds that it is clearly in the child's best interests.

8.21 Written judgments are not produced in the family court as a matter of course. If it is thought that a judgment will be helpful, consideration should be given to making an application seeking production at public expense. Alternatively, a note of the judgment signed by the barrister or solicitor representing may be useful.

8.22 There may be occasions where despite the consent of the parties (which would usually mean that no order is made[13]) an order is seen to be in the best interests of a child. For example, if it is known or feared that a parent will be removed or deported from the UK, courts are usually willing to make an order formalising contact (or access as it used to be called and still is in the Immigration Rules), so that the parent can seek leave to enter to have contact (access).[14]

---

12 *Re F (Child Case: Disclosure of Documents)* [1995] 1 FCR 589.
13 See para 1.26.
14 Under Immigration Rules (HC 395 as amended) para 246.

Section 8 orders[15]

8.23   If removal directions are made in respect of either an adult or a child covered by a contact order, it can be argued that this disruption interferes with the court's intentions.

8.24   If there is a residence order in force the child cannot be removed from the jurisdiction of England and Wales without either the written consent of every person who has parental responsibility or the leave of the court.[16] When the Home Secretary sets removal directions this is frequently overlooked and this can be used as a reason to challenge removal of the child along with the parent.[17]

8.25   A prohibited steps order[18] prohibiting contact with particular individuals who are in the country to which the child will be returned or a specific issue order requiring specific medical treatment that is not available in that country can be referred to in representations to the Home Office. If the order cannot or will not be enforced in the country to which it is proposed to send the child, this can militate against removal of the child and could form the basis of a challenge.

Care proceedings

8.26   There may be circumstances where an order is not considered necessary in terms of the threshold criteria[19] but may be of considerable assistance when arguing against removal. For example, a supervision order,[20] requiring involvement by a local authority in order to protect the child, where there is no comparable system in the country of origin, could delay or extinguish the possibility of removal from the UK. It may, in some circumstances, be in the interests of a family for the parents not to resist a care or supervison order.

8.27   Where a care plan[21] provides for on-going contact with the child it can be argued that the family court clearly concluded that on-going contact between the child and the parent or carer was in the child's best interests. There is likely to be some concern on the part of both the local authority and the family court about giving a parent without

---

15   See paras 1.65–1.71.
16   CA 1989 s13.
17   It may be appropriate to draw an analogy with the requirements to be met to remove from the jurisdiction a child who is subject to a care order.
18   See para 1.70.
19   See para 1.89.
20   See para 1.73.
21   See para 1.98.

secure immigration status an integral part in a care plan, when he or she may not be in the country to undertake the allotted role. In this situation, it may be preferable to keep the Home Office fully informed about the progress of the family case in an effort to build sympathy for the client by showing that he or she is acting in a responsible manner in relation to the child, even though the child has been removed from his/her care.

Use of the European Convention on Human Rights

8.28 It is important to consider the relevance of the European Convention on Human Rights (ECHR) in determining the form of the application. The principles set out in chapter 4 should be applied to the facts in formulating the application.

Use of other international conventions

8.29 Other than the UN Convention on Refugees 1951 and the ECHR, international conventions to which the UK is a signatory are not incorporated into UK law. This does not however mean that the principles of the conventions should not be drawn upon to support an argument or as illustrative of good practice. A failure correctly to interpret or apply principles could lead to administrative challenge and can assist in making persuasive representations.

How to make the application

8.30 Any application to the Immigration and Nationality Department (IND) must be made on the relevant application form whether the application is for exercise of discretion or is an application within the Immigration Rules. The forms are free and are available from the Home Office or can be downloaded from the IND website free of charge.[22] The application form must be fully and correctly completed and submitted with all relevant original documents. If the required documents are not available an explanation must be given. Failure to comply with these instructions will result in the application being rejected for technical failure with no consideration of the merits.

8.31 If the applicant is a port applicant, for example, and he or she has an outstanding asylum claim or there are family members with

---

22 See www.homeoffice.gov.uk/ind.

8.32 Where the applicant is abroad, an application for entry clearance[23] must be submitted[24] to the nearest British consulate[25] to where the applicant habitually lives. Supporting documentation can be posted or emailed from the UK. Full details should accompany the application together with certified copies of any documents relied upon. Alternatively, representations should be submitted very soon after the application form has been submitted. If the sponsor is a refugee there is no fee. If the sponsor is not a refugee, the fee will, in practice, be waived on production of evidence of receipt of benefits although the instructions to ECOs state that 'the long term non-settlement fee should be charged'.[26] If one of the criteria for grant of entry clearance is an ability of the sponsor to maintain and accommodate then production of benefit evidence could in itself lead to a refusal of the application.

Preparing an application

8.33 There is no requirement on the Home Secretary to take decisions on the basis that the welfare of the child is paramount. But the Home Secretary is required to take the order and the views of the family court into account in coming to a decision on applications to remain in the UK or whether to remove.[27] This is the case whether the order in question is a residence or care order where the leave of the court is required to remove the child from the jurisdiction, or where further court directions will be required if the responsible adult is being removed, or whether there is a specific issue order, for example, for specific treatment or education.

8.34 Where family proceedings (for instance, for a residence order) are issued involving a child who is subject to immigration control, the

---

23 See *Macdonald's Immigration Law and Practice* (5th edn, Butterworths, 2001) for further details.
24 Specified forms must be used. They are available free of charge from the British post abroad or can be downloaded from the Joint Entry Clearance Unit (JECU) website at www.fco.gov.uk/ukvisas/dynpage.asp?Page=336.
25 Not all British consulates are authorised to issue entry clearance. The current list of authorised consulates can be found on the JECU website.
26 Entry Clearance General Instructions Vol 1, para 16.9. See Appendix B.
27 See paras 6.18 and 4.54.

family court will make its decision in accordance with the provisions of the CA 1989 and in the best interests of the child. Whether the application is a device to avoid an adverse immigration decision is a matter to which the court would have regard, but it is not a matter that would determine the outcome of the application. It may be necessary in some cases to show that there are circumstances that take the case outside the usual considerations of welfare.[28] This does not mean that, for example, a residence order cannot be applied for in circumstances where there would usually be no order made. It is necessary to be aware that such issues may be raised.

8.35 An order made in the family court does not fetter the discretion of the Home Secretary to deport or remove but must be taken into account in any exercise of his powers.[29] In *Lamuratur Mbatude v Home Secretary*[30] it was held that, in determining his/her discretion, the Home Secretary was permitted a wide margin of appreciation. In *R v Home Secretary ex p Begum*,[31] it was confirmed that the Home Secretary is not obliged to view the child's interest as paramount. In practice, family court orders play an important role in persuading the Home Secretary to exercise his discretion favourably in cases concerning children.

8.36 When a child who was subject to an order made under the CA 1989 reaches the age of 18, the order ceases to have effect. Where a child was accommodated or subject to a care order, the local authority retains responsibility for advice and assistance for those children it had previously looked after, that is, those who were accommodated or subject to a care order or supervision order, until the child reaches the age of 21.[32]

8.37 When drafting representations, be as detailed as possible. Build the application around the client's instructions. In some cases it may be advisable to incorporate the bulk of the factual information in a statement from the client and refer to that as supporting evidence in the submission. Reference to the supporting reports from those involved with the family (such as teachers), expert reports and letters of support provides substance to the assertions of the legal position and the matters that the Home Secretary is required to take into account.

28 *Re Matondo* [1993] Imm AR 541; also *Re K and S (minors)* [1992] 1 FLR 432 and *Re A (a minor) (wardship: immigration)* [1992] 1 FLR 432.
29 *Re T* [1994] Imm AR 368.
30 [1996] Imm AR 184.
31 [1996] Imm AR 582.
32 See paras 1.82 and 4.58, and Children (Leaving Care) Act 2000.

8.38 Ensure that the representations include a full analysis of the history of the individuals and the family,[33] the background to the application, the current situation and the consequences of removal. Reference should be drawn to the positive consequences for the individuals concerned and to the community of the applicant being allowed to remain in the UK.

8.39 The application of current policies and guidelines, legislation, the ECHR and international conventions to the client's case should form the conclusion to the representations. Place the information about the individual's claim within the context of the relevant policy or convention to enable the application to be fully considered.

> **Example: Children with different status, asylum**
>
> Helen had seven children, six of whom were under 18 and one was 19. All were in the UK. Two of the children were British citizens: the four-year-old was born in the UK and had not left since birth; the ten-year-old was also born in the UK but left when she was two, returning with her mother four years ago. The remaining three children, including the 19-year-old, were overstayers like their mother, having arrived four years ago as visitors and overstayed their leave. Helen stated that she was prevented from practising birth control by her husband and that she was unable to leave him and live by herself with her children in Nigeria. She stated that her husband and his family would have taken the children from her and she would have had no rights to obtain custody.
>
> This complex case requires consideration of the potential applications for British citizenship by some of the children, whether the 19-year-old leads a separate life and should thus submit a separate application, the likely success of an asylum application by Helen, the relevance of ECHR art 8 (sibling group, moral and psychological integrity of the children as individuals and as a group), whether there is another home, the separation of the family group in the event of removal. All elements should be considered and detailed written representations should cover all the issues.

---

33 For example, the development of a child to adolescent or from an adolescent to a young adult, whether there are any additional children born, whether a child is approaching seven years' residence in the UK, or a child who was born in the UK is approaching 10 years' residence, etc.

> **Example: Family unit, under-18 and over-18 child abroad**
>
> Maria came to the UK as a visitor and overstayed. She left two young children in the care of her mother. While an overstayer she married a British citizen and became pregnant. She was granted one year's leave to remain. The child, a British citizen, suffered from cerebral palsy and was quadriplegic. Her husband left her and had no further contact with either her or the child. Maria continued to work at a school, her child attending a specialist centre during the day while she was at work. An application was submitted for her to be given indefinite leave to remain which was refused. Deportation proceedings were served. Her appeal against deportation was rejected on the basis that there was power in law to deport. However, a recommendation was made that she be granted leave to remain. Following the intervention of her MP she was granted indefinite leave to remain in 1996. She then travelled to Nigeria, in 1996, to see her two older children. She was unable to take her youngest son with her as he was too seriously ill to travel, requiring continuous care and sometimes requiring urgent emergency medical treatment that was not readily available in Nigeria. While there it became apparent that Maria's mother was no longer physically able to look after the two children; she was suffering from dementia and was physically weak.
>
> On return to the UK an application for entry clearance was submitted for the two children to come to the UK for settlement. The application was refused and an appeal lodged. Maria's solicitors advised her that because she had not been sending money on a regular basis the appeal was bound to fail and withdrew the appeal.
>
> Maria sought further advice. By this time Maria's mother had died and the older child was aged over 18, although the younger child was only 16. A detailed application was submitted for the younger child and he was successful. He arrived in the UK.
>
> Maria was then diagnosed with cancer and had to undergo a series of operations. She needed considerable help with her youngest son, some of which assistance was provided by the 16-year-old. She was no longer able to work full time and became more reliant on benefits.
>
> The issue raised was what to do about the older boy, who was still only 18 years old, alone, at school and dependent on his mother for financial support. There was no other relative willing or able to assist him in Nigeria. Detailed written representations were sent to

> an MP, providing full medical reports on Maria and her youngest child; social services provided full reports of the help given by the middle son and the care provided by social services; estimates of the savings to social services if her eldest son were granted leave to enter were given; reference was made to family life in terms of the benefit to the youngest son having all siblings with him and the unity of the family; reference was made to the private life of the two children in the UK and to Maria, her physical integrity and that of her youngest son and the benefit the eldest child would have; confirmation was provided that once Maria recovered she could return to work full time and details of her excellent work record were provided.
>
> A request was made for an indication that, were an entry clearance to be applied for it would be granted, such request being made to attempt to avoid a refusal and thus a lengthy appeal process as well as to save money. A positive response was received, an entry clearance application made and the eldest son arrived in the UK.

Appeal rights

8.40 If the application is refused the relevant notices should be served enabling an appeal to be lodged in accordance with Immigration and Asylum Act 1999 s65. The port, or IND, may not have considered the application in accordance with the relevant article and the breach will have to be further asserted to enable the appeal process to commence.[34]

---

34 See *Macdonald's Immigration Law and Practice* for further detail.

APPENDICES

A   Immigration Directorate Instructions on adoption   179

B   Extract from Entry Clearance General Instructions Vol 1 Chapter 16 and Annex 16   205

C   Extract from Asylum Policy Instructions   209

D   Some relevant Concessions   215

E   Extracts from European Convention on Human Rights   227

F   International Covenant on Civil and Political Rights (selected articles)   233

G   Other International Conventions   237

H   Convention of the Rights of the Child   243

I   Universal Declaration of Human Rights 1948 (selected articles)   255

J   Practice Notes   257

K   Letter from Barbara Roche to Lord Archer of Sandwell QC, 30 June 2000   263

L   Extracts from Marriages Handbook for Registration Officers (produced by General Register Office)   265

M   Useful resources   269

APPENDIX A

Immigration Directorate Instructions on adoption

Immigration Directorates' Instructions
Chapter 8 section 5 Annexe Q and Annexe S

**Immigration Directorates' Instructions
Chapter 8 section 5 – Adopted children
Annex Q
September 2001**

Validity of adoptions under United Kingdom law and general guidance relating to adoption cases which fall to be considered under the immigration rules

1 **Introduction**

Following the implementation of the Adoption (Intercountry Aspects) Act 1999 on 30/4/2001, it is now an offence for prospective adoptive parents to bring a child into the United Kingdom for the purposes of adoption, unless they have complied with requirements prescribed in law. The penalty for non-compliance is a fine of up to £5000 and/or up to three months imprisonment. This legislation does not apply to parents, guardians or relatives of a child coming for adoption through the UK courts.

The Adoption of Children from Overseas Regulations 2001 and the Adoption from Children from Overseas (Scotland) Regulations 2001 aim to deter people from bringing children into the United Kingdom for the purpose of adoption unless they have first been assessed and approved by a local council or a voluntary adoption agency (VAA) and had their suitability endorsed by the Secretary of State. In order to avoid committing an offence, the Regulations require prospective adoptive parents in England, Scotland and Wales, to have first:

- applied for their suitability to adopt a child to be approved by a local council or VAA; and
- complied with the assessment process; and
- received confirmation, in writing, of the agency's decision to approve them as suitable to be an adoptive parent; and
- received written notification from the Secretary of State that he is prepared to issue a certificate of eligibility.

2 Actions on arrival

Within 14 days of the prospective adoptive parents' arrival in the United Kingdom with a child, they must notify their local council of their intention to adopt or not. Once this notification has been received, the child will be a protected child under section 22 of the Adoption Act 1976 or in Scotland, section 22 of the Adoption (Scotland) Act 1978, and his/her placement will be monitored by the council under sections 32 to 37 of whichever Act is appropriate.

Adopters who claim to have completed the adoption process in a designated country (see paragraph 10, below), ie, those countries whose adoption orders are recognised by the UK courts, are not treated as 'prospective adopters'. It is unlikely that parents of a child who hold a designated country adoption order would bring a child to the UK for the purpose of adopting the child here. Extreme vigilance must be exercised if a person(s) resident in the UK arrives with a child, whom the [Immigration Officer] IO suspects is not the person(s)'s own and claims that the child is here for 'a visit', where no evidence of the child's parent(s)/guardian(s)'s consent for travel and entry to the UK is produced.

3 On entry – advice to Immigration Officers

(This should be read in conjunction with IDI Chapter 8 section 5 – Adopted Children):

3.1 For immigration purposes, there are several categories of intercountry adoption

Adopted children; Rule 310/311/314, IDI ref Ch8, s5. These Rules apply to children who are adopted in countries whose adoption orders are recognised under UK law according to the Adoption (Designation of Overseas Adoptions) Order 1973, with the child usually coming here for settlement. A list of these countries, the 'designated list', can be found at paragraph 10, below.

Children coming to the UK for adoption through the courts here; Rule 316A, IDI ref Ch8, Annex S. This would normally only apply to those people who have followed the correct intercountry adoption process in a non-designated country and who want the parent-child relationship to be legally recognised in the UK by adopting the child through the courts here.

The 'De Facto' adoption concession; Concession outside the Rules, IDI ref Ch8, Annex R. This is applicable for those cases where a child has been brought into a family unit and is now an integral part, even if no formal adoption has taken place, whether this took place in a designated or non-designated country.

3.2 Parents arriving at a port with an 'adopted' child

High profile media interest in January 2000 raised the profile of intercountry adoptions, leading to the early implementation of the new regulations. The regulations are designed to act as a deterrent for would-be adoptive parents who wish to speed up the process of adoption, by taking matters into their own hands and bypassing the safeguards in the system. A person(s) (British or EEA nationals or those with settled status in the UK) who adopts a child in a designated country will not be caught by the regulations, as adoptions carried out in designated countries are recognised by the UK courts. The regulations are designed to prevent a parent(s) from bringing a child from a non-designated country to the UK for the purpose of adoption without having followed proper procedures. IOs should be extremely vigilant where a parent(s) claims to be bringing a child to the UK solely for a visit, when the actual intention may be to adopt the child once admitted to the UK. If there is any doubt in such circumstances, the DoH/local authority should be contacted as appropriate. If possible, a statement concerning the intent of the person(s) bringing the child to the UK for the 'visit' should be taken. This would help with DoH prosecution if the person(s) subsequently decide(s) to adopt the child.

Difficulties could arise where 'parents' present themselves to IOs on entry and state that they wish to adopt 'their' child through the UK courts, if an adoption order from a designated country has not already been obtained. IOs would then be in the difficult situation of having to refuse entry to the child (the child would not hold prior entry clearance), which may not be in the child's best interests and would be presentationally difficult. However, if IOs were to grant entry to the child, the parents would then be potentially liable to prosecution, under the terms of the new regulations for intercountry adoption (the parents are unlikely to have obtained entry clearance or followed the new DoH procedures, in such cases). The advice to IOs, therefore, is to notify immediately the prospective adoptive parent(s) that they may be in breach of section 14 of the Adoption (Intercountry Aspects) Act 1999. The prospective adoptive parent(s) should be told to contact their local authority of their intention to adopt the child (within 14 days of arrival with the child in the UK). This should lead to an early decision concerning the welfare of the child and any potential prosecution of the parents. If the prospective adoptive parent(s) still wish to enter the UK with the child once they have learnt of their legal position, the child should be granted temporary admission. If they do enter, the IO should also notify the appropriate local authority and the police, then inform the DoH that this action has been taken. As with all such cases, speed is of the essence for a beneficial resolution. This will be to the benefit of the child's welfare, always the prime consideration, and the avoidance of media attention, which is unlikely to be in the child's best interest.

3.3 Parents arriving at a port with a 'de facto' adopted child

'De facto' adoptions will usually present more difficulty for [entry clearance officers] ECOs rather than IOs when 'parents' arrive at a port with a child. However, IOs must still be satisfied that the 'parents' do not intend to adopt the child through the UK courts. ECOs will normally have undertaken checks as far as possible in such cases before issuing entry clearance to the child. In a situation where 'parents' arriving at a port with a de facto adopted child subsequently state that adoption of the child through the UK courts is the intention, the same procedures as outlined in paragraph 3.2 (above) should be followed.

If the IO is satisfied that the 'parents' do not intend to adopt through the UK courts, it may still be necessary to remind 'parents' that they are under an obligation to inform their local authority (if they have not already done this prior to travelling), within 3 days of the child's arrival in the UK. This is in accordance with the Children Act 1989 guidance on private fostering arrangements and if the 'parents' do not notify their local authority, they will be committing an offence under section 70(1)(a) of the Children Act 1989 or, in Scotland, under section 15 (1) (a) of the Foster Children (Scotland) Act 1984.

Cases involving de facto adoptions arriving at port without entry clearance for the child are less clear cut. They should be treated in the same way as if the child had been brought to the country for the purpose of adoption here, even if 'parents' state that there is no intention to adopt the child in the UK (see paragraph 3.2. above). The DoH/local authority is unlikely to have any knowledge of the children or 'parents' in such cases, but these departments should be informed nevertheless. This is to ensure that the best interests of the child are served in all cases and that no trafficking or kidnapping has taken place.

4 After entry – advice to caseworkers

There should be very few situations in which in-country applications to adopt a child occur following the introduction of the new intercountry adoption regulations. If procedures have been followed correctly, all parents should have obtained the appropriate entry clearance for the child in question.

The Department of Health [DoH](or other relevant authority) will usually become aware of an intention to adopt a child who was not initially brought into the UK for that purpose. The parents who therefore intend to adopt would not have followed the correct procedures and would be liable to prosecution. In all circumstances involving in-country applications for adoption, the Department of Health should be contacted and made aware of the circumstances of the case, to determine if prosecution is necessary. It may also be necessary to remind 'parents' that they are liable to prosecution if adoption is their intention. In such instances, the case will usually be referred to the High Court for determination and limited leave to remain should be granted to the child pending the outcome of the court hearing.

5 Department of Health guidance taken from the 'intercountry adoption guide – practice and procedures' concerning bringing a child to the UK

When bringing a child to live in the UK, adopters must seek entry clearance for the child.

If an adoption order has been made in one of the countries or territories known as designated countries (according to the Adoption (Designation of Overseas Adoptions) Order 1973) the adoption order is recognised under UK law.

Where adopters have an adoption order that is recognised in the UK, the Entry Clearance Officer (ECO) will consider the application and if he is satisfied that the immigration requirements have been met then a visa for indefinite leave to enter will be granted. The requirements are set out in the Home Office leaflet 'Intercountry Adoption'. Occasionally the ECO will refer the case to the Joint Entry Clearance Unit in London for advice.

When the UK does not recognise an adoption order made for a child under the law of their home country (non-designated countries), the ECO will consider the application. If he is satisfied that the immigration requirements have been met he will ask the lead Home Department for advice as to the likelihood of a court in England, Scotland and Wales granting an adoption order.

Before the Department of Health, Scottish Executive or National Assembly for Wales can give any advice it must see:
- The child's original birth certificate (if available) and new certificate.
- A medical report on the child. It is recommended that a British Agencies for Adoption and Fostering (BAAF) intercountry adoption medical form is used. This can be obtained from BAAF.
- A parental consent form. This is only valid if it is given when the child is 6 weeks old or over. It must also be notarised in the birth parents' own country. If a child is an orphan, proof of their parents' death is required. If the child is abandoned, a certificate of abandonment is required.
- An adoption/guardianship order.
- Confirmation from the relevant authorities of the country concerned that they are content for the child to leave the country for the purpose of adoption.
- A report from the overseas authority detailing the child's parentage and history, the degree of contact with the birth parents, the date and reasons for the child's entry into an institution or foster placement and when, how and why the child came to be offered to the prospective adoptive parents.
- If the child is seven years of age or over, a report of an interview with the child, in which his/her view and understanding of the proposed adoption is clearly stated.

This information should be provided by the overseas authorities and the applicants to the ECO who will send it to the lead department. If all the documents are satisfactory, the ECO will issue a visa for the child which gives leave to enter the UK for 12 months for the purpose of adoption.

Full details of the Department of Health's entry clearance procedure can be found on the Department of Health's website on www.doh.gov.uk/adoption. Further information on entry clearance procedures can be obtained from the Home Office leaflet 'Intercountry Adoption' on www.ind.homeoffice.gov.uk and from the Foreign and Commonwealth Office on www.fco.gov.uk.

After arrival in the UK

On arrival in the UK, if the child's country of origin is not on the designated country list, the Adoption of Children from Overseas Regulations 2001 require prospective adopters in England and Wales to notify the local council of their intention to adopt within 14 days. The child will then be treated as a protected child and the placement monitored by the Council under sections 32 to 37 of the Adoption Act 1976 or in Scotland the Adoption (Scotland) Act 1978. Until the council has been notified by the adopters of their intention to adopt the placement should be treated as a private fostering arrangement under section 66 of the Children Act 1989 or in Scotland section 1 of the Foster Children (Scotland) Act 1984.

To seek an adoption order the prospective adopters need to lodge an application to adopt the child in a British court. They also need to notify the Home Office of the application for an adoption order. Under section 22 of the 1976

Act or in Scotland the Adoption (Scotland) Act 1978 the applicants must make an application for an adoption order within two years of giving notice of the intention to adopt the child to the council. However by virtue of section 13(2) of the 1976 or 1978 Act an order cannot be made until the child has lived with the adopter(s) for at least 12 months.

Once the Court has received an application they will ask the council to write a Schedule 2 report. This must include information on a range of issues including:
- The suitability of the applicant.
- The needs and wishes of the child, having regard to his age and understanding.
- Whether the child was placed with the applicants lawfully.
- Whether the applicants circumvented the usual procedures for adopting a child overseas.

Where the applicants have circumvented the usual procedures for adopting a child overseas and the application has been made to the County Court, the case is likely to be transferred to the High Court. This is in accordance with the Practice Direction on the Transfer of Intercountry Adoptions between the County Court and the High Court issued in 1993. In such circumstances the council should notify the relevant law enforcement agencies.

When an adoption order is made in the UK it automatically confers British Citizenship on the child provided one of the adoptive parents is a British Citizen at the time the adoption order is made.

If the child's country of origin is on the designated list there is no need to apply for an adoption order in the British Courts. However, where a child is subject to an interim adoption order and not to a full adoption order, the prospective adopters should notify the council that the child is with them. The council must then treat the child as a privately fostered child under section 66 of the Children Act 1989 or in Scotland section 1 of the Foster Children (Scotland) Act 1984 and carry out monitoring visits to protect the child's welfare.

Where the adopters have a full adoption order recognised under UK law the council does not have a role in monitoring the placement other than under their normal child protection functions and, where agreed, to produce post-placement reports.

Adoption orders recognised in the UK but made overseas do not automatically confer British Citizenship on the child. Adoptive parents should apply to the Nationality Department of the Home Office for citizenship on behalf of their child. In such cases, applications for citizenship would usually fall to be considered under section 3(1) of the British Nationality Act 1981. Registration as a British Citizen under this provision would be at the discretion of the Secretary of State.

Action to be taken where the procedures have not been followed correctly
Where agencies become aware of a child who has been brought into the UK for the purposes of adoption without the proper procedures being followed they should:
- Take action to ensure that the welfare of the child is protected.

6 Guidance as to whether or not a case should be considered under the Immigration Rules as a case where a child is already adopted or is coming to the United Kingdom to be adopted through the courts here

The Immigration Rules make provision for children who have been adopted abroad to be granted entry clearance to this country, admitted and/or allowed to remain here with an adoptive parent or parents for settlement or for a limited period with a view to settlement, provided certain requirements are first satisfied.

However, before giving consideration to an application from a child under these provisions, it must first be determined whether or not the child's circumstances warrant the application being looked at in this way. With this in mind, therefore, there are two questions which initially have to be asked:
- has an adoption order already been granted? and
- if so, is the order valid under United Kingdom law?

Ultimately, only the courts here can determine whether an adoption order granted overseas in a particular case is valid. However, should an adoption order be issued in a country or territory specified in the Adoption (Designation of Overseas Adoptions) Order, 1973 (a 'designated' country), following the completion of the due legal process there, it will normally be recognised as valid for the purposes of United Kingdom law. A list of 'designated' countries can be found at paragraph 4 (below).

If an adoption order has been granted, and it was issued in a 'designated' country following the completion of due legal process there, (see paragraph 3.1 below), the application will fall for consideration under the adoption provisions of HC 395, paragraphs 310–316 as appropriate. It must be emphasised though, that for such a child to be granted entry clearance, admitted to this country, or allowed to remain here for settlement or with a view to settlement, he will still have to satisfy all the particular adoption requirements of the Rules. If the adoption order is not valid at UK law or the child has not yet been adopted, the family should be advised to apply for entry clearance for the child to come to the UK as a child coming for adoption under paragraphs 316A–C of the Immigration Rules. For more details see Annex S.

Such applications are dealt with in the main part of this section (above); and further guidance relating to these provisions of the Rules is provided in paragraph 3 to this Annex and in Annex M to section 3.

7 Interim adoption orders

Some 'designated' countries, such as the US, will issue an interim adoption order to allow the child to live with the adopting parents. This can be converted to a full order at a later date (normally twelve months after the interim order, but this period can differ depending on the State in which they are adopting). An interim adoption order is not valid under United Kingdom law.

If an interim adoption order from a 'designated' country has been issued, and all the other requirements of the Rules relating to adoption can be met, an entry clearance can be granted to the child. Where the parents intend to adopt a child, (who is the subject of the interim adoption order in another country), through the Courts in the United Kingdom, the case should be considered under paragraphs 316A–C of HC 395 relating to 'for adoption'. Where the parents are waiting for the interim adoption order to be made final in the 'designated' country, the case should be considered exceptionally outside the Rules. The appropriate entry clearance will be 'Adoption CYR'. A child holding such an entry clearance should be granted 12 months leave to enter on arrival. An application may be made for the time limit on a child's stay to be removed on completion of the adoption proceedings.

8 Recognition of overseas adoptions at common law

There may be instances where an application is received on behalf of a child who has been 'adopted', and it is claimed that a court in this country would recognise the 'adoption' as common law. This may be even though the 'adoption' has not been completed in a 'designated' country or territory or, if it has, an order has not been granted following the completion of the due legal process there. One of the factors that will have a bearing will be the domicile of the adoptive parent(s) at the time the overseas 'adoption' is granted or completed. However, any case where it is claimed that the adoption is recognisable here under common law is to be referred to INPD for guidance. Such cases are likely to be very rare.

Where the adoption is not recognised as valid in the United Kingdom, see Annex R.

9 General guidance relating to adoption cases which fall to be considered under the Immigration Rules as a child who is already adopted or is coming to the United Kingdom to be adopted through the courts here

9.1 Child to have been adopted in accordance with a decision taken by the competent administrative authority or court

Where it is claimed that a child has already been adopted overseas by a particular person/couple, it will need to be satisfactorily demonstrated that the adoption order was granted either by the administrative authority or by a court which has the legal power to consider and decide such applications, and that it was issued in the child's country of origin, or in which he is living.

If a particular overseas country has two forms of adoption, a religious one which is purely for ceremonial purposes, and a separate one recognised in law which requires the granting of an order by a court, care should be exercised to ensure that the adoption process completed has resulted in an adoption order being issued by the court. Generally, the provision of the adoption order as issued by the court or appropriate administrative authority should be sufficient to show that the due legal process has been completed.

9.2 Cases where an adoption order has been issued in a 'designated' country but there is evidence of deception, etc.

It should be noted that where an adoption order has been issued by the appropriate administrative authority or court in a 'designated' country, we are not able to refuse to accept its validity, even if for example, we have information which indicates that deception has been exercised by the adoptive parent(s) to obtain the adoption order. Legal advice is that where such an order is granted, it remains valid for our purposes unless and until revoked by the appropriate authority in the country in which it was issued.

The above, however, must not be confused with situations where it is established that an adoption order has not been granted, or where the documentation presented to us to support an application for entry clearance, etc. is found to be forged. In such a case, action should follow on the basis that an adoption order has not been issued.

9.3 Child to have the same rights and obligations as any other child of the marriage

Where a child has been adopted, he should be treated and considered by his adoptive parent(s) in exactly the same way as if he were their natural child, and in line with any other natural or adopted child they may have.

9.4 Child adopted due to the inability of the original parent(s) or current carer(s) to care

These are important considerations, both where applications are received on behalf of children who have already been adopted, and where children are effectively to be adopted through the courts in this country.

The widely accepted objective of adoption, including inter-country adoption, is to provide a child with a parent(s) and a family where he does not already have one or, if he does already have parent(s) and/or a family but they are unable to care for him, to provide him with a new family. It is not the objective to provide a childless person or couple with a child.

Particularly where a child has for some time been adequately cared for and brought up by his parents, by other members of his natural family, by family friends, or by foster parents, it must be satisfactorily demonstrated that a child's adoption or proposed adoption was/is as a result of the inability of his original parent(s) or those currently caring for him to continue to adequately do so. In line with internationally recognised objectives concerning inter-country adoption, the inability to care for the child must be one of necessity and not one of choice.

9.5 Children from children's homes or orphanages

The consideration of the current carer(s) inability to care for a child should only apply where a child is being cared for by individuals, and not to cases where a child is in the care of a children's home, institution or orphanage. However, where a child has been placed in such an institution for a relatively short period of time, or since the adoptive parent(s) came to know of him, extra care should be exercised in assessing the true inability of the original parent(s) or previous carer(s) to care, through necessity, for him.

9.6 Genuine transfer of parental responsibility

It will not only have to be shown that there is an inability to care by the original parent(s) or the current carer(s) for the child, but also that parental responsibility has been genuinely transferred to the adoptive parent(s). In this regard, the adoptive parent(s) will have to be able to show that they have day to day responsibility for the child, and provide the child with all the emotional, financial and other needs which he may and does have. Furthermore, it will have to be satisfactorily demonstrated that they can and do exercise full control over the major aspects of the child's life, such as schooling, religion, medical care etc. Such control and responsibility is to be to the exclusion of any other person, including the child's original parent(s), and family.

However, where the adoptive parent(s) are temporarily back in this country without the child, perhaps due to the fact that an entry clearance application cannot be decided prior to their return date, they will obviously have to delegate day to day responsibility for the child to others in their absence. While this may be the case, the expectation is that this will only be for a limited period, with the overall responsibility for the child being retained by the adoptive parent(s) and the decisions being made by them on matters of importance.

9.7 Severance of ties with family of origin

Upon the making of an adoption order in the United Kingdom, the adopted child is deemed to be the child of the adopter(s) to the exclusion of the original parent(s).

Where the adoptive parent(s) have decided to maintain some contact with the birth parent(s) or where a blood relationship between original and adoptive parent(s) exists and future contact between child and original parent(s) is likely, this would be acceptable provided that it is clear that all parties concerned accept that it is the adoptive parent(s) who exercise full parental responsibility for the child and that the child himself considers himself to be the adopters' child to the exclusion of his original parent(s).

9.8 Adoption not to be of convenience arranged to facilitate the child's admission

In deciding whether or not a proposed adoption is one of convenience, the following points should be addressed:

(1) Have all the other immigration requirements been met?
(2) Would the child qualify for leave to remain in the United Kingdom on any other basis?
(3) Were the adoption proceedings started after an application for leave to remain on behalf of the child had been refused?
(4) On what basis was the child admitted to the United Kingdom? If possible, obtain a copy of the Visa Application Form and/or landing card to ascertain the original family's circumstances.
(5) Where do the child's parents live, what accommodation and income do they have and why have they given the child up for adoption?
(6) How old is the child? If he has lived with his birth parents for several years and there has been no appreciable change in their circumstances, are there ulterior motives for the adoption such as a better standard of living and/or advanced educational and employment prospects?
(7) Does the child have any siblings? If so, what are their ages and where and with whom do they live?

If the answers to any or all of the above questions suggest that the child would not qualify for leave to enter or remain for the purpose of adoption or on any other basis, then the adoption proceedings may have been instigated solely to facilitate the child's admission to or stay in the United Kingdom.

Further guidance for interpreting the requirements of the Rules is provided in Annex M to section 3,'Children' .

10 Countries and territories specified in the Adoption (Designation of Overseas Adoptions) Order 1973

10.1 Commonwealth Countries and Territories

Anguilla
Australia
Bahamas
Barbados
Belize
Bermuda
Botswana
British Virgin Islands
Canada
Cayman Islands
Cyprus (both Greek and Turkish sides)
Dominica
Fiji
Ghana
Gibraltar
Guyana
Hong Kong
Jamaica
Kenya
Lesotho
Malawi
Malaysia
Malta
Mauritius
Montserrat
Namibia (previously known as South West Africa)
New Zealand
Nigeria
Pitcairn Island
St Christopher and Nevis
St Vincent
Seychelles
Singapore
South Africa
Sri Lanka
Swaziland
Tanzania
Tonga
Trinidad and Tobago
Uganda
Zambia
Zimbabwe (previously known as Rhodesia)

10.2 Other Countries and Territories

Austria
Belgium
China (but only where the child was adopted on or after 5 April, 1993, and will be living in England or Wales or adopted on or after 10 July 1995 and will be living in Scotland)
Denmark (including the Faroe Islands and Greenland)
Finland
France (including French Guyana, Guadeloupe, Martinique, and Reunion)
Germany
Greece
Iceland
Israel
Italy
Luxembourg
The Netherlands (including the Antilles)
Norway
Portugal
Republic of Ireland
Spain (including the Balearic Islands and Canary Islands)
Surinam
Sweden

Switzerland
Turkey
United States of America
Yugoslavia (but not any of the States which now make up the former Yugoslavia)

10.3 Further enquiries in respect of the Adoption (Designation of Overseas Adoptions) Order 1973

The responsibility for the Adoption (Designation of Overseas Adoptions) Order 1973 rests entirely with the territorial health departments, namely the Department of Health for England and Wales, the Scottish Office for Scotland, and the Department of Health and Social Services for Northern Ireland. Any specific enquiries concerning the Order therefore, including whether a particular country or territory should be added or removed from it, the reasons for a particular country's inclusion etc. should be directed to the territorial health department which covers the area where the enquirer lives. Enquiries from those living outside the United Kingdom should normally be directed to the Department of Health. Addresses for the territorial health departments can be found in Annex S.

11 Information for applicants

11.1 The public information leaflet

The public information leaflet, 'Intercountry Adoption', details the procedures and requirements involved in bringing children to this country who have been adopted overseas and/or are being brought to this country for the purpose of adoption through the courts here. It is widely available from local social services, citizens' advice bureaux etc, as well as IND, and is issued free of charge to anybody who requests it.

11.2 Documents to be produced in adoption cases

A list of documents which should accompany any application on behalf of a child who has been adopted abroad or is coming to this country for adoption is to be found in the 'Intercountry Adoption' leaflet. The list should not be considered as exhaustive or in any order of priority. Any additional documents or details which may be helpful should also be requested. Where documents are not in English, the sponsors should be asked to provide certified translations.

**Immigration Directorates' Instructions
Chapter 8 section 5 – Adopted children
Annex S
July 2001**

Children coming for adoption and children adopted through courts in the United Kingdom

1 Introduction

A concession for children coming to the UK for adoption has existed for some time. In line with the Home Secretary's commitment to incorporate concessions into the Immigration Rules wherever possible, this concession is being withdrawn in favour of a specific provision in the Immigration Rules. Applications for entry clearance may be made on behalf of children to travel here effectively for the purpose of adoption through the courts in this country. An application will fall into this category where:
- a child has not been adopted overseas by his sponsors; or
- a child has been adopted following the completion of the due legal process overseas, but the Order granted is not recognised as valid for the purposes of United Kingdom law, (ie, the adoption took pace in a 'non-designated' country).

Annex Q provides guidance relating to cases involving countries whose adoption orders are recognised in the United Kingdom.

Entry clearance for entry in this capacity should first be obtained from the nearest designated British Diplomatic Post to the child's overseas address before he travels here. Entry clearance officers must first be satisfied on certain conditions before a child is admitted for adoption through the courts here.

2 Information for the public

The public information leaflet, 'Intercountry Adoption', details the requirements and procedures involved in obtaining entry clearance to bring a child here 'for adoption' through the courts in this country. It is issued free of charge to anyone who requests it.

Page 4 of the 'Intercountry Adoption' leaflet provides a list of documents which should accompany any application on behalf of a child who has already been adopted, or who is coming to this country for adoption through the courts here. The list should not, however, be considered as exhaustive or in any order of priority. Any additional documents or details that may be helpful should also be supplied. It is important to bear in mind that the majority of the documents on the list will be required by the courts here when considering an application to adopt, and therefore are not solely for the benefit of entry clearance officers in considering the immigration application.

3 Procedures for handling 'for adoption' applications

3.1 Documents needed by entry clearance officers

All applications should be accompanied by the documentation specified in page 4 of the 'Intercountry Adoption' leaflet, the child's original birth certificate and, if the child has not been adopted in the courts, permission from the court or administrative authority of that country that the child may come to the United Kingdom for adoption.

All documents produced should be the originals but if they are not, they must be certified by the entry clearance officer or some other professional person, (such as a judge), that they are true copies of the original. Where documents are in a foreign language, the sponsors or their representatives should have arranged for certified translations to have been prepared and presented to the entry clearance officer when the application for entry clearance was being lodged.

3.2 Initial consideration of the case on immigration grounds

Applications are to be considered in the first instance on immigration grounds alone. The factors which are to be taken into account and which have to be satisfied are based on those applied to all adoption cases which fall within the Rules.

3.3 Requirements for limited leave to enter 'for adoption'

The requirements to be satisfied in the case of a child seeking limited leave to enter for the purpose of adoption through the courts here are that he:

(i) is seeking limited leave to enter to accompany or join a person or persons who wish to adopt him in the United Kingdom (the 'prospective parent(s)'), in one of the following circumstances:

(a) both prospective parents are present and settled in the United Kingdom; or

(b) both prospective parents are being admitted for settlement on the same occasion that the child is seeking admission; or

(c) one prospective parent is present and settled in the United Kingdom and the other is being admitted for settlement on the same occasion that the child is seeking admission; or

(d) one prospective parent is present and settled in the United Kingdom and the other is being given limited leave to enter or remain in the United Kingdom with a view to settlement on the same occasion that the child is seeking admission, or has previously been given such leave; or

(e) one prospective parent is being admitted for settlement on the same occasion that the other is being granted limited leave to enter with a view to settlement, which is also on the same occasion that the child is seeking admission; or

(f) one prospective parent is present and settled in the United Kingdom or is being admitted for settlement on the same occasion that the child is seeking admission, and has had sole responsibility for the child's upbringing; or

(g) one prospective parent is present and settled in the United Kingdom or is being admitted for settlement on the same occasion that the child is seeking admission, and there are serious and compelling family or other considerations which would make the child's exclusion undesirable, and suitable arrangements have been made for the child's care; and

(ii) is under the age of 18; and
(iii) is not leading an independent life, is unmarried, and has not formed an independent family unit; and
(iv) can, and will, be maintained and accommodated adequately without recourse to public funds in accommodation which the prospective parent or parents own or occupy exclusively; and
(v) will have the same rights and obligations as any other child of the marriage; and
(vi) is being adopted due to the inability of the original parent(s) or current carer(s) (or those looking after him immediately prior to him being physically transferred to his prospective parent or parents) to care for him, and there has been a genuine transfer of parental responsibility to the prospective parent or parents; and
(vii) has lost or broken or intends to lose or break his ties with his family of origin; and
(viii) will be adopted in the United Kingdom by his prospective parent or parents, but the proposed adoption is not one of convenience arranged to facilitate his admission to the United Kingdom; and
(ix) holds a valid United Kingdom entry clearance for entry in this capacity.

Guidance in respect of (i)–(iv) above is provided in Annex M to section 3 of this chapter.

Guidance in respect of (v)–(viii) is provided in Annex Q

4 Children already in the United Kingdom

There is no provision in the Immigration Rules which permits a child to remain in the United Kingdom for adoption proceedings to take place. However, discretion to depart from the Immigration Rules may be exercised to children seeking leave to remain in this category provided certain criteria are met. Where a child was admitted with entry clearance endorsed 'for adoption', it is not necessary to recheck that the requirements are met and leave may be granted on application as set out in paragraph 4.2.

In all other cases, full enquiries must be made and documentation requested (see paragraph 8) to confirm that all of the requirements in paragraph 4.2 below are met.

4.1 Referral of cases to the Immigration and Nationality Policy Directorate

Caseworkers should refer to [Immigration and Nationality Policy Directorate] INPD all cases that involve a child who has been brought to or is now in the United Kingdom for adoption without entry clearance. Before referring, the following information must be on file;
(a) the child's full name at birth, date and place of birth and nationality; and
(b) the full names, dates of birth, nationalities or immigration status and address of the prospective adoptive parent(s); and
(c) the date and method of entry of the child to the United Kingdom and the period of leave granted if applicable; and
(d) an explanation from the prospective adoptive parent(s) for their failure to obtain entry clearance or the appropriate entry clearance for the child – an explanation is not required from the prospective adoptive

parents(s) of children who have been placed in their care by the social services.

4.2 Requirements for limited leave to remain 'for adoption'
A child may be granted leave to remain exceptionally, outside of the Immigration Rules, on the basis of ongoing adoption proceedings if he:
(i) is seeking limited leave to remain with a person or persons who wish to adopt him in the United Kingdom (the 'prospective parent(s)'), in one of the following circumstances:
(a) both prospective parents are present and settled in the United Kingdom; or
(b) one prospective parent is present and settled in the United Kingdom and the other parent is dead; or
(c) one prospective parent is present and settled in the United Kingdom and has had sole responsibility for the child's upbringing; or
(d) one prospective parent is present and settled in the United Kingdom and there are serious and compelling family or other considerations which would make the child's exclusion undesirable, and suitable arrangements have been made for the child's care; and
(ii) is under the age of 18; and
(iii) is not leading an independent life, is unmarried, and has not formed an independent family unit; and
(iv) can, and will, be maintained and accommodated adequately without recourse to public funds in accommodation which the prospective parent or parents own or occupy exclusively; and
(v) will have the same rights and obligations as any other child of the marriage; and
(vi) is being adopted due to the inability of the original parent(s) or current carer(s) (or those looking after him immediately prior to him being physically transferred to his prospective parent or parents) to care for him, and there has been a genuine transfer of parental responsibility to the prospective parent or parents; and
(vii) has lost or broken or intends to lose or break his ties with his family of origin; and
(viii) will be adopted in the United Kingdom by his prospective parent or parents, but the proposed adoption is not one of convenience arranged to facilitate his admission to the United Kingdom.

Guidance in respect of (1)–(4) above is in Annex M to section 3 of this chapter.

Guidance in respect of (5)–(8) is in Annex Q.

4.3 Granting leave to remain
If the child was admitted with entry clearance endorsed 'for adoption' or all of the requirements of paragraph 4.2 are met, then leave to remain may be granted. If confirmation is received from a court here that they have received and will be processing an application from the prospective adoptive parent(s) to adopt, then 12 months leave may be granted to enable the adoption proceedings to be finalised. Otherwise, only 3 months leave should be granted (INDECS code X3).

For action to take upon the making of an adoption order, see paragraph 6 below.

4.4 Refusing leave to remain

Where the requirements in paragraph 4.2 are not met, the application should be refused (INDECS code X6). It is worth bearing in mind that we would not expect a child to leave the United Kingdom until any adoption proceedings had been concluded but this should not preclude caseworkers from refusing applications.

See paragraph 8.7 below for guidance on refusing applications in this category.

Caseworkers should also give consideration to intervening in the adoption proceedings when invited to do so by the court (see paragraph 5 below).

5 Intervention

5.1 Background

Under Rule 15(3) of the Adoption Rules 1984, the Secretary of State may apply to the courts to be made party to adoption proceedings involving children who are subject to immigration control and who would become British citizens if an adoption order were made. Normally, British citizenship can only be acquired under the British Nationality Act 1981.

Whilst the courts' first duty is to consider what the best interests of the child are, it has been held that it also has a duty to consider the public interest in maintaining an effective immigration control. For this reason, the Secretary of State may set out his objections to the court in particular cases, including those where a child will still remain subject to immigration control following adoption in the United Kingdom courts.

5.2 Policy

All decisions on whether or not to intervene should be made at Grade 7/AD level.

IND should intervene in all cases where it is not prepared to grant leave to remain for the purpose of adoption (see paragraph 4.4 above).

5.3 Notification

IND should be informed by the courts of all adoption applications involving children who are subject to immigration control. They will either write to us direct or instruct the prospective adoptive parent(s), their solicitors or the guardian ad litem to do so. The guardian ad litem is a person appointed by the court to defend the interests of the child being adopted. The letter will ask us to advise them if the Secretary of State wishes to be made party to the proceedings.

Where an adoption hearing is imminent and we have been unable to make a decision due to the short notice given by the court or the fact that any enquiries we may have begun to make are still in progress, Treasury Solicitors may be asked to seek an adjournment.

5.4 Cases not warranting intervention
The Secretary of State should not intervene in cases where the child:
(1) is being adopted by a couple one of whom is a natural parent; or
(2) was admitted in possession of entry clearance endorsed 'for adoption'; or
(3) has been granted or would qualify for indefinite leave to remain or leave in some other capacity where it is accepted that the child's original family is unable to care for him, eg, as a minor dependant relative or in the absence of parents; or
(4) has been granted or would qualify for leave to remain for the purpose of adoption (see paragraph 4 above).

In these cases, a short letter should be sent to the court advising that the Secretary of State does not wish to intervene.

5.5 Cases warranting intervention
In all cases where we are not prepared to grant leave to remain for the purpose of adoption, the Secretary of State should intervene.

5.6 Procedure
Once it has been agreed at Grade 7/AD level that IND should intervene, a letter should be sent by the SEO to Treasury Solicitors as soon as possible with two copies of the IND file. The letter should set out the full immigration history of the child and why it is considered appropriate to intervene and instruct them to make the necessary arrangements for the Secretary of State to be made party to the application.

The letter should be copied to Legal Adviser's Branch with a short covering note inviting them to contact us if they need a copy of the file or any documents.

Treasury Solicitors may advise against proceeding on a particular case. If this is so, the case should be reviewed again at Grade 7/AD level and the decision conveyed to the Treasury Solicitors. If it is agreed not to intervene, the court should be advised of the decision.

If IND is to intervene, the Treasury Solicitors will make an application to the court on the Secretary of State's behalf. An affidavit, which sets out the Secretary of State's concerns, will need to be sworn by us at not less than SEO level. The Treasury Solicitors will draft the affidavit in consultation with the official who will swear it. This will be placed before the court at any subsequent hearing. Treasury Solicitors will advise if the official who swore the affidavit is required to attend court. The official may be called upon to answer questions.

Treasury Solicitors will keep caseworkers advised of any developments, change of circumstances and hearing dates. Similarly, caseworkers should advise Treasury Solicitors of any developments by copying to them correspondence which has not already been copied to them.

Where an application or representations are made on behalf of the child after we have intervened, a copy of any proposed refusal or reply should be forwarded to Treasury Solicitors for clearance before being sent out.

Treasury Solicitors will advise us of the outcome of the final adoption hearing. If an adoption order is made, they will let us know if there are any grounds on which to appeal. If an adoption order is not made, then the judge will normally direct the responsible social services department to make arrangements for the child's return to his original family.

5.7 Notifying the Immigration and Nationality Policy Directorate
Caseworkers must notify INPD of all cases where the Secretary of State is invited to intervene using form AD1 (a copy of which is attached at the end of this Annex and stocks of which should be kept locally).

Where a decision has been taken to intervene, caseworkers should keep INPD informed of developments by completing the relevant parts of section 3 as and when appropriate.

6 Adoption orders issued by courts in the United Kingdom
Under section 1(5) of the British Nationally Act 1981, a child who has been adopted through the courts in this country automatically acquires British Citizenship if his adoptive parent (or, if he was adopted by a couple, one or both of his adoptive parents) is a British Citizen on the date the order was made.

INDECS should be notified when children whose stay in the United Kingdom was subject to conditions become British Citizens through adoption in the United Kingdom, otherwise the children will appear as overstayers. The INDECS record should be cleared by inputting a decision with INDECS code 3CA.

This action does not constitute a grant of settlement and no mention of settlement should be made to the child's parents or representatives. If the adoptive parents forward the child's passport for endorsement, a letter should be sent advising them that their child became a British citizen on the date the adoption order was made by virtue of their British citizenship and that the child now qualifies for a British passport, obtainable from the Passport Office. If they travel abroad before they have obtained a British passport, they should take the letter and a copy of the adoption order as evidence that the child is a British citizen for their return to the United Kingdom.

If a child's adoptive parents were not British Citizens on the date the adoption order was issued by a court here, he may, upon application, be granted leave in line with whichever adoptive parent has the lesser period of leave. Should such a child subsequently leave this country and then at a later stage wish to return or, after arrival, remain on the basis of his relationship to his adoptive parent(s), his application should be considered and decided as if he were the natural child of his parent(s).

7 Residence orders
Residence orders represent a less final relationship than adoption and vest legal custody of a child in the adult caring for him. The carer has most of the rights and duties of a parent and is able to take nearly all the important decisions about the child's upbringing and day to day care. Unlike an adoption order, however, a residence order does not sever a child's legal ties with his

natural parents, nor does it involve a change of name. In certain circumstances, if it is felt to be in the child's best interest, the courts may grant a residence order instead of an adoption order.

When an adoption order is made by a court in the United Kingdom in respect of a child from overseas, the child automatically acquires British citizenship on the date of the order providing at least one of the adoptive parents is a British citizen on that date. This is not the case with a residence order. After a residence order has been made the child will remain subject to immigration control.

A court may revoke residence orders at any time on application by the carer, the child's original parent(s), the child's guardian or a local authority. Otherwise the order has effect until the child leaves full-time education.

Usually a residence order involves a clause prohibiting the child's removal from the United Kingdom other than accompanying the carer for a period not exceeding 1 month.

Residence orders have replaced custodianship orders which routinely remained in force until the child reached 18.

7.1 Children already in the United Kingdom – Residence Order already made

On receipt of an application consideration should first be given as to whether the child has any claim to remain in the United Kingdom under paragraph 298(i)(d) of HC 395, (see the main part of this section).

If the requirements of the Rules cannot be met it may be appropriate to exercise discretion and grant the child leave to remain outside the Rules if the following requirements are met:
- the child is under the age of 18, is unmarried, is not leading an independent life and has not formed an independent family unit;
- the adult carer is present and settled in the United Kingdom;
- there will be a genuine transfer of parental responsibility due to the natural parents' inability to care for the child;
- the residence order proceedings were not a matter of convenience arranged to facilitate the child's admission or stay in the United Kingdom; and
- there is adequate maintenance and accommodation for the child without recourse to public funds.

When all of the above criteria are met, it will normally be appropriate to grant leave to remain. If the residence order is intended to be in place for over 4 years it is appropriate to grant leave to remain for 4 years on Code 1 (INDECS code X3).

Cases may arise where the residence order is intended to be of only limited duration. In such circumstances it will be appropriate to grant the child limited leave on Code 1 (INDECS code X3) for 12 months at a time, reviewing the situation after 4 years.

After 4 years if there is no prospect of the child's removal from the United Kingdom in the immediate future indefinite leave to remain should be granted [INDECS code 7DA].

If the above criteria are not met, then the application should be refused. The refusal wording must relate only to the decision taken under the Rules (Paragraph 321). A covering letter should be sent with the refusal notice advising that consideration has been given to the application on an exceptional basis but the Secretary of State is not satisfied that there are any grounds for treating the case exceptionally.

7.2 Children already in the United Kingdom – Residence Order proceedings not yet resolved

Consideration should first be given as to whether the child has any claim to remain here under the Immigration Rules. If the child has no claim to remain, a decision must be made as to whether the Secretary of State should intervene in the residence order proceedings. If the hearing is imminent and it is not possible to make a final decision on intervention because enquiries are incomplete, Treasury Solicitors may be asked to seek an adjournment.

All decisions on whether or not to intervene should be taken at Grade 7/AD level. IND should intervene in all cases where it is not prepared to grant leave to remain for the purpose of residence order proceedings.

It is not appropriate to intervene in cases where the child was admitted in possession of entry clearance endorsed 'for adoption' or he has been granted or would qualify for indefinite leave to remain or leave in some other capacity where it is accepted that the child's original family is unable to care for him, eg. as a minor dependant relative or in the absence of parents.

In all other cases, consideration should be restricted to whether the requirements in paragraph 7.1 above are or can be met. If they can, it would not be appropriate to intervene. If they cannot, the Secretary of State should intervene.

See paragraph 5 above for the procedures which should be followed when intervening.

8 Enquiries and documentation for referred cases and children arriving without entry clearance

The following enquiries should be carried out by IND for all cases referred by entry clearance officers and by INPD for all cases where the child has arrived in the United Kingdom without entry clearance. Entry Clearance Officers contact the appropriate Health Authority directly to obtain consideration and advice on 'for adoption' cases.

8.1 Referral to appropriate Health Department

- If it is satisfactorily demonstrated that the immigration requirements have been met, the file should be clearly minuted to that effect and then forwarded to the appropriate 'territorial' health department for consideration and advice (see paragraph 8.2 below).
- Applications must not be referred to the territorial health departments for their action before the case has been considered on immigration grounds. If a file is forwarded to any of the health departments prior to the immigration aspects being considered and deemed to have been satisfied, and the file minuted accordingly, it will be returned unactioned.

- If the immigration requirements are not satisfied, the application should be refused on immigration grounds alone without referral to the appropriate territorial health department.

8.2 Referral to the territorial health departments

The territorial health departments comprise of the Department of Health in England, the Scottish Office in Scotland, the Welsh Office in Wales, and the Department of Health and Social Services in Northern Ireland. The file should be sent to the territorial health department appropriate to where the sponsoring 'parent' or 'parents' live. For instance, if the 'parents' live in Swansea, the file should be sent to the Welsh Office, while if they live in Belfast, it should be sent to the Department of Health and Social Services there. A list of the addresses and telephone numbers of the territorial health departments where the files should be sent is provided in paragraph 9 below.

8.3 Action by the territorial health departments

The appropriate health department considers the 'welfare' aspects of an application. They assess whether or not it would be in the child's best interests to be brought to or to remain in this country for the purpose of adoption by this particular person/couple, and the likelihood of a court in this country granting an adoption order for this child to the 'parent' or 'parents'.

8.4 Home study reports

The appropriate health department normally liaises with the appropriate local social services and requests them to provide a 'home study report' on the 'parent' or 'parents'. It may well be that the local social services have been able to prepare a report for this purpose in advance, for example where the 'parent' or 'parents' have commissioned one and paid any fee charged. If this is the case, the time taken by the health department to consider and advise entry clearance officers or IND on an individual case will undoubtedly be greatly shortened.

Whether or not a local authority chooses to carry out an assessment on the 'parent' or 'parents' in advance, and if so, to charge a fee, is entirely for the appropriate local authority to decide. It is not something that IND has any direct involvement in, or any influence over. Likewise, a local authority does not require our permission to undertake an assessment, or need to have an entry clearance application first referred to them.

It is also entirely up to the local authority to decide whether or not to in any way endorse or accept a home study report which has been completed by a private individual, perhaps a social worker acting in a private capacity, or a non-accredited organisation (such reports are usually referred to as 'private home study reports').

There may be instances where a home study report of some kind either accompanies a referred entry clearance application, or is presented to us prior to the immigration aspects being deemed to be satisfied. Should this occur, the case is still to be forwarded to the appropriate health department if the immigration requirements are first satisfied, irrespective of whom has completed the report or its contents. The information contained in such a report is not sufficient on its own to enable a thorough assessment to be made by the health department, and for them to provide us with a carefully considered response. Furthermore, we do not have any means of accurately assessing the report, finding out how recent it is, whether it is genuine, and whether any such recommendation contained is still applicable given the information contained within our file on the particular child in question.

8.5 Cases of exceptional urgency

If exceptional urgency is warranted in a particular case, and most but not all of the required documents are on file, the health department may be prepared to instigate their action before all the outstanding documents are received. The case will first, however, need to be discussed with the appropriate health department to explain why the case needs to be considered so urgently, why the documents have not yet been produced, and when they are likely to be provided. This course of action should only be contemplated when it is clear that the immigration requirements have been satisfied.

8.6 Priority for a child who is approaching or is 17 years old

Once a child reaches the age of 18, he cannot be adopted through the courts here irrespective of the stage the proceedings have reached.

By virtue of section 13(2) of the Adoption Act 1976, an adoption order cannot be made by a United Kingdom court in respect of a child where that child is not related to his prospective adoptive parent(s), unless he has been living with them in the United Kingdom at all times during the 12 months immediately prior to the date on which the court may grant an adoption order. Thus, where a child is not related to his 'parent' or 'parents' and was not in any way related to them prior to any overseas adoption order being granted, he will have to live with his 'parent' or 'parents' in this country for at least 12 months before an adoption order can be granted.

With this in mind, note should be taken of any application involving a child approaching 17 and action taken accordingly so that it does not fall for refusal simply because of the passage of time. A child who has passed his 17th birthday and is not related to his 'parent' or 'parents' must therefore have his application refused as it will not be possible to achieve the purpose for which he would be coming here.

Where a child is related to his 'parent' or 'parents' prior to any overseas adoption order being granted, an adoption order may be granted by a United Kingdom court by virtue of section 13(1)(a) of the Adoption Act 1976, where he is living in this country with his 'parent' or 'parents' at all times during the 13 weeks immediately prior to the date on which it is proposed that the order is to be granted. A case can, therefore, in an instance such as this, continue to be considered until a child is much closer to his 18th birthday.

8.7 Children already related to the 'parent' or 'parents'

If the child is a blood relative of the prospective adoptive parents, then the application should firstly be considered under the provisions of paragraphs 297–303 of HC 395 relating to children joining a parent or relatives other than parents. Only if the application falls to be refused should the case be considered under the 'for adoption' procedures.

8.8 Authorisation of entry clearance

Irrespective of any advice offered to us by any health department, the final decision as to whether or not to authorise entry clearance rests with ECOs or with IND to authorise leave to remain in referred cases. However, it will usually follow that the advice offered by them regarding whether it is in a child's best interests to come here or remain for adoption by the person/couple concerned, and the likelihood of a court here granting an adoption order for a child to the 'parent' or 'parents', will be accepted.

Provided that the immigration requirements of a particular case are met, and the appropriate health department provide us with a positive recommendation, it will normally follow that entry clearance should be authorised for a child to travel here `for adoption', or leave to remain to be granted 'for adoption' through the UK courts. The endorsement should be:

'HO/ HOF no. / 360 /FOR ADOPTION'

8.9 Refusal of entry clearance application

If it is decided it would not be appropriate to grant the child entry clearance to travel here or leave to remain for the purpose of adoption through the courts in this country, and he does not qualify for admission under a provision of the Rules, consideration should be given as to whether he can qualify exceptionally outside the Rules on another basis – see Annex R to this section.

When it is decided to refuse an application, refusal of a child coming for adoption through the UK Courts should be under paragraph 316C of HC 395 if it is not satisfactorily demonstrated that the requirements of 316A (i)–(viii) are met, unless the child is a blood relative (see below).

Annex U provides examples of refusal formulae.

For leave to remain 'for adoption' cases, a covering letter should accompany the refusal notice making it clear that the application has been considered by the Secretary of State exceptionally outside the Immigration Rules as there are no provisions within the Rules which allow for a child to remain here for the purpose of adoption through the courts in this country. If some form of adoption order has previously been granted overseas, and/or it is has been claimed that the child has already been adopted and is seeking to join or accompany his adoptive 'parent(s)' here, reference should be made to the fact that, as the adoption took place in a country whose adoption orders the United Kingdom does not recognise, the sponsor(s) are not, for the purposes of the Immigration Rules, recognised as the child's adoptive parent(s).

The refusal letter should clearly state the basis upon which the application has been considered exceptionally outside the Rules, and the reason(s) why discretion is not being exercised. For instance, if refusal is considered appropriate because the Secretary of State is not satisfied that there is an inability to care for the child through necessity by his original parent(s) or those currently caring for him, and that if he now in the UK, he would be adequately maintained and accommodated without recourse to public funds in accommodation which the 'parent(s)' own or occupy exclusively, those reasons should be given. Likewise, if refusal is as a result of advice received from the territorial health department, their reasons must be given in the letter.

An application should only be refused on the advice of the territorial health departments where specific reasons have been provided, for instance, the local authority have found the 'parent' or 'parents' to be unsuitable to adopt a child under 8 years of age, and the child in question is only 9 months old. Furthermore, as there will be a right of appeal against any such refusal, a report detailing this information must be provided by the territorial health department prior to refusal, and be one which can be made public at any appeal hearing. If such a report is not forthcoming, there will be no option but to set aside the advice of the territorial health department and grant leave to remain as any refusal at appeal could not be defended.

On the rare occasion that an application is made for a child adopted in a 'non designated' country to settle with his 'adoptive parents' in the United Kingdom and no de facto dependency has arisen, and there is no intention to adopt the child again in the United Kingdom, the application should be refused under paragraphs 310 and 320(1) of HC 395 (for the refusal wording, see Annex U).

Where the child's application also falls to be refused under the Rules relating to minor dependant relatives, the refusal wording should include a reference to paragraphs 300 and 297 of HC395.

The appropriate British Diplomatic Post, the 'parent' or 'parents', and the appropriate territorial health department should all be notified of the decision as soon as possible.

9 List of addresses and telephone numbers of the territorial health departments

England:
Adoption and Permanence Team
Social Care Group
Department of Health
Room 122 Wellington House Via IDS
133–155 Waterloo Road
LONDON
SE1 8UG

Tel No: 020 7972 4014/4082   Fax No: 020 7972 4179

Scotland:
Children and Young People's Group
Scottish Executive
Room 43B, Area 2B-S
Victoria Quay By Post
EDINBURGH
EH1 3BA

Tel No: 0131 244 5480   Fax No: 0131 244 5347

Wales:
Children and Families Division
The National Assembly for Wales
Cathays Park By Post
CARDIFF
CF10 3NQ

Tel No: 02920 823676   Fax No: 02920 823142

Northern Ireland:
Department of Health and Social Services and Public Safety
Child and Community Care Directorate
Dundonald House By Post
Upper Newtownards Road
BELFAST
BT4 3SF

Tel No: 02890 524762   Fax No: 02890 524196

Isle of Man:
Department Of Health and Social Security
Social Services Division
Hillary House
Prospect Hill
Douglas
Isle of Man
IM1 1EQ

Tel No: 01624 686179   Fax No: 01624 686198

Guernsey:
States of Guernsey Children Board
Homefinding Services
Garden Hill Resource Centre
The Rohais
St Peter Port
Guernsey
GY1 1FB

Tel No: 01481 713320   Fax No: 01481 700951

Jersey:
States of Jersey Health and Social Services
Children's Services
Maison Le Pape
The Parade
St Helier
Jersey
JE2 3PU

Tel No: 01534 623500   Fax No: 01534 623598

APPENDIX B

Extract from Entry Clearance General Instructions Volume 1 Chapter 16 and Annex 16

Entry Clearance General Instructions Volume 1 Chapter 16

Family reunion for dependants of those with exceptional leave or refugee status

16.1 Definitions of exceptional leave

Exceptional leave to remain (ELR) and exceptional leave to enter (ELE) in the UK are given to people who do not qualify for asylum but have been allowed to remain in the UK outside the Immigration Rules.

16.2 Background to exceptional leave

ELR/ELE following a failed asylum application will usually have been granted to a person in response to conditions in a particular country or because there are genuinely compelling humanitarian reasons for not enforcing removal of that person from the UK. ELR/ELE may also be given because removal from the UK would breach our obligations under the European Convention on Human Rights (ECHR).

Since July 1998, ELR/ELE is normally granted for a period of 4 years, after which the holder becomes eligible for the grant of Indefinite Leave to Remain (ILR). Once ILR has been granted, any dependants are eligible to apply to join the sponsor under the usual settlement paragraphs of the Rules.

Prior to 27 July 1998 the arrangements for granting ELR/ELE were different in that the holder would normally expect to complete seven years' ELR/ELE before becoming eligible for ILR. Annex 16.1 gives further details and shows how the transition from ELR/ELE to ILR is now handled. The transitional arrangements mean that someone granted ELR/ELE before 27 July 1998 may not be eligible for ILR until 27 July 2002. Although applications from dependants to join such a sponsor will be few the procedure to follow is described in paragraph 16.3 below.

Evidence of ELR/ELE will normally be in the form of a Home Office status letter.

16.3 Spouse/dependants of sponsors with ELR/ELE

There is no provision in the Immigration Rules for any person to join a sponsor with ELR/ELE in the UK. A sponsor who is eligible for ILR (see Annex

16.1) should, therefore, obtain it before applications from dependants are made. In cases where the sponsor is not yet eligible for ILR, the spouse and minor dependent children may qualify for entry clearance under Home Office policy 'outside the rules' if certain conditions are met. These conditions relate to spouses and minor dependent children irrespective of whether the marriage or births took place before or after the sponsor left his/her normal country of residence.

The requirements for a spouse are that:
(a) the sponsor has completed at least 4 years' ELR/ELE (and is not yet eligible for ILR);
(b) the marriage is genuine and subsisting;
(c) each of the parties intend to live permanently with the other as his/her spouse (see below);
(d) there will be adequate accommodation for the parties without recourse to public funds in accommodation which they own or occupy exclusively;
(e) the parties will be able to maintain and accommodate themselves and any dependants adequately without any recourse to public funds

With (c) care should be taken to allow for the fact that in many cases applicants will not have seen the sponsor in recent years in view of the requirement for the sponsor to have completed four years' ELR. Refusal on these grounds should only be considered if there is strong evidence to suggest that the intention to live together may be in doubt (eg, the known existence of a long-term partner of the sponsor).

The requirements for dependants are the same as those detailed in chapter 14.3 and paragraph 297 of the Rules.

16.4 Determining applications

Entry Clearance may be issued locally without referral to the Home Office as long as all the requirements in 16.3 above have been met.

Applications may be deferred pending further enquiries with the Evidence and Enquiries Section of ICD if it is considered necessary to establish facts, eg, the sponsor's status or the claimed relationship to the applicants. Sponsors with ELR/ELE will have completed a detailed Home Office questionnaire when they first sought to remain in the UK. This may contain details of all claimed family members and in cases of doubt can be checked against the information provided by the present applicants.

16.5 Those who do not qualify under the policy

Where it is clear from the outset that an application clearly does not meet the requirements set out above (eg, where the sponsor has not had ELR/ELE for at least 4 years, the children are over the age of 18 or the applicants are related in some other way to the sponsor), ECOs should advise the applicants that there is no provision in the Rules for the application, that they do not meet the policy criteria and that their applications might not be successful. If in spite of this advice the applicants decide to proceed, the fee should be taken and an interview conducted to establish the background and circumstances to the application with a view to determining whether there are compelling compassionate circumstances involved.

16.6 Referrals

If you consider there are compelling and compassionate circumstances involved and the applicants do not meet the requirements in 16.3 above, you should refer the application to ICD, Home Office for a decision. You should say why the application falls outside the normal criteria and explain clearly the compassionate circumstances to be taken into account.

16.7 Refusal

If an applicant does not qualify under the family reunion policy and you do not consider referral appropriate the application should be refused on an APP 200 under paragraph 320(1) of the Rules '... but I am not satisfied that entry is being sought for a purpose covered by the Immigration Rules'. You should ensure that the applicants are fully aware of the reasons why entry clearance cannot be issued. The applicants have the right of appeal.

16.8 Endorsements

Entry clearance for successful applicants should be endorsed 'to join spouse/parent' with leave to enter given in line with the sponsor.

16.9 Fees

The long-term non-settlement fee should be charged.

ANNEX 16.1

Transition from ELR to ILR

Prior to the 27 July 1998 exceptional leave to enter/remain (ELE/R) was normally granted for a period of 12 months followed by two periods of 3 years. From 27 July 1998 (publication date of the Government White Paper on Immigration and Asylum) ELE/R will normally be granted for a period of 4 years, after which the holder will become eligible for the grant of indefinite leave to remain (ILR).

To ensure that this change in practice does not result in unfairnes, the following transition arrangements have been agreed for handling applications for further LTR/settlement (ILR) from those with ELE/R. The aim is to ensure that no advantage is afforded to those granted ELE/R immediately after the change over those granted ELE/R before, and that all those granted before 27 July 1998 are considered for settlement by 27 July 2002 (4 years after the change).

Under the transition arrangements people will be required to complete varying periods of leave before being eligible to apply for settlement. These periods are determined by the year in which they were initially granted ELE/R and are set out in the centre row in the table below.

ELR granted	1992	1993	1994	1995	1996	1997	1998	1999
Years of leave before ILR to be considered	7	7	7	6	6	5	4	4
ILR	1999	2000	2001	2001	2002	By 27.02.02	By 27.7.02	27.7.02

When an application for further ELR is received it will normally be appropriate for caseworkers to grant leave to allow the applicant to complete the normal qualifying period for settlement (ILR). This will vary according to the year in which ELE/R was first granted and no one granted ELE/R before 27 July 1998 should be given leave beyond 27 July 2002.

APPENDIX C

Extract from Asylum Policy Instructions[1]

API Chapter 2 section 7 – Concurrent applications
API Chapter 5 section 1 – Exceptional leave

API Chapter 2 section 7 – Concurrent applications

1 Introduction
This instruction gives guidance on the procedures for assessing an *in country* asylum application when the applicant also has an application for leave to remain under another category of the Immigration Rules.

Where an applicant at port or illegal entrant has made concurrent application for asylum and under another category of the rules, caseworkers should follow the standard procedures for considering such claims. The Port or ISED will then deal with the other applications once it has received the decision on the asylum application.

2 Procedures for considering concurrent non-asylum and asylum applications

2.1 Order of consideration
The non-asylum application should normally be considered before the asylum application, although there may be occasions (eg, a likely grant of asylum or difficulties in concluding the non-asylum application) where the asylum claim may be considered first.

Unless it is decided to grant leave following a non-asylum application in a category leading to settlement or to refuse an out of time non-asylum application, the decisions should be served simultaneously. This is in order to enable appeals to be heard at the same hearing, and to avoid difficulties with VOLO leave.

- Both the non-asylum and asylum applications must be notified to INDECS and the asylum application to the Refugee Index. This should be done by AD if the file is with AD when an application is received for linking.

---

1 This extract was published prior to December 2001 and is currently being revised.

3 Invitations to withdraw: grants of non-asylum applications leading to settlement

All asylum applications remain outstanding until finally determined or withdrawn. In order to resolve asylum applications swiftly, where it is unlikely that the applicant will be required to leave the country in the near future, it is normally appropriate to invite the applicant to withdraw his asylum application if he is granted a period of leave in a category leading to settlement.

3.1 Invitation to withdraw the asylum application

If it is decided to grant an asylum-seeker a period of leave to enter/remain in another category leading to settlement (eg, as a spouse/fiancé, as a businessman, or as a person of independent means), AEAD should endorse the passport and return in to the applicant with the usual notification.

He should be invited, by the section granting the leave, to withdraw the outstanding asylum application using the letter at Annex A. A Lunar House address label should be enclosed, marked with the title of the section dealing with the asylum application.

The file will, at the same time, be returned to AD, via ASU, to await any notice of withdrawal or to continue consideration of the asylum application as set out below.

3.2 Refusal of asylum

If the applicant does not withdraw the application, action should be taken as in paragraph 3.2 of the instructions on *Implementation: Mixed Applications*.

3.3 Re-applications and appeals against the refusal of asylum claims

Where the applicant re-applies or appeals, substantive consideration should then be given to the asylum claim, if it has not already been substantively considered.

3.4 United Nations' travel document

Where the person argues that he has been disadvantaged because he has lost his entitlement to a UN travel document, the file should be referred to APU for advice.

4 Non-simultaneous service: non-asylum decisions to be served prior to consideration of the asylum application

4.1 Grants of non-asylum leave not leading to settlement

If the asylum application has been granted leave in a category not leading to settlement, one of the probable requirements he had to meet to qualify for that leave is an intention to leave the country at the end of that period of stay.

AEAD should therefore inform the applicant of the outcome of his non-asylum application, and invite a withdrawal of the asylum claim, but inform him that consideration of the asylum claim will continue if he decides against withdrawal. AD should continue to consider the claim substantively against the normal criteria, as paragraph 334(iii) of HC 395 (as amended) is not applicable in these cases.

If the asylum application was made in time during ordinary leave and it remains undecided when the leave granted as above expires, VOLO will automatically extend that leave to protect the section 8(2) right of appeal.

However, if the asylum application was made during a period of leave extended by VOLO (triggered by the in-time non-asylum application) and it remains undecided when the leave granted as above expires, there will not be a further extension of leave by virtue of VOLO and the asylum application should be dealt with as being out of time.

4.2 Refusals of out-of-time non-asylum applications

AEAD should issue the refusal, informing the applicant that his application is now being considered and he will be informed of the result in due course. AEAD then record the decision on INDECS, before sending the file to ASU. The claim will then be considered in accordance with normal procedures by the asylum caseworker and implemented as a decision solely on the asylum application. (See also paragraph 5 of the instruction on *Implementation: Mixed Applications*.)

5 Simultaneous service: refusals of in-time non-asylum applications

If AEAD decide to refuse an in-time non-asylum application, and there is an outstanding asylum claim, they will not send out the refusal notice and appeal forms in respect of their decision. Instead the file will be forwarded to the ASU with:

(i) A completed MIX1 form containing the refusal wording and quoting the paragraphs of the Immigration Rules under which the decision to refuse was made.

(ii) All relevant documents flagged and marked and the file flagged to show whether it is an AEAD or AD application/

Where appropriate, ASU will screen the applicant and obtain the SCQ before forwarding the file to the caseworking team. If screening has already taken place, the file will be passed directly to the caseworking team to consider the asylum application.

AD should give priority to cases where the decision is to refuse the non-asylum application. Any delay might result in the need to consider the non-asylum aspects afresh in the event of an asylum refusal, negating the work already completed.

5.1 Granting asylum

Action should be taken as in paragraph 4.2 of the instruction on Implementation: Mixed Applications.

5.2 Refusing asylum

If it is decided to refuse the asylum application and that a grant of exceptional leave is not merited, action should be taken as in paragraph 4.1 of the instruction on *Implementation: Mixed Applications*.

5.3 Refusing asylum but granting exceptional leave

Action should be taken as in paragraph 4.3 of the instruction on *Implementation: Mixed Applications*.

API Chapter 5 section 1 – Exceptional leave

1 Introduction
This instruction outlines the criteria to be applied in deciding whether an asylum applicant should be granted exceptional leave to enter/remain (ELE/R) in the UK. It also sets out the circumstances in which a grant of ELE/R may not be appropriate. This chapter should be considered together with Chapter 1 section 2 – Assessing the Claim.

Guidance on granting ELE/R to dependants is included in the instruction on *Dependants*.

2 Criteria for granting exceptional leave
Exceptional leave should normally be granted to asylum applicants only *after* their application has been substantively considered, and it has been decided that asylum should be refused.

If the case is to be refused without substantive consideration (eg, for reasons of non-compliance), the caseworker should consider whether the applicant qualifies for ELE/R on the basis of the information already provided.

2.1 Eligibility criteria
ELE/R *must* be granted to asylum applicants if they fall under one of the following criteria:
- Where the 1951 UN Convention requirements are not met in the individual case but return to the country of origin would result in the applicant being subjected to torture or other cruel, inhuman or degrading treatment, or where the removal would result in an unjustifiable break up of family life. For example,
- Where there are *substantial* grounds for believing that someone will suffer a serious and wholly disproportionate punishment for a criminal offence, eg, execution for draft evasion.
- Where there is *credible* medical evidence that return, due to the medical facilities in the country concerned, would reduce the applicant's life expectancy and subject him to acute physical and mental suffering, in circumstances where the UK can be regarded as having assumed responsibility for his care. In cases of doubt, a second opinion should be sought from a credible source.
- Where the applicant does not satisfy the 1951 UN Convention criteria for refugee status but there are compassionate or humanitarian reasons which merit not requiring the person to return to their country of origin or habitual residence.
- Where ministers have agreed that, for humanitarian reasons, a general country policy will apply. These countries are reviewed by ministers at appropriate intervals – see Annex A for the current list. Please note that the periods of exceptional leave granted in these cases may not accord with the general practice, and may not be granted to all unsuccessful asylum applicants. If there is any doubt concerning a specific country, the Country Information and Policy Unit should be contacted for clarification.

In addition, exceptional leave *may* be granted in cases where a decision has *not* been taken seven years after the application was made.

2.2 Disqualifying criteria

A person should *never* be disqualified from ELE/R if there are substantial reasons for believing that he or she would be tortured or otherwise subjected to inhuman or degrading treatment if they were to be returned to their country of origin.

However, if in the individual case the person concerned would not face torture or other cruel or inhuman treatment an asylum applicant who meets the eligibility criteria set out in paragraph 2.1 above may be refused ELE/R if any of the following criteria apply:

- The applicant has committed a serious non-political crime in the UK or overseas.
- The applicant is a major political figure or there are other obvious political or security sensitivities. (Although exceptional leave is not automatically ruled out, it may be necessary to seek the views of other government departments first, eg, FCO.)
- The application is so clearly unfounded and abusive that any prolongation of stay would be inappropriate.

2.3 Enforcement difficulties

Caseworkers should *not* grant, or propose granting exceptional leave simply because they consider there may be practical difficulties in enforcing departure. It is a matter for ISED to decide whether removal action should be pursued.

3 Application for exceptional leave following refusal of asylum and exhaustion of appeal rights

Occasions may arise when, following the refusal of asylum and exhaustion of all appeal rights, and application is nonetheless made requesting ELE/R outside the Immigration Rules.

By the time all rights of appeal have been brought before the Appellate Authorities, there will not be many cases that would merit the grant of ELE/R. However, caseworkers should give full and careful consideration to the reasons given for requesting exceptional leave, and decide whether the grant of ELE/R would be appropriate.

3.1 Refusing

AD caseworkers should inform the applicant by form ADL 43 (see Annex B) that the Secretary of State is not prepared to exercise his discretion in the applicant's favour. The file should then be forwarded to the appropriate Directorate for their continued action.

3.2 Further representations

If the request for exceptional leave reiterates the asylum claim as previously made, or if the request for exceptional leave provides new information that would oblige the Directorate to consider it under the terms of the 1951 Convention, the application for ELE/R should be treated in accordance with the instructions given in *Further Representations and Fresh Applications*.

4 Procedures

4.1 Granting

For information on granting ELE/R please see the instruction on *Implementation: Grants*.

4.2 Upgrade of status

For information on requests by those granted ELE/R to be upgraded to refugee status, please see the instruction on *Upgrade of Status*.

4.3 Refusal/revocation

For information on the circumstances when it may be appropriate not to grant further exceptional leave, or when it may be appropriate to revoke ELE/R status, please see the instruction on *Termination of Refugee Status and Exceptional Leave*.

APPENDIX D

Some relevant Concessions

DP 4/95 – Deportation and removal of children whose parent or parents are subject to deportation action

DP 3/96 – Marriage policy

DP 4/95 – Children

DP 5/96 – Deportation in cases where there are children with long residence

Concession outside the Immigration Rules for victims of domestic violence and bereaved spouses

DP 4/95 – Deportation and removal of children whose parent or parents are subject to deportation action

Introduction

1 In cases where a child (ie, a minor under 18) is in the United Kingdom and his/her parents are to be deported, the current practice is to allow the child to accompany his/her parents on departure at public expense. Ministers have recently reviewed this practice and have agreed that in future consideration should be given to taking action against children under either sections 3(5)(a) or 3(5)(c) of the Immigration Act 1971.

Policy

2 The purpose of this notice is, therefore, to advise caseworkers that deportation action against children should in future be considered *at the outset* with a view to serving notices of intention to deport at the same time as notices are served on the parent or parents, rather than waiting to see whether or not the parents are willing to see whether or not the parents are willing to take their children with them when they are deported.

3 Where a child is 16 or over and is *liable to deportation as an overstayer* consideration should be given to taking action against him/her under Immigration Act 1971 s3(5)(a) in his/her own right.

4 Where are child is under 16 or is not an overstayer (eg, the child was born here but does not have the right of abode) consideration should be given to serving the child with a notice of intention of deportation under section 3(5)(c) of the Immigration Act 1971. The service of a notice of intention to deport will leave parents in no doubt as to the status of their children and might discourage them from attempting to use their children as a means of delaying or avoiding removal. An example of the APP 104 to be served is at Annex A.

5 Where a decision to take Immigration Act 1971 s3(5)(c) action is taken full account must be taken of paragraph 366 of HC 395 which sets out the circumstances in which the Secretary of State will not normally take deportation action against a child, *as well as* the factors set out in paragraph 364. Parents *must* be notified in writing that there remains the opportunity for the child to leave voluntarily as required by paragraph 368 of the Rules.

6 It goes without saying that Immigration Act 1971 s3(5)(c) action is not to be used against British citizen children and in considering whether to take such action caseworkers must bear in mind that a child *born in the United Kingdom* after 1 January 1983 will be entitled to British citizenship once he/she has completed 10 years' residence – paragraph 1(4) of the British Nationality Act 1981 refers.

7 Appeals against deportation under section 3(5)(c0 of the Immigration Act 1971 are heard in the first instance by the Tribunal and any appeal by the parent(s) will be heard at the same time by the Tribunal. Where a child was given leave to enter less than 7 years before the date of decision the appeal will nonetheless be restricted to whether there us in law power to make the deportation order for the reasons stated in the notice. However, a child born in the United Kingdom who has not subsequently been granted leave to enter will have a full right of appeal against the decision to deport him/her.

8 It should be noted that a deportation order cannot be made against a dependant if more that weeks have elapsed since the parent has left the United Kingdom after the making of a deportation made against him. However, in calculating the 8 week period any period during which there is an appeal pending against the decision to make the order shall be disregarded.

9 For the purposes of section 3(5)(c) of the Immigration Act 1971 an adopted child, whether legally adopted or not, may be treated as the child of the adopter and an illegitimate child shall be regarded as the child of the mother.

Children who are on their own in the United Kingdom

10 The current policy that enforcement action against children under 16 years of age who are overstayers and *who are on their own* in the United Kingdom should only be contemplated when the child's voluntary departure cannot be arranged in unaffected by this notice. Guidance on this is set out in DP 2/93.

Enquiries about this instruction should be addressed to the Enforcement Policy Group.

DP 3/96 – Marriage policy

Introduction
1 This notice provides guidance, in general terms, on the consideration of cases of those persons liable to be removed as illegal entrants or deported who have married a person settled in the United Kingdom. *This notice supersedes DP2/93 which is hereby cancelled*, subject to the transitional provisions set out in paragraph 10 of this instruction. Deportation cases fall to be considered within the framework of the Immigration Rules and the attached guidance should be read in conjunction with those Rules. Although illegal entry cases are considered outside the Rules, any relevant compassionate circumstances, including those referred to below, should be considered before a decision to remove is taken.

Policy
2 Paragraph 364 of the Immigration Rules explains that deportation will normally be the proper course where a person has failed to comply with or has contravened a condition or has remained here without authority but that all the known relevant factors must be taken into account before a decision is reached. These include:
   (i)   age;
   (ii)   length of residence in the United Kingdom;
   (iii) strength of connections with the United Kingdom;
   (iv)   personal history, including character, conduct and employment record;
   (v)   domestic circumstances;
   (vi)   previous criminal record and the nature of any offence;
   (vii) compassionate circumstances;
   (viii) any representations.

3 Where persons do not qualify for leave to remain under the Immigration Rules and are to be considered for deportation, or where they are illegal entrants liable to removal, but seek nevertheless to remain on the basis of marriage in the United Kingdom, the following paragraphs of this guidance apply.

4 Where enforcement action is under consideration and the offender is married to someone settled here a judgement will need to be reached on the weight to be attached to the marriage as a compassionate factor. Caseworkers should bear in mind that paragraph 284 of the Immigration Rules, which sets out the requirements to be met for an extension of stay as the spouse of a person present and settled in the United Kingdom, specifically requires, amongst other things, a person to have a limited leave to remain here and to have not remained here in breach of the immigration laws, in order to obtain leave to remain on that basis. Therefore, the fact that an offender is married to a person settled here does not give him/her any right to remain under the Rules.

Marriage that pre-date enforcement action
5 As a *general rule*, deportation action under sections 3(5)(a) or 3(5)(b) of the Immigration Act 1971 (in non-criminal cases) or illegal entry action should not normally be initiated in the following circumstances (but see notes below):

Some relevant Concessions 219

(a) where the subject has a genuine and subsisting marriage with someone settled here and the couple have lived together in this country continuously since their marriage for at least 2 years before the commencement of enforcement action;

and

(b) it is unreasonable to expect the settled spouse to accompany his/her spouse on removal.

Notes

(i) In this instruction, 'settled' refers to British citizens who live in the United Kingdom or to other nationals who have ILE or ILR here.

(ii) In considering whether or not, under paragraph 5(b) above, it would be unreasonable for a settled spouse to accompany the subject of enforcement action on removal the onus rests with the settled spouse to make out a case with supporting evidence as to why it is unreasonable for him/her to live outside the United Kingdom. Factors which caseworkers should take into account, if they are made known to them, will include whether the United Kingdom settled spouse:
(a) has very strong and close family ties in the United Kingdom such as older children from a previous relationship that form part of the family unit; or
(b) has been settled and living in the United Kingdom for at least the preceding 10 years;
(c) suffers from ill-health and medical evidence conclusively shows that his/her life would be significantly impaired or endangered if he/she were to accompany his/her spouse on removal.

(iii) In this instruction commencement of enforcement action is to be taken as either:
(a) a specific instruction to leave with a warning of liability to deportation if the subject fails to do so; or
(b) service of a notice of intention to deport or service of illegal entry papers (including the service of papers during a previous stay in the United Kingdom where the subject has returned illegally); or
(c) a recommendation by a court that a person should be deported following a conviction.

(iv) The commencement of enforcement action 'stops the clock' in terms of the 2 year qualifying period referred to in paragraph 5a) above in which a marriage must have subsisted. No further time can then be accrued to meet this criterion, eg, whilst making representations, appealing against the decision or applying for judicial review.

(v) This notice contains guidance as to the approach to be adopted in the generality of cases but it must be remembered that each case is to be decided on its individual merits and, for instance, a particularly poor immigration history may warrant the offender's enforced departure from the UK notwithstanding the factors referred to above.

Criminal convictions

6 In cases where someone liable to immigration control has family ties here which would normally benefit him/her under paragraph 4 above but has

criminal convictions, the severity of the offence should be balanced against the strength of the family ties. Serious crimes which are punishable with imprisonment or a series of lesser crimes which show a propensity to re-offend, would normally outweigh the family ties. A very poor immigration history may also be taken into account. Caseworkers must use their judgement to decide what is reasonable in any individual case.

Children

7 The presence of children with the right of abode in the UK (see note below) is a factor to be taken into account. In cases involving children who have the right of abode, the crucial question is whether it is reasonable for the child to accompany his/her parents abroad. Factors to be considered include:
   (a) the age of the child (in most cases a child of 10 or younger could reasonably be expected to adapt to life abroad);
   (b) serious ill-health for which treatment is not available in the country to which the family is going.

Note
(i) Children will have the right of abode most commonly as a result of having been born in the United Kingdom to a parent settled here. It should be noted that under the British Nationality Act 1981 an illegitimate child born in the United Kingdom obtains British citizenship only if the mother is a British citizen or is settled in the United Kingdom. Under the 1981 Act the status of the nationality of the child unless he subsequently marries the mother and thus legitimises the child.

Marriages that post-date enforcement action

8 Where a person marries *after* the commencement of enforcement action removal should normally be enforced. The criteria set out in paragraph 5 do *not* apply in such cases. Paragraph 284 of the Immigration Rules makes it clear that one of the requirements for an extension of stay as the spouse of a person present and settled in the United Kingdom is that 'the marriage has not taken place after a decision has been made to deport the applicant or he has been recommended for deportation or has been given notice under section 6(2) of the Immigration Act 1971'. Marriage cannot therefore in itself be considered a sufficiently compassionate factor to militate against removal. Detailed enquiries in order to ascertain whether the marriage is genuine and subsisting should *not* normally be undertaken. The onus is on the subject to put forward any compelling compassionate factors that he/she wishes to be considered which must be supported by documentary evidence. Only in the most *exceptional circumstances* should removal action be stopped and the person allowed to stay.

Marriage to European Economic Area (EEA) nationals

9 Any foreign national who contracts a marriage to an EEA national should have his/her case considered in the first instance by EC group, B6 Division to whom the case must be referred, irrespective of whether the marriage took place before or after the initiation of enforcement action.

Transitional Arrangements

10 This instruction will not apply retrospectively. It has immediate effect in cases where the marriage came to the notice of the Immigration and Nationality Department after 13 March 1996 irrespective of the date on which the marriage took place. Cases where the marriage came to notice on or prior to 13 March 1996 should be considered under the terms of DP 2/93.

Enquiries

11 Any enquiries about this instruction should be addressed to the Enforcement Policy Group.

Enforcement Policy Group
13 March 1996

FLOW CHART

This flow chart should be used as a *guide* only. There will occasionally be cases which fall outside the guidelines.

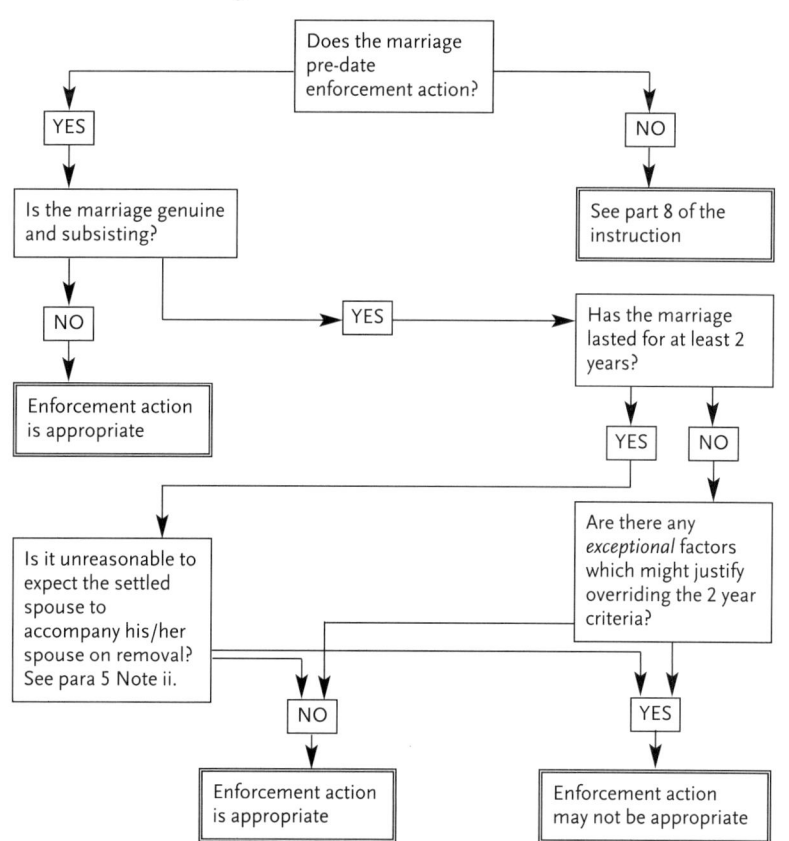

```
                    Does the marriage
                    pre-date
                    enforcement action?
         ┌──────────────┴──────────────┐
        YES                            NO
         │                             │
         ▼                             ▼
  Is the marriage genuine      See part 8 of the
  and subsisting?              instruction
         │
   ┌─────┴─────┐
  NO          YES ─────────►  Has the marriage
   │                          lasted for at least 2
   ▼                          years?
  Enforcement action              │
  is appropriate            ┌─────┴─────┐
                           YES          NO
                            │            │
                            ▼            ▼
  Is it unreasonable to              Are there any
  expect the settled                 *exceptional* factors
  spouse to                          which might justify
  accompany his/her                  overriding the 2 year
  spouse on removal?                 criteria?
  See para 5 Note ii.
         │                            │
    ┌────┴────┐                  ┌────┴────┐
   NO        YES                NO        YES
    │                                      │
    ▼                                      ▼
  Enforcement action              Enforcement action
  is appropriate                  may not be appropriate
```

DP 4/95 – Children

Introduction

1 This notice provides guidance, an general terms, on the consideration of cases of those persons liable to be removed as illegal entrants or deported who are either children on their own here or who are parents who have children present in the United Kingdom. It supplements the advice given in DP 3/96 about the consideration of marriage cases involving children with the right of abode, DP 4/95 which gives guidance on the user if section 3(5)(c) of the Immigration Act 1971.

Policy

2 There is no bar to taking deportation/illegal entry action against children of any age who are liable to such action. However, enforcement action against children and young persons under the age of 16 *who are on their own* in the United Kingdom should only be contemplated when the child's voluntary departure cannot be arranged. In all cases removal must not be enforced unless we are satisfied that the child will be met on arrival in his/her home country and that care arrangements are in place thereafter. To this end, caseworkers should contact the Welfare Section of the appropriate Embassy of High Commission as well as the local Social Services Department.

3 If there is any evidence, not just a suspicion, that the care arrangements are seriously below the standard normally provided in the country concerned or that they are so inadequate that the child would face serious risk of harm if returned, consideration should be given to abandoning enforcement action. Where deportation or removal remains the right course, consideration will need to be given to whether an escort is necessary on the journey.

4 Where deportation/removal action is being considered against a parent or parents the existence of children in the United Kingdom is a factor which must be taken into account when assessing the merits of such action. The weight to be attached to children as a compassionate factor which will vary from case to case and has to be balanced against or along with the other factors.

5 In all cases the longer the child has been here the greater will be the weight to be attached to this as a factor; but the general presumption will be that a child who has spent less than 10 years in the United Kingdom would be able to adapt to life abroad. (See DP 5/96 for cases involving children who have been here for 10 years or more.)

Divorced and separated children

6 Deportation or illegal entry action should not necessarily be conceded where a person is liable to deportation or removal as an illegal entrant, whose marriage has broken down, has access rights to his/her child (who is entitled to remain here) and seeks to remain in order to exercise those rights. He/she should be advised that such an application should be made from abroad. Paragraphs 246–248 of the Immigration Rules provide a specific category for those who wish to enter the United Kingdom to exercise access rights to children. Entry clearance is required for this purpose which must be applied

for from abroad, and there is a right to appeal against refusal. Recent legal advice indicates that in this type of case there is unlikely to be a breach of article 8 of the ECHR as 'family life' has already broken down and that as there is no bar to someone applying to return to the United Kingdom for access visits and as a right of appeal is provided for, there can be no breach of article 13 (the right to legal redress).

7   Enforcement action should normally proceed in these cases if, notwithstanding the advice provided, the offender fails to leave. A person who then becomes the subject of a deportation order should be informed that before he/she can apply to return in accordance with paragraphs 246–248 of the Rules, he/she will need to apply for revocation of the deportation order. Again, this must be done from *abroad*. Only in the *most exceptional* circumstances will it be right to concede a case to enable a parent to continue access visits, with agreement at no less than A/D level.

8   It should be noted that paragraphs 246–248 of the Rules apply only in cases where the parents of the child were married. It should also be noted that in cases where the parent is already to subject of a deportation order it may be unreasonable to expect him or her to return abroad to apply for entry clearance as he or she would normally be barred from re-entry for 3 years. In these cases it will be important to assess the quality and the regularity of access to the child in deciding how much weight should be attached to it as a compassionate factor.

Adoption, wardship, custodianship and residence orders

9   The following paragraphs provide advice on the handling of cases where there is reason to believe that the purpose of one or more of the above proceedings is to frustrate enforcement action. The definition of these proceedings are:

Adoption	A child adopted by order of a court in the United Kingdom is a British citizen (and thus not liable to immigration control) from the date of the order if an adoptive parent is a British citizen at that date. An adoption by order of a foreign court may not be recognised in United Kingdom law: in such cases advice should be sought from B2 Division.
Custodianship	This represents a less final relationship than adoption and vests legal custody of a child in the adult(s) caring for him/her. Where a custodianship order is made the child's immigration status is unchanged but he/she should not removed from the jurisdiction of the court while the order remains in force.
Wardship	Children who are wards of court should not be removed from the United Kingdom without the court's leave.
Residence orders	Residence orders are very similar in effect to wardship and children subject to a residence order should not be removed from the United Kingdom without the leave of the court.
Contact order	A court order allowing a person contact with a child and specifying the terms under which the contact is to take place.

Intervention in the above proceedings

10 The Family Court will generally attach much more weight to the child's welfare than to the irregularities surrounding the immigration status of the child or a parent. Where, however, it is clear that the court proceedings are designed purely to enable the child or the parent to evade immigration control consideration may be given to instructing the Treasury Solicitor with a view to intervention in the proceedings. *There must be evidence, not just a suspicion, that there has been a serious attempt to circumvent the immigration control* and decisions to intervene must be taken at not less than SEO level.

11 Where intervention had been agrees the papers should be copied to the Treasury Solicitor's office as soon as possible. Their normal practice is then to apply for the Secretary of State to be joined as a respondent, and to file an affidavit setting out the child's and/or parents' immigration history and the Secretary of State's objections.

12 It should be noted that where an order has been made under the Children Act this cannot in itself deprive the Secretary of State of the power conferred by the Immigration Act 1971 to remove or deport any party to the proceeding although it may be something to which he should have regard when deciding whether to exercise his powers under the Act.

Enquiries

13 Any enquiries about this instruction should be addressed to the Enforcement Policy Group.

Enforcement Policy Group
March 1996

DP 5/96 – Deportation in cases where there are Children with Long Residence

Introduction
1 The purpose of this instruction is to define more clearly the criteria to be applied when considering whether enforcement action should proceed or be initiated against parents who have children who were either born here and are aged 10 or over or where, having come to the United Kingdom at an early age, they have accumulated 10 years or more continuous residence.

Policy
2 Whilst it is important that each individual case must be considered on its merits, the following are factors which may be of particular relevance:
   (a) the length of the parents' residence without leave;
   (b) whether removal has been delayed through protracted (and often repetitive) representations or by the parents going to ground;
   (c) the age of the children;
   (d) whether the children were conceived at a time when either of the parents had leave to remain;
   (e) whether return to the parents' country of origin would cause extreme hardship for the children or put their health seriously at risk;
   (f) whether either of the parents has a history of criminal behaviour or deception.

3 When notifying a decision to either concede or proceed with enforcement action it is important that full reasons be given making clear that each cases is considered on its individual merits.

Enquiries
4 Any enquiries about this instruction should be addressed to the Enforcement Policy Group.

Enforcement Policy Group
March 1996

Concession outside the Immigration Rules for victims of domestic violence and bereaved spouses

Mr O'Brien announced the concession on 16 June 1999 at it came into force with immediate effect. Any application outstanding on 16 June 1999 for further leave to remain or indefinite leave to remain in the United Kingdom where the applicant has been granted limited leave to enter or remain as the spouse or unmarried partner of a person who is present and settled in the United Kingdom and the relationship has broken down during the probationary period as a result of domestic violence, or the sponsor has died, will be considered outside the Immigration Rules under this concession.

The concession

An applicant who has limited leave to enter or remain in the United Kingdom as the spouse or unmarried partner of a person who is present and settled in the United Kingdom as the spouse or unmarried partner of a person who is present in the UK and whose relationship breaks down during the probationary period as a result of domestic violence, maybe granted indefinite leave to remain in the United Kingdom exceptionally outside the Immigration Rules provided that the domestic violence occurred during the probationary period whilst the marriage or relationship was subsisting and the applicant is able to produce one of the following forms of evidence that domestic violence has taken place:

(i) an injunction, non-molestation order or other protection order against the sponsor (other than an ex-parte or interim order); or
(ii) a relevant court conviction against the sponsor; or
(iii) full details of a relevant police caution issued against the sponsor.

Where a prosecution is pending against the sponsor the applicant may be granted further periods of 6 months limited leave to remain, subject to the same conditions, until the outcome of the criminal prosecution is known. Where a hearing seeking an injunction, non-molestation order or other protection order is pending, a decision on the application will be delayed pending the outcome of that hearing.

Where an applicant is widowed during the probationary period they may be granted indefinite leave to remain exceptionally outside the Immigration Rules provided that the Secretary of State is satisfied that the marriage was subsisting at the time of the sponsor's death.

APPENDIX E

Extracts from European Convention on Human Rights

Article 1 – Obligation to respect human rights
The High Contracting Parties shall secure to everyone within their jurisdiction the rights and freedoms defined in Section I of this Convention.

SECTION I – RIGHTS AND FREEDOMS
Article 2 – Right to life
1. Everyone's right to life shall be protected by law. No one shall be deprived of his life intentionally save in the execution of a sentence of a court following his conviction of a crime for which this penalty is provided by law.
2. Deprivation of life shall not be regarded as inflicted in contravention of this article when it results from the use of force which is no more than absolutely necessary:
   a in defence of any person from unlawful violence;
   b in order to effect a lawful arrest or to prevent the escape of a person lawfully detained;
   c in action lawfully taken for the purpose of quelling a riot or insurrection.

Article 3 – Prohibition of torture
No one shall be subjected to torture or to inhuman or degrading treatment or punishment.

Article 4 – Prohibition of slavery and forced labour
1. No one shall be held in slavery or servitude.
2. No one shall be required to perform forced or compulsory labour.
3. For the purpose of this article the term 'forced or compulsory labour' shall not include:
   a any work required to be done in the ordinary course of detention imposed according to the provisions of Article 5 of this Convention or during conditional release from such detention;
   b any service of a military character or, in case of conscientious objectors in countries where they are recognised, service exacted instead of compulsory military service;
   c any service exacted in case of an emergency or calamity threatening the life or well-being of the community;
   d any work or service which forms part of normal civic obligations.

Article 5 – Right to liberty and security
1. Everyone has the right to liberty and security of person. No one shall be

deprived of his liberty save in the following cases and in accordance with a procedure prescribed by law:
   a   the lawful detention of a person after conviction by a competent court;
   b   the lawful arrest or detention of a person for non-compliance with the lawful order of a court or in order to secure the fulfilment of any obligation prescribed by law;
   c   the lawful arrest or detention of a person effected for the purpose of bringing him before the competent legal authority on reasonable suspicion of having committed an offence or when it is reasonably considered necessary to prevent his committing an offence or fleeing after having done so;
   d   the detention of a minor by lawful order for the purpose of educational supervision or his lawful detention for the purpose of bringing him before the competent legal authority;
   e   the lawful detention of persons for the prevention of the spreading of infectious diseases, of persons of unsound mind, alcoholics or drug addicts or vagrants;
   f   the lawful arrest or detention of a person to prevent his effecting an unauthorised entry into the country or of a person against whom action is being taken with a view to deportation or extradition.
2 Everyone who is arrested shall be informed promptly, in a language which he understands, of the reasons for his arrest and of any charge against him.
3 Everyone arrested or detained in accordance with the provisions of paragraph 1c of this article shall be brought promptly before a judge or other officer authorised by law to exercise judicial power and shall be entitled to trial within a reasonable time or to release pending trial. Release may be conditioned by guarantees to appear for trial.
4 Everyone who is deprived of his liberty by arrest or detention shall be entitled to take proceedings by which the lawfulness of his detention shall be decided speedily by a court and his release ordered if the detention is not lawful.
5 Everyone who has been the victim of arrest or detention in contravention of the provisions of this article shall have an enforceable right to compensation.

Article 6 – Right to a fair trial
1 In the determination of his civil rights and obligations or of any criminal charge against him, everyone is entitled to a fair and public hearing within a reasonable time by an independent and impartial tribunal established by law. Judgment shall be pronounced publicly but the press and public may be excluded from all or part of the trial in the interests of morals, public order or national security in a democratic society, where the interests of juveniles or the protection of the private life of the parties so require, or to the extent strictly necessary in the opinion of the court in special circumstances where publicity would prejudice the interests of justice.
2 Everyone charged with a criminal offence shall be presumed innocent until proved guilty according to law.
3 Everyone charged with a criminal offence has the following minimum rights:
   a   to be informed promptly, in a language which he understands and in detail, of the nature and cause of the accusation against him;
   b   to have adequate time and facilities for the preparation of his defence;
   c   to defend himself in person or through legal assistance of his own choos-

ing or, if he has not sufficient means to pay for legal assistance, to be given it free when the interests of justice so require;
d   to examine or have examined witnesses against him and to obtain the attendance and examination of witnesses on his behalf under the same conditions as witnesses against him;
e   to have the free assistance of an interpreter if he cannot understand or speak the language used in court.

Article 7 – No punishment without law

1   No one shall be held guilty of any criminal offence on account of any act or omission which did not constitute a criminal offence under national or international law at the time when it was committed. Nor shall a heavier penalty be imposed than the one that was applicable at the time the criminal offence was committed.
2   This article shall not prejudice the trial and punishment of any person for any act or omission which, at the time when it was committed, was criminal according to the general principles of law recognised by civilised nations.

Article 8 – Right to respect for private and family life

1   Everyone has the right to respect for his private and family life, his home and his correspondence.
2   There shall be no interference by a public authority with the exercise of this right except such as is in accordance with the law and is necessary in a democratic society in the interests of national security, public safety or the economic well-being of the country, for the prevention of disorder or crime, for the protection of health or morals, or for the protection of the rights and freedoms of others.

Article 9 – Freedom of thought, conscience and religion

1   Everyone has the right to freedom of thought, conscience and religion; this right includes freedom to change his religion or belief and freedom, either alone or in community with others and in public or private, to manifest his religion or belief, in worship, teaching, practice and observance.
2   Freedom to manifest one's religion or beliefs shall be subject only to such limitations as are prescribed by law and are necessary in a democratic society in the interests of public safety, for the protection of public order, health or morals, or for the protection of the rights and freedoms of others.

Article 10 – Freedom of expression

1   Everyone has the right to freedom of expression. This right shall include freedom to hold opinions and to receive and impart information and ideas without interference by public authority and regardless of frontiers. This article shall not prevent States from requiring the licensing of broadcasting, television or cinema enterprises.
2   The exercise of these freedoms, since it carries with it duties and responsibilities, may be subject to such formalities, conditions, restrictions or penalties as are prescribed by law and are necessary in a democratic society, in the interests of national security, territorial integrity or public safety, for the prevention of disorder or crime, for the protection of health or morals, for the protection of the reputation or rights of others, for preventing the disclosure

of information received in confidence, or for maintaining the authority and impartiality of the judiciary.

Article 11 – Freedom of assembly and association

1. Everyone has the right to freedom of peaceful assembly and to freedom of association with others, including the right to form and to join trade unions for the protection of his interests.
2. No restrictions shall be placed on the exercise of these rights other than such as are prescribed by law and are necessary in a democratic society in the interests of national security or public safety, for the prevention of disorder or crime, for the protection of health or morals or for the protection of the rights and freedoms of others. This article shall not prevent the imposition of lawful restrictions on the exercise of these rights by members of the armed forces, of the police or of the administration of the State.

Article 12 – Right to marry

Men and women of marriageable age have the right to marry and to found a family, according to the national laws governing the exercise of this right.

Article 13 – Right to an effective remedy

Everyone whose rights and freedoms as set forth in this Convention are violated shall have an effective remedy before a national authority notwithstanding that the violation has been committed by persons acting in an official capacity.

Article 14 – Prohibition of discrimination

The enjoyment of the rights and freedoms set forth in this Convention shall be secured without discrimination on any ground such as sex, race, colour, language, religion, political or other opinion, national or social origin, association with a national minority, property, birth or other status.

Article 15 – Derogation in time of emergency

1. In time of war or other public emergency threatening the life of the nation any High Contracting Party may take measures derogating from its obligations under this Convention to the extent strictly required by the exigencies of the situation, provided that such measures are not inconsistent with its other obligations under international law.
2. No derogation from Article 2, except in respect of deaths resulting from lawful acts of war, or from Articles 3, 4 (paragraph 1) and 7 shall be made under this provision.
3. Any High Contracting Party availing itself of this right of derogation shall keep the Secretary General of the Council of Europe fully informed of the measures which it has taken and the reasons therefor. It shall also inform the Secretary General of the Council of Europe when such measures have ceased to operate and the provisions of the Convention are again being fully executed.

Article 16 – Restrictions on political activity of aliens

Nothing in Articles 10, 11 and 14 shall be regarded as preventing the High Contracting Parties from imposing restrictions on the political activity of aliens.

Protocol to the Convention for the Protection of Human Rights and Fundamental Freedoms

Article 2 – Right to education

No person shall be denied the right to education. In the exercise of any functions which it assumes in relation to education and to teaching, the State shall respect the right of parents to ensure such education and teaching in conformity with their own religious and philosophical convictions.

Protocol No 6 to the Convention for the Protection of Human Rights and Fundamental Freedoms concerning the abolition of the death penalty

Article 1 – Abolition of the death penalty

The death penalty shall be abolished. No-one shall be condemned to such penalty or executed.

Article 2 – Death penalty in time of war

A State may make provision in its law for the death penalty in respect of acts committed in time of war or of imminent threat of war; such penalty shall be applied only in the instances laid down in the law and in accordance with its provisions. The State shall communicate to the Secretary General of the Council of Europe the relevant provisions of that law.

Article 3 – Prohibition of derogations

No derogation from the provisions of this Protocol shall be made under Article 15 of the Convention.

APPENDIX F

International Covenant on Civil and Political Rights (selected articles)

Part III
Article 6
1. Every human being has the inherent right to life. This right shall be protected by law. No one shall be arbitrarily deprived of his life.
2. In countries which have not abolished the death penalty, sentence of death may be imposed only for the most serious crimes in accordance with the law in force at the time of the commission of the crime and not contrary to the provisions of the present Covenant and to the Convention on the Prevention and Punishment of the Crime of Genocide. This penalty can only be carried out pursuant to a final judgement rendered by a competent court.
3. When deprivation of life constitutes the crime of genocide, it is understood that nothing in this article shall authorise any State Party to the present Covenant to derogate in any way from any obligation assumed under the provisions of the Convention on the Prevention and Punishment of the Crime of Genocide.
4. Anyone sentenced to death shall have the right to seek pardon or commutation of the sentence. Amnesty, pardon or commutation of the sentence of death may be granted in all cases.
5. Sentence of death shall not be imposed for crimes committed by persons below eighteen years of age and shall not be carried out on pregnant women.
6. Nothing in this article shall be invoked to delay or to prevent the abolition of capital punishment by any State Party to the present Covenant.

Article 8
1. No one shall be held in slavery; slavery and the slave-trade in all their forms shall be prohibited.
2. No one shall be held in servitude.
3. a No one shall be required to perform forced or compulsory labour;
   b Paragraph 3 (a) shall not be held to preclude, in countries where imprisonment with hard labour may be imposed as a punishment for a crime, the performance of hard labour in pursuance of a sentence to such punishment by a competent court;
   c For the purpose of this paragraph the term 'forced or compulsory labour' shall not include:
      (i) Any work or service, not referred to in subparagraph (b), normally required of a person who is under detention in consequence of a lawful order of a court, or of a person during conditional release from such detention;

(ii) Any service of a military character and, in countries where conscientious objection is recognised, any national service required by law of conscientious objectors;
(iii) Any service exacted in cases of emergency or calamity threatening the life or well-being of the community;
(iv) Any work or service which forms part of normal civil obligations.

Article 10

1 All persons deprived of their liberty shall be treated with humanity and with respect for the inherent dignity of the human person.
2 a Accused persons shall, save in exceptional circumstances, be segregated from convicted persons and shall be subject to separate treatment appropriate to their status as unconvicted persons;
  b Accused juvenile persons shall be separated from adults and brought as speedily as possible for adjudication. 3. The penitentiary system shall comprise treatment of prisoners the essential aim of which shall be their reformation and social rehabilitation. Juvenile offenders shall be segregated from adults and be accorded treatment appropriate to their age and legal status.

Article 14

1 All persons shall be equal before the courts and tribunals. In the determination of any criminal charge against him, or of his rights and obligations in a suit at law, everyone shall be entitled to a fair and public hearing by a competent, independent and impartial tribunal established by law. The press and the public may be excluded from all or part of a trial for reasons of morals, public order (ordre public) or national security in a democratic society, or when the interest of the private lives of the parties so requires, or to the extent strictly necessary in the opinion of the court in special circumstances where publicity would prejudice the interests of justice; but any judgement rendered in a criminal case or in a suit at law shall be made public except where the interest of juvenile persons otherwise requires or the proceedings concern matrimonial disputes or the guardianship of children.
2 Everyone charged with a criminal offence shall have the right to be presumed innocent until proved guilty according to law.
3 In the determination of any criminal charge against him, everyone shall be entitled to the following minimum guarantees, in full equality:
  a To be informed promptly and in detail in a language which he understands of the nature and cause of the charge against him;
  b To have adequate time and facilities for the preparation of his defence and to communicate with counsel of his own choosing;
  c To be tried without undue delay;
  d To be tried in his presence, and to defend himself in person or through legal assistance of his own choosing; to be informed, if he does not have legal assistance, of this right; and to have legal assistance assigned to him, in any case where the interests of justice so require, and without payment by him in any such case if he does not have sufficient means to pay for it;
  e To examine, or have examined, the witnesses against him and to obtain

the attendance and examination of witnesses on his behalf under the same conditions as witnesses against him;
- f   To have the free assistance of an interpreter if he cannot understand or speak the language used in court;
- g   Not to be compelled to testify against himself or to confess guilt.

4 In the case of juvenile persons, the procedure shall be such as will take account of their age and the desirability of promoting their rehabilitation.
5 Everyone convicted of a crime shall have the right to his conviction and sentence being reviewed by a higher tribunal according to law.
6 When a person has by a final decision been convicted of a criminal offence and when subsequently his conviction has been reversed or he has been pardoned on the ground that a new or newly discovered fact shows conclusively that there has been a miscarriage of justice, the person who has suffered punishment as a result of such conviction shall be compensated according to law, unless it is proved that the non-disclosure of the unknown fact in time is wholly or partly attributable to him.
7 No one shall be liable to be tried or punished again for an offence for which he has already been finally convicted or acquitted in accordance with the law and penal procedure of each country.

Article 17

1 No one shall be subjected to arbitrary or unlawful interference with his privacy, family, home or correspondence, nor to unlawful attacks on his honour and reputation.
2 Everyone has the right to the protection of the law against such interference or attacks.

Article 18

1 Everyone shall have the right to freedom of thought, conscience and religion. This right shall include freedom to have or to adopt a religion or belief of his choice, and freedom, either individually or in community with others and in public or private, to manifest his religion or belief in worship, observance, practice and teaching.
2 No one shall be subject to coercion which would impair his freedom to have or to adopt a religion or belief of his choice.
3 Freedom to manifest one's religion or beliefs may be subject only to such limitations as are prescribed by law and are necessary to protect public safety, order, health, or morals or the fundamental rights and freedoms of others. 4. The States Parties to the present Covenant undertake to have respect for the liberty of parents and, when applicable, legal guardians to ensure the religious and moral education of their children in conformity with their own convictions.

Article 23

1 The family is the natural and fundamental group unit of society and is entitled to protection by society and the State.
2 The right of men and women of marriageable age to marry and to found a family shall be recognised.

3 No marriage shall be entered into without the free and full consent of the intending spouses.
4 States Parties to the present Covenant shall take appropriate steps to ensure equality of rights and responsibilities of spouses as to marriage, during marriage and at its dissolution. In the case of dissolution, provision shall be made for the necessary protection of any children.

APPENDIX G

Other International Conventions

Convention on the Elimination of all Forms of Discrimination Against Women (CEDAW) 18 December 1979

Optional Protocol to the Convention of the Elimination of all Forms of Discrimination Against Women 6 October 1999

International Covenant on Civil and Political Rights (ICCPR) 16 December 1966

International Covenant on Economic, Social and Cultural Rights (ICESCR) 16 December 1966

Convention Against Torture and Other Cruel, Inhuman or Degrading Treatment or Punishment (UNCAT) 10 December 1984

Declaration on the Elimination of Violence Against Women 20 December 1993 UN General Assembly Resolution 48/104

These extracts are taken from the United Nations website at www.un.org

Convention on the Elimination of All Forms of Discrimination Against Women (CEDAW) 18 December 1979

The Convention on the Elimination of All Forms of Discrimination against Women is the most comprehensive treaty on women's human rights, establishing legally binding obligations to end discrimination. Often described as the international bill of rights for women, the Convention provides for equality between women and men in the enjoyment of civil, political, economic, social and cultural rights. Discrimination against women is to be eliminated through legal, policy and programmatic measures and through temporary special measures to accelerate women's equality, which are defined as non-discriminatory.

Key Provisions

States parties are required to end all forms of discrimination against women and to ensure their equality with men in political and public life with regard to nationality, education, employment, health and economic and social benefits. Obligations are also imposed to eliminate discrimination against women in marriage and family life and to ensure that women and men are treated equally before the law. States are required to take account of the particular problems of women in rural areas, and their special roles in the economic survival of the family.

The Convention is the only human rights treaty to affirm the reproductive rights of women. In addition, it obliges States parties to modify the social and cultural patterns of conduct of men and women in order to eliminate prejudices and customs and all other practices which are based on the idea of the inferiority or superiority of either of the sexes or on stereotyped roles for men and women.

Optional Protocol to the Convention on the Elimination of All Forms of Discrimination against Women 6 October 1999

The objective of the Optional Protocol is to allow individuals or groups of individuals who have exhausted national remedies to petition the Committee directly about alleged violations of the Convention by their Governments

Key Provisions

States parties to the Optional Protocol undertake to make the Convention and the Protocol widely known and to facilitate access to information about the views and recommendations of the Committee. They are also required to take all appropriate measures to ensure that individuals under their jurisdiction are not subjected to ill-treatment or intimidation when they take advantage of the Protocol's procedure or provide information associated with these procedures. States which ratify or accede to the Optional Protocol may not enter reservations to its terms, but they are able to opt-out of the inquiry procedure.

International Covenant on Civil and Political Rights (ICCPR) 16 December 1966

The Covenant is a landmark in the efforts of the international community to promote human rights. It defends the right to life and stipulates that no individual can be subjected to torture, enslavement, forced labour and arbitrary detention or be restricted from such freedoms as movement, expression and association.

Key Provisions

The Covenant is divided into six parts. Part I reaffirms the right of self-determination. Part II formulates general obligations by States parties, notably to implement the Covenant through legislative and other measures, to provide effective remedies to victims and to ensure gender equality, and it restricts the possibility of derogation. Part III spells out the classical civil and political rights, including the right to life, the prohibition of torture, the right to liberty and security of person, the right to freedom of movement, the right to a fair hearing, the right to privacy, the right to freedom of religion, freedom of expression, freedom of peaceful assembly, the right to family life, the rights of children to special protection, the right to participate in the conduct of public affairs, the over-arching right to equal treatment, and the special rights of persons belonging to ethnic, religious and linguistic minorities.

International Covenant on Economic, Social and Cultural Rights (ICESCR) 16 December 1966

Economic, social and cultural rights are designed to ensure the protection of people as full persons, based on a perspective in which people can enjoy rights, freedoms and social justice simultaneously. In a world where, according to the United Nations Development Programme (UNDP), 'a fifth of the developing world's population goes hungry every night, a quarter lacks access to even a basic necessity like safe drinking water, and a third lives in a state of abject poverty at such a margin of human existence that words simply fail to describe it' (UNDP, *Human Development Report 1994*, Oxford University Press, 1994, p2) the importance of renewed attention and commitment to the full realisation of economic, social and cultural rights is self-evident.

Despite significant progress since the establishment of the United Nations in addressing problems of human deprivation, well over 1 billion people live in circumstances of extreme poverty, homelessness, hunger and malnutrition, unemployment, illiteracy and chronic ill-health. More than 1.5 billion people lack access to clean drinking water and sanitation: some 500 million children don't have access to even primary education; and more than 1 billion adults cannot read and write. This massive scale of marginalisation, in spite of continued global economic growth and development, raises serious questions, not only in relation to development, but also in relation to basic human rights.

Of all the basic human rights standards, the International Covenant on Economic, Social and Cultural Rights provides the most important international legal framework for protecting basic human rights.

Key Provisions
The Covenant contains some of the most significant international legal provisions establishing economic, social and cultural rights, including rights relating to work in just and favourable conditions, to social protection, to an adequate standard of living, to the highest attainable standards of physical and mental health, to education and to enjoyment of the benefits of cultural freedom and scientific progress. It also provides for the right of self-determination; equal rights for men and women; the right to work; the right to just and favourable conditions of work; the right to form and join trade unions; the right to social security and social insurance; protection and assistance to the family; the right to adequate standard of living; the right to the highest attainable standard of physical and mental health; the right to education; the right to take part in cultural life; and the right to enjoy the benefits of scientific progress and its applications.

Convention against Torture and Other Cruel, Inhuman or Degrading Treatment or Punishment (UNCAT) 10 December 1984

Torture and other cruel, inhuman or degrading treatment or punishment are particularly serious violations of human rights and, as such, are strictly condemned by international law. Based upon the recognition that such practices are outlawed, the Convention strengthens the existing prohibition by a number of supporting measures. The Convention provides for several forms of international supervision in relation to the observance by States parties of their obligations under the Convention including the creation of an international supervisory body – the Committee against Torture – which can consider complaints from a State party or from or on behalf of individuals.

Key Provisions
The prohibition against torture is absolute and, according to the Convention, no exceptional circumstances whatsoever, including state of emergency or war or an order from a public authority may be invoked as a justification of torture. 'Torture' is defined as:

> ... any act by which severe pain or suffering, whether physical or mental, is intentionally inflicted on a person for such purposes as obtaining from him or a third person information or a confession, punishing him for an act he or a third person has committed or is suspected of having committed, or intimidating or coercing him or a third person, or for any reason based on discrimination of any kind, when such pain or suffering is inflicted by or at the instigation of or with the consent or acquiescence of a public official or other person acting in an official capacity. It does not include pain or suffering arising only from, inherent in or incidental to lawful sanctions.

States parties have the obligation to prevent and punish not only acts of torture as defined in the Convention, but also other acts of cruel, inhuman or degrading treatment or punishment, when such acts are committed by or at the instigation of or with the consent or acquiescence of a public official or other person acting in an official capacity.

States parties have an obligation to take effective legislative, administrative, judicial or other measures to prevent acts of torture from occurring on their territories. Measures mentioned in the Convention include the prohibition and punishability by appropriate penalties of all acts of torture in domestic criminal law; education and information regarding the prohibition against torture to be fully integrated into the training of law enforcement personnel, civil or military, medical personnel, public officials and others; the systematic review by State parties of interrogation rules, instructions, methods and practices as well as of arrangements for the custody and treatment of suspects, detainees and prisoners; guarantees for the prompt and impartial investigation by competent authorities into allegations of torture; the protection of witnesses; and the possibility for victims to obtain redress and fair and adequate compensation and rehabilitation.

In addition, States parties have an obligation not to expel, return or extradite a person to another State where he or she would be in danger of being subjected to torture.

Declaration on the Elimination of Violence against Women 20 December 1993. UN General Assembly Resolution 48/104

This is a short declaration that recognises that violence against women is a manifestation of historically unequal power relations between men and women, which have led to domination over and discrimination against women by men and to the prevention of the full advancement of women, and that violence against women is one of the crucial social mechanisms by which women are forced into a subordinate position compared with men. It sets out to provide a comprehensive definition of violence against women, a statement of the rights to be applied to ensure elimination of violence and the commitment of States and the international community to eliminate violence against women.

APPENDIX H

Convention on the Rights of the Child

The full text of the convention can be found at www.unhchr.ch. There are 54 clauses. The first 41 clauses are reproduced here. The UK has entered reservations on the interpretation of the Convention which include:

...the right to apply such legislation, in so far as it relates to the entry into, stay in and departure from the UK of those who do not have the right under the law of the UK to enter and remain in the UK, and to the acquisition and possession of citizenship, as it may deem necessary from time to time.

Article 1
For the purposes of the present Convention, a child means every human being below the age of eighteen years unless, under the law applicable to the child, majority is attained earlier.

Article 2
1 States Parties shall respect and ensure the rights set forth in the present Convention to each child within their jurisdiction without discrimination of any kind, irrespective of the child's or his or her parent's or legal guardian's race, colour, sex, language, religion, political or other opinion, national, ethnic or social origin, property, disability, birth or other status.
2 States Parties shall take all appropriate measures to ensure that the child is protected against all forms of discrimination or punishment on the basis of the status, activities, expressed opinions, or beliefs of the child's parents, legal guardians, or family members.

Article 3
1 In all actions concerning children, whether undertaken by public or private social welfare institutions, courts of law, administrative authorities or legislative bodies, the best interests of the child shall be a primary consideration.
2 States Parties undertake to ensure the child such protection and care as is necessary for his or her well-being, taking into account the rights and duties of his or her parents, legal guardians, or other individuals legally responsible for him or her, and, to this end, shall take all appropriate legislative and administrative measures.
3 States Parties shall ensure that the institutions, services and facilities responsible for the care or protection of children shall conform with the standards established by competent authorities, particularly in the areas of safety, health, in the number and suitability of their staff, as well as competent supervision.

Article 4
States Parties shall undertake all appropriate legislative, administrative, and other measures for the implementation of the rights recognized in the present Convention. With regard to economic, social and cultural rights, States Parties shall undertake such measures to the maximum extent of their available resources and, where needed, within the framework of international cooperation.

Article 5
States Parties shall respect the responsibilities, rights and duties of parents or, where applicable, the members of the extended family or community as provided for by local custom, legal guardians or other persons legally responsible for the child, to provide, in a manner consistent with the evolving capacities of the child, appropriate direction and guidance in the exercise by the child of the rights recognized in the present Convention.

Article 6
1 States Parties recognize that every child has the inherent right to life.
2 States Parties shall ensure to the maximum extent possible the survival and development of the child.

Article 7
1 The child shall be registered immediately after birth and shall have the right from birth to a name, the right to acquire a nationality and, as far as possible, the right to know and be cared for by his or her parents.
2 States Parties shall ensure the implementation of these rights in accordance with their national law and their obligations under the relevant international instruments in this field, in particular where the child would otherwise be stateless.

Article 8
1 States Parties undertake to respect the right of the child to preserve his or her identity, including nationality, name and family relations as recognized by law without unlawful interference.
2 Where a child is illegally deprived of some or all of the elements of his or her identity, States Parties shall provide appropriate assistance and protection, with a view to speedily re-establishing his or her identity.

Article 9
1 States Parties shall ensure that a child shall not be separated from his or her parents against their will, except when competent authorities subject to judicial review determine, in accordance with applicable law and procedures, that such separation is necessary for the best interests of the child. Such determination may be necessary in a particular case such as one involving abuse or neglect of the child by the parents, or one where the parents are living separately and a decision must be made as to the child's place of residence.
2 In any proceedings pursuant to paragraph 1 of the present article, all interested parties shall be given an opportunity to participate in the proceedings and make their views known.
3 States Parties shall respect the right of the child who is separated from one or

both parents to maintain personal relations and direct contact with both parents on a regular basis, except if it is contrary to the child's best interests.
4 Where such separation results from any action initiated by a State Party, such as the detention, imprisonment, exile, deportation or death (including death arising from any cause while the person is in the custody of the State) of one or both parents or of the child, that State Party shall, upon request, provide the parents, the child or, if appropriate, another member of the family with the essential information concerning the whereabouts of the absent member(s) of the family unless the provision of the information would be detrimental to the well-being of the child. States Parties shall further ensure that the submission of such a request shall of itself entail no adverse consequences for the person(s) concerned.

Article 10
1 In accordance with the obligation of States Parties under article 9, paragraph 1, applications by a child or his or her parents to enter or leave a State Party for the purpose of family reunification shall be dealt with by States Parties in a positive, humane and expeditious manner. States Parties shall further ensure that the submission of such a request shall entail no adverse consequences for the applicants and for the members of their family.
2 A child whose parents reside in different States shall have the right to maintain on a regular basis, save in exceptional circumstances personal relations and direct contacts with both parents. Towards that end and in accordance with the obligation of States Parties under article 9, paragraph 1, States Parties shall respect the right of the child and his or her parents to leave any country, including their own, and to enter their own country. The right to leave any country shall be subject only to such restrictions as are prescribed by law and which are necessary to protect the national security, public order (order public), public health or morals or the rights and freedoms of others and are consistent with the other rights recognized in the present Convention.

Article 11
1 States Parties shall take measures to combat the illicit transfer and non-return of children abroad.
2 To this end, States Parties shall promote the conclusion of bilateral or multilateral agreements or accession to existing agreements.

Article 12
1 States Parties shall assure to the child who is capable of forming his or her own views the right to express those views freely in all matters affecting the child, the views of the child being given due weight in accordance with the age and maturity of the child.
2 For this purpose, the child shall in particular be provided the opportunity to be heard in any judicial and administrative proceedings affecting the child, either directly, or through a representative or an appropriate body, in a manner consistent with the procedural rules of national law.

Article 13
1 The child shall have the right to freedom of expression; this right shall include freedom to seek, receive and impart information and ideas of all kinds,

regardless of frontiers, either orally, in writing or in print, in the form of art, or through any other media of the child's choice.
2   The exercise of this right may be subject to certain restrictions, but these shall only be such as are provided by law and are necessary:
   a   For respect of the rights or reputations of others; or
   b   For the protection of national security or of public order (ordre public), or of public health or morals.

Article 14
1   States Parties shall respect the right of the child to freedom of thought, conscience and religion.
2   States Parties shall respect the rights and duties of the parents and, when applicable, legal guardians, to provide direction to the child in the exercise of his or her right in a manner consistent with the evolving capacities of the child.
3   Freedom to manifest one's religion or beliefs may be subject only to such limitations as are prescribed by law and are necessary to protect public safety, order, health or morals, or the fundamental rights and freedoms of others.

Article 15
1   States Parties recognize the rights of the child to freedom of association and to freedom of peaceful assembly.
2   No restrictions may be placed on the exercise of these rights other than those imposed in conformity with the law and which are necessary in a democratic society in the interests of national security or public safety, public order (ordre public), the protection of public health or morals or the protection of the rights and freedoms of others.

Article 16
1   No child shall be subjected to arbitrary or unlawful interference with his or her privacy, family, home or correspondence, nor to unlawful attacks on his or her honour and reputation.
2   The child has the right to the protection of the law against such interference or attacks.

Article 17
States Parties recognize the important function performed by the mass media and shall ensure that the child has access to information and material from a diversity of national and international sources, especially those aimed at the promotion of his or her social, spiritual and moral well-being and physical and mental health. To this end, States Parties shall:
   a   the mass media to disseminate information and material of social and cultural benefit to the child and in accordance with the spirit of article 29;
   b   Encourage international co-operation in the production, exchange and dissemination of such information and material from a diversity of cultural, national and international sources;
   c   Encourage the production and dissemination of children's books;
   d   Encourage the mass media to have particular regard to the linguistic needs of the child who belongs to a minority group or who is indigenous;
   e   Encourage the development of appropriate guidelines for the protection

of the child from information and material injurious to his or her well-being, bearing in mind the provisions of articles 13 and 18.

Article 18
1 States Parties shall use their best efforts to ensure recognition of the principle that both parents have common responsibilities for the upbringing and development of the child. Parents or, as the case may be, legal guardians, have the primary responsibility for the upbringing and development of the child. The best interests of the child will be their basic concern.
2 For the purpose of guaranteeing and promoting the rights set forth in the present Convention, States Parties shall render appropriate assistance to parents and legal guardians in the performance of their child-rearing responsibilities and shall ensure the development of institutions, facilities and services for the care of children.
3 States Parties shall take all appropriate measures to ensure that children of working parents have the right to benefit from child-care services and facilities for which they are eligible.

Article 19
1 States Parties shall take all appropriate legislative, administrative, social and educational measures to protect the child from all forms of physical or mental violence, injury or abuse, neglect or negligent treatment, maltreatment or exploitation, including sexual abuse, while in the care of parent(s), legal guardian(s) or any other person who has the care of the child.
2 Such protective measures should, as appropriate, include effective procedures for the establishment of social programmes to provide necessary support for the child and for those who have the care of the child, as well as for other forms of prevention and for identification, reporting, referral, investigation, treatment and follow-up of instances of child maltreatment described heretofore, and, as appropriate, for judicial involvement.

Article 20
1 A child temporarily or permanently deprived of his or her family environment, or in whose own best interests cannot be allowed to remain in that environment, shall be entitled to special protection and assistance provided by the State.
2 States Parties shall in accordance with their national laws ensure alternative care for such a child.
3 Such care could include, inter alia, foster placement, kafalah of Islamic law, adoption or if necessary placement in suitable institutions for the care of children. When considering solutions, due regard shall be paid to the desirability of continuity in a child's upbringing and to the child's ethnic, religious, cultural and linguistic background.

Article 21
States Parties that recognize and/or permit the system of adoption shall ensure that the best interests of the child shall be the paramount consideration and they shall:
    a Ensure that the adoption of a child is authorized only by competent authorities who determine, in accordance with applicable law and procedures

and on the basis of all pertinent and reliable information, that the adoption is permissible in view of the child's status concerning parents, relatives and legal guardians and that, if required, the persons concerned have given their informed consent to the adoption on the basis of such counselling as may be necessary;
b Recognize that inter-country adoption may be considered as an alternative means of child's care, if the child cannot be placed in a foster or an adoptive family or cannot in any suitable manner be cared for in the child's country of origin;
c Ensure that the child concerned by inter-country adoption enjoys safeguards and standards equivalent to those existing in the case of national adoption;
d Take all appropriate measures to ensure that, in inter-country adoption, the placement does not result in improper financial gain for those involved in it;
e Promote, where appropriate, the objectives of the present article by concluding bilateral or multilateral arrangements or agreements, and endeavour, within this framework, to ensure that the placement of the child in another country is carried out by competent authorities or organs.

Article 22

1 States Parties shall take appropriate measures to ensure that a child who is seeking refugee status or who is considered a refugee in accordance with applicable international or domestic law and procedures shall, whether unaccompanied or accompanied by his or her parents or by any other person, receive appropriate protection and humanitarian assistance in the enjoyment of applicable rights set forth in the present Convention and in other international human rights or humanitarian instruments to which the said States are Parties.
2 For this purpose, States Parties shall provide, as they consider appropriate, co-operation in any efforts by the United Nations and other competent intergovernmental organizations or non-governmental organizations co-operating with the United Nations to protect and assist such a child and to trace the parents or other members of the family of any refugee child in order to obtain information necessary for reunification with his or her family. In cases where no parents or other members of the family can be found, the child shall be accorded the same protection as any other child permanently or temporarily deprived of his or her family environment for any reason, as set forth in the present Convention.

Article 23

1 States Parties recognize that a mentally or physically disabled child should enjoy a full and decent life, in conditions which ensure dignity, promote self-reliance and facilitate the child's active participation in the community.
2 States Parties recognize the right of the disabled child to special care and shall encourage and ensure the extension, subject to available resources, to the eligible child and those responsible for his or her care, of assistance for which application is made and which is appropriate to the child's condition and to the circumstances of the parents or others caring for the child.

3 Recognizing the special needs of a disabled child, assistance extended in accordance with paragraph 2 of the present article shall be provided free of charge, whenever possible, taking into account the financial resources of the parents or others caring for the child, and shall be designed to ensure that the disabled child has effective access to and receives education, training, health care services, rehabilitation services, preparation for employment and recreation opportunities in a manner conducive to the child's achieving the fullest possible social integration and individual development, including his or her cultural and spiritual development.

4 States Parties shall promote, in the spirit of international co-operation, the exchange of appropriate information in the field of preventive health care and of medical, psychological and functional treatment of disabled children, including dissemination of and access to information concerning methods of rehabilitation, education and vocational services, with the aim of enabling States Parties to improve their capabilities and skills and to widen their experience in these areas. In this regard, particular account shall be taken of the needs of developing countries.

Article 24

1 States Parties recognize the right of the child to the enjoyment of the highest attainable standard of health and to facilities for the treatment of illness and rehabilitation of health. States Parties shall strive to ensure that no child is deprived of his or her right of access to such health care services.

2 States Parties shall pursue full implementation of this right and, in particular, shall take appropriate measures:
   a To diminish infant and child mortality;
   b To ensure the provision of necessary medical assistance and health care to all children with emphasis on the development of primary health care;
   c To combat disease and malnutrition, including within the framework of primary health care, through, inter alia, the application of readily available technology and through the provision of adequate nutritious foods and clean drinking water, taking into consideration the dangers and risks of environmental pollution;
   d To ensure appropriate pre-natal and post-natal health care for mothers;
   e To ensure that all segments of society, in particular parents and children, are informed, have access to education and are supported in the use of basic knowledge of child health and nutrition, the advantages of breastfeeding, hygiene and environmental sanitation and the prevention of accidents;
   f To develop preventive health care, guidance for parents and family planning education and services.

3 States Parties shall take all effective and appropriate measures with a view to abolishing traditional practices prejudicial to the health of children.

4 States Parties undertake to promote and encourage international co-operation with a view to achieving progressively the full realization of the right recognized in the present article. In this regard, particular account shall be taken of the needs of developing countries.

Article 25
States Parties recognize the right of a child who has been placed by the competent authorities for the purposes of care, protection or treatment of his or her physical or mental health, to a periodic review of the treatment provided to the child and all other circumstances relevant to his or her placement.

Article 26
1   States Parties shall recognize for every child the right to benefit from social security, including social insurance, and shall take the necessary measures to achieve the full realization of this right in accordance with their national law.
2   The benefits should, where appropriate, be granted, taking into account the resources and the circumstances of the child and persons having responsibility for the maintenance of the child, as well as any other consideration relevant to an application for benefits made by or on behalf of the child.

Article 27
1   States Parties recognize the right of every child to a standard of living adequate for the child's physical, mental, spiritual, moral and social development.
2   The parent(s) or others responsible for the child have the primary responsibility to secure, within their abilities and financial capacities, the conditions of living necessary for the child's development.
3   States Parties, in accordance with national conditions and within their means, shall take appropriate measures to assist parents and others responsible for the child to implement this right and shall in case of need provide material assistance and support programmes, particularly with regard to nutrition, clothing and housing.
4   States Parties shall take all appropriate measures to secure the recovery of maintenance for the child from the parents or other persons having financial responsibility for the child, both within the State Party and from abroad. In particular, where the person having financial responsibility for the child lives in a State different from that of the child, States Parties shall promote the accession to international agreements or the conclusion of such agreements, as well as the making of other appropriate arrangements.

Article 28
1   States Parties recognize the right of the child to education, and with a view to achieving this right progressively and on the basis of equal opportunity, they shall, in particular:
  a   Make primary education compulsory and available free to all;
  b   Encourage the development of different forms of secondary education, including general and vocational education, make them available and accessible to every child, and take appropriate measures such as the introduction of free education and offering financial assistance in case of need;
  c   Make higher education accessible to all on the basis of capacity by every appropriate means;
  d   Make educational and vocational information and guidance available and accessible to all children;

e Take measures to encourage regular attendance at schools and the reduction of drop-out rates.
2 States Parties shall take all appropriate measures to ensure that school discipline is administered in a manner consistent with the child's human dignity and in conformity with the present Convention.
3 States Parties shall promote and encourage international co-operation in matters relating to education, in particular with a view to contributing to the elimination of ignorance and illiteracy throughout the world and facilitating access to scientific and technical knowledge and modern teaching methods. In this regard, particular account shall be taken of the needs of developing countries.

Article 29
1 States Parties agree that the education of the child shall be directed to:
   a The development of the child's personality, talents and mental and physical abilities to their fullest potential;
   b The development of respect for human rights and fundamental freedoms, and for the principles enshrined in the Charter of the United Nations;
   c The development of respect for the child's parents, his or her own cultural identity, language and values, for the national values of the country in which the child is living, the country from which he or she may originate, and for civilizations different from his or her own;
   d The preparation of the child for responsible life in a free society, in the spirit of understanding, peace, tolerance, equality of sexes, and friendship among all peoples, ethnic, national and religious groups and persons of indigenous origin;
   e The development of respect for the natural environment.
2 No part of the present article or article 28 shall be construed so as to interfere with the liberty of individuals and bodies to establish and direct educational institutions, subject always to the observance of the principles set forth in paragraph 1 of the present article and to the requirements that the education given in such institutions shall conform to such minimum standards as may be laid down by the State.

Article 30
In those States in which ethnic, religious or linguistic minorities or persons of indigenous origin exist, a child belonging to such a minority or who is indigenous shall not be denied the right, in community with other members of his or her group, to enjoy his or her own culture, to profess and practise his or her own religion, or to use his or her own language.

Article 31
1 States Parties recognize the right of the child to rest and leisure, to engage in play and recreational activities appropriate to the age of the child and to participate freely in cultural life and the arts.
2 States Parties shall respect and promote the right of the child to participate fully in cultural and artistic life and shall encourage the provision of appropriate and equal opportunities for cultural, artistic, recreational and leisure activity.

Article 32

1. States Parties recognize the right of the child to be protected from economic exploitation and from performing any work that is likely to be hazardous or to interfere with the child's education, or to be harmful to the child's health or physical, mental, spiritual, moral or social development.
2. States Parties shall take legislative, administrative, social and educational measures to ensure the implementation of the present article. To this end, and having regard to the relevant provisions of other international instruments, States Parties shall in particular:
   a   Provide for a minimum age or minimum ages for admission to employment;
   b   Provide for appropriate regulation of the hours and conditions of employment;
   c   Provide for appropriate penalties or other sanctions to ensure the effective enforcement of the present article.

Article 33

States Parties shall take all appropriate measures, including legislative, administrative, social and educational measures, to protect children from the illicit use of narcotic drugs and psychotropic substances as defined in the relevant international treaties, and to prevent the use of children in the illicit production and trafficking of such substances.

Article 34

States Parties undertake to protect the child from all forms of sexual exploitation and sexual abuse. For these purposes, States Parties shall in particular take all appropriate national, bilateral and multilateral measures to prevent:
a   The inducement or coercion of a child to engage in any unlawful sexual activity;
b   The exploitative use of children in prostitution or other unlawful sexual practices;
c   The exploitative use of children in pornographic performances and materials.

Article 35

States Parties shall take all appropriate national, bilateral and multilateral measures to prevent the abduction of, the sale of or traffic in children for any purpose or in any form.

Article 36

States Parties shall protect the child against all other forms of exploitation prejudicial to any aspects of the child's welfare.

Article 37

States Parties shall ensure that:
a   No child shall be subjected to torture or other cruel, inhuman or degrading treatment or punishment. Neither capital punishment nor life imprisonment without possibility of release shall be imposed for offences committed by persons below eighteen years of age;
b   No child shall be deprived of his or her liberty unlawfully or arbitrarily.

The arrest, detention or imprisonment of a child shall be in conformity with the law and shall be used only as a measure of last resort and for the shortest appropriate period of time;
c   Every child deprived of liberty shall be treated with humanity and respect for the inherent dignity of the human person, and in a manner which takes into account the needs of persons of his or her age. In particular, every child deprived of liberty shall be separated from adults unless it is considered in the child's best interest not to do so and shall have the right to maintain contact with his or her family through correspondence and visits, save in exceptional circumstances;
d   Every child deprived of his or her liberty shall have the right to prompt access to legal and other appropriate assistance, as well as the right to challenge the legality of the deprivation of his or her liberty before a court or other competent, independent and impartial authority, and to a prompt decision on any such action.

Article 38
1   States Parties undertake to respect and to ensure respect for rules of international humanitarian law applicable to them in armed conflicts which are relevant to the child.
2   States Parties shall take all feasible measures to ensure that persons who have not attained the age of fifteen years do not take a direct part in hostilities.
3   States Parties shall refrain from recruiting any person who has not attained the age of fifteen years into their armed forces. In recruiting among those persons who have attained the age of fifteen years but who have not attained the age of eighteen years, States Parties shall endeavour to give priority to those who are oldest.
4   In accordance with their obligations under international humanitarian law to protect the civilian population in armed conflicts, States Parties shall take all feasible measures to ensure protection and care of children who are affected by an armed conflict.

Article 39
States Parties shall take all appropriate measures to promote physical and psychological recovery and social reintegration of a child victim of: any form of neglect, exploitation, or abuse; torture or any other form of cruel, inhuman or degrading treatment or punishment; or armed conflicts. Such recovery and reintegration shall take place in an environment which fosters the health, self-respect and dignity of the child.

Article 40
1   States Parties recognize the right of every child alleged as, accused of, or recognized as having infringed the penal law to be treated in a manner consistent with the promotion of the child's sense of dignity and worth, which reinforces the child's respect for the human rights and fundamental freedoms of others and which takes into account the child's age and the desirability of promoting the child's reintegration and the child's assuming a constructive role in society.
2   To this end, and having regard to the relevant provisions of international instruments, States Parties shall, in particular, ensure that:

a   No child shall be alleged as, be accused of, or recognized as having infringed the penal law by reason of acts or omissions that were not prohibited by national or international law at the time they were committed;
b   Every child alleged as or accused of having infringed the penal law has at least the following guarantees:
(i) To be presumed innocent until proven guilty according to law;
(ii) To be informed promptly and directly of the charges against him or her, and, if appropriate, through his or her parents or legal guardians, and to have legal or other appropriate assistance in the preparation and presentation of his or her defence;
(iii) To have the matter determined without delay by a competent, independent and impartial authority or judicial body in a fair hearing according to law, in the presence of legal or other appropriate assistance and, unless it is considered not to be in the best interest of the child, in particular, taking into account his or her age or situation, his or her parents or legal guardians;
(iv) Not to be compelled to give testimony or to confess guilt; to examine or have examined adverse witnesses and to obtain the participation and examination of witnesses on his or her behalf under conditions of equality;
(v) If considered to have infringed the penal law, to have this decision and any measures imposed in consequence thereof reviewed by a higher competent, independent and impartial authority or judicial body according to law;
(vi) To have the free assistance of an interpreter if the child cannot understand or speak the language used;
(vii) To have his or her privacy fully respected at all stages of the proceedings.
3   States Parties shall seek to promote the establishment of laws, procedures, authorities and institutions specifically applicable to children alleged as, accused of, or recognized as having infringed the penal law, and, in particular:
a   The establishment of a minimum age below which children shall be presumed not to have the capacity to infringe the penal law;
b   Whenever appropriate and desirable, measures for dealing with such children without resorting to judicial proceedings, providing that human rights and legal safeguards are fully respected.
4   A variety of dispositions, such as care, guidance and supervision orders; counselling; probation; foster care; education and vocational training programmes and other alternatives to institutional care shall be available to ensure that children are dealt with in a manner appropriate to their well-being and proportionate both to their circumstances and the offence.

APPENDIX I

Universal Declaration of Human Rights 1948 (selected articles)

Article 1
All human beings are born free and equal in dignity and rights. They are endowed with reason and conscience and should act towards one another in a spirit of brotherhood.

Article 2
Everyone is entitled to all the rights and freedoms set forth in this Declaration, without distinction of any kind, such as race, colour, sex, language, religion, political or other opinion, national or social origin, property, birth or other status. Furthermore, no distinction shall be made on the basis of the political, jurisdictional or international status of the country or territory to which a person belongs, whether it be independent, trust, non-self-governing or under any other limitation of sovereignty.

Article 3
Everyone has the right to life, liberty and security of person.

Article 4
No one shall be held in slavery or servitude; slavery and the slave trade shall be prohibited in all their forms.

Article 5
No one shall be subjected to torture or to cruel, inhuman or degrading treatment or punishment.

Article 12
No one shall be subjected to arbitrary interference with his privacy, family, home or correspondence, nor to attacks upon his honour and reputation. Everyone has the right to the protection of the law against such interference or attacks.

Article 16
1. Men and women of full age, without any limitation due to race, nationality or religion, have the right to marry and to found a family. They are entitled to equal rights as to marriage, during marriage and at its dissolution.
2. Marriage shall be entered into only with the free and full consent of the intending spouses.
3. The family is the natural and fundamental group unit of society and is entitled to protection by society and the State.

Article 25

1 Everyone has the right to a standard of living adequate for the health and well-being of himself and of his family, including food, clothing, housing and medical care and necessary social services, and the right to security in the event of unemployment, sickness, disability, widowhood, old age or other lack of livelihood in circumstances beyond his control.
2 Motherhood and childhood are entitled to special care and assistance. All children, whether born in or out of wedlock, shall enjoy the same social protection.

Article 26

1 Everyone has the right to education. Education shall be free, at least in the elementary and fundamental stages. Elementary education shall be compulsory. Technical and professional education shall be made generally available and higher education shall be equally accessible to all on the basis of merit.

Article 30

Nothing in this Declaration may be interpreted as implying for any State, group or person any right to engage in any activity or to perform any act aimed at the destruction of any of the rights and freedoms set forth herein.

APPENDIX J

Practice Notes

CAFCASS Practice Notes March 2001
Official Solicitor Practice Notes

CAFCASS Practice Notes March 2001, 2 April 2001

15 CAFCASS PRACTICE NOTE
Officers of CAFCASS legal services and special casework:
Appointment in family proceedings

Practice notes – CAFCASS legal services and special casework – appointment of officer as children's guardian – terms of appointment

1 This Practice Note comes into effect on 1 April 2001 and supersedes the Practice Note dated 4 December 1998 issued by the Official Solicitor in relation to the representation of children in family proceedings. It is issued in conjunction with a Practice Note dealing with the appointment of the Official Solicitor in family proceedings. This Practice Note is intended to be helpful guidance, but always subject to Practice Directions, decisions of the courts and other legal guidance.

The Children and Family Court Advisory and Support Service
Appointment as children's guardian

2 The Children and Family Court Advisory and Support Service (CAFCASS) has responsibilities in relation to children in family proceedings as defined in section 12 of the Criminal Justice and Court Services Act 2000. CAFCASS has established CAFCASS Legal Services and Special Casework ('CAFCASS Legal') principally to take over the Official Solicitor's responsibilities of representing children who are the subject of family proceedings.

3 Generally it is only where it appears to the court that the child ought to have party status and be legally represented that the question of the involvement of CAFCASS Legal may arise. Normally an officer of CAFCASS in the area in which the case is proceeding will be appointed as the children's guardian, but all private law cases where it is felt necessary for the child to be joined as a party, and all High Court adoption cases, should be referred to CAFCASS Legal. CAFCASS Legal may represent children in family proceedings either in the High Court or in a county court (but not in a family proceedings court).

Private Cases

4 The court will normally at the first directions appointment consider whether the child should be made a party to the proceedings. In most private law cases (non-specified proceedings), a child's interests will be sufficiently safeguarded by the commissioning of a report under section 7 of the Children Act 1989 from a children and family reporter. Children who need someone to orchestrate an investigation of the case on their behalf may need party status and legal representation: *Re A* (2001), Times 28 February. Particular examples are where:

   a there is a significant foreign element such as a challenge to the English court's jurisdiction or a need for enquiries to be conducted abroad;
   b there is a need for expert medical or other evidence to be adduced on behalf of a child in circumstances where a joint instruction by the parties is impossible;
   c where a child wants to instruct a solicitor direct but has been refused leave pursuant to Family Proceedings Rules r9.2A to instruct a solicitor.
   d an application is made for leave to seek contact with an adopted child
   e there are exceptionally difficult, unusual or sensitive issues making it necessary for the child to be granted party status within the proceedings: such cases are likely to be High Court matters.

5 CAFCASS Legal will almost invariably accept cases where case law has pointed to the need for a child to be granted party status and to be legally represented, for instance in 'special category' medical treatment cases, notably in those cases involving an application to authorise sterilisation and cases concerning disputed life sustaining treatment. Applications in such cases should be made under the inherent jurisdiction of the High Court. The Official Solicitor will have a continuing role in such cases for adult patients and for some older children who are also patients.

Public Law Cases

6 In most public law cases (specified proceedings) an officer of CAFCASS in the area in which the case is proceeding will be appointed as the children's guardian. It will only be appropriate for an officer of CAFCASS Legal to be appointed as children's guardian in public law cases in the High Court or the county court which are exceptionally difficult, unusual or sensitive or where either he or she, or the Official Solicitor, previously acted for the child in related public law or private law proceedings.

Adoption and Surrogacy

7 Proceedings under the Adoption Act 1976 should be commenced in the High Court or transferred there and referred to CAFCASS Legal if they are exceptionally difficult, unusual or sensitive. Circumstances warranting transfer will include difficult issues about parental agreement or compliance with the law. Reference should be made to Practice Directions, decisions of the courts and other guidance. In relation to inter country adoptions, the case of *Re R (Inter-Country Adoptions: Practice)* [1999] 1 FLR 1042 is particularly instructive. Generally only High Court adoptions will be accepted by CAFCASS Legal and not those straightforward cases where the natural parents consent (unless the Official Solicitor or an officer in CAFCASS Legal previously acted for the child in family proceedings).

8 Only exceptionally difficult, unusual or sensitive cases under s30 of the Human Fertilisation and Embryology Act 1990 should be referred to CAFCASS Legal.

Non-subject children

9 Exceptionally, CAFCASS Legal may accept appointment on behalf of child applicants (typically seeking contact with siblings) or children who are otherwise parties to family proceedings, such as a minor mother of a child who is the subject of the proceedings. This may be appropriate to allow continuity of representation following earlier proceedings in which the child was the subject. In all cases where the child is the applicant, CAFCASS Legal will need to be satisfied that the proposed proceedings would benefit that child before proceeding.

Advising the Court

10 CAFCASS Legal may be invited to act or instruct counsel as friend of the court (amicus).

Liaison with the Official Solicitor

11 In cases of doubt or difficulty, staff of CAFCASS Legal will liaise with staff of the Official Solicitor's office to avoid duplication and ensure the most suitable arrangements are made.

Appointment of an officer of CAFCASS Legal Services and Special Casework

12 Where the court considers that a child should be made a respondent to an application and represented by CAFCASS Legal it should make an order in the following terms:
 a The Director of Legal Services, CAFCASS, is invited to nominate one of his officers to act as children's guardian for [name(s)]
 b Upon an officer of CAFCASS Legal Services and Special Casework consenting to act as children's guardian [name(s)] will be made respondent(s) to the applications before the court.

CAFCASS Legal will normally provide a response to any invitation within 10 working days of receiving the papers referred to in paragraph 15 below.

13 It is often helpful to discuss the question of appointment with the duty divisional manager or a lawyer at CAFCASS Legal by telephoning 020 7904 0867. It is particularly important to do so in urgent cases.

14 Save in the most urgent cases a substantive hearing date should not normally be fixed before the next directions hearing following the invitation to act.

15 The following documents should be forwarded to CAFCASS Legal without delay:
 a a copy of the order and a note of the reasons for approaching CAFCASS Legal approved by the judge;
 b the court file;
 c whenever practicable, a bundle with summary, statement of issues and chronology (in the form required by the President's Direction of 10 March 2000).

The address of CAFCASS Legal Services and Special Casework is:

Newspaper House
8–16 Great New Street
London EC4A 3BN
Telephone:020 7904 0867
Fax: 020 7904 0868/9
e-mail: legal@cafcass.gsi.gov.uk

March 2001
Charles Prest
Director of Legal Services
CAFCASS

OFFICIAL SOLICITOR PRACTICE NOTE
Official Solicitor: Appointment in family proceedings

Practice directions and notes – Official Solicitor – Appointment as guardian ad litem – Appointment as next friend – Terms of appointment

This Practice Note supersedes the Practice Note dated 4 December 1998 issued by the Official Solicitor in relation to his appointment in family proceedings. It is issued in conjunction with a Practice Note dealing with the appointment of Officers of CAFCASS Legal Services and Special Casework in family proceedings. This Practice Note is intended to be helpful guidance, but always subject to Practice Directions, decisions of the court and other legal guidance.

The Children and Family Court Advisory and Support Service (CAFCASS) has responsibilities in relation to children in family proceedings in which their welfare is or may be in question (Criminal Justice and Court Services Act 2000, section 12). From 1 April 2001 the Official Solicitor will no longer represent children who are the subject of family proceedings (other than in very exceptional circumstances and after liaison with CAFCASS).

This Practice Note summarises the continuing role of the Official Solicitor in family proceedings. Since there are no provisions for parties under disability in the Family Proceedings Courts (Children Act 1989) Rules 1991, the Official Solicitor can only act in the High Court or in a county court, pursuant to Part IX of Family Proceedings Rules 1991. The Official Solicitor will shortly issue an updated Practice Note about his role for adults under disability who are the subject of declaratory proceedings in relation to their medical treatment or welfare.

Adults under disability

The Official Solicitor will, in the absence of any other willing and suitable person, act as next friend or guardian ad litem of an adult party under disability, a 'patient'. 'Patient' means someone who is incapable by reason of mental disorder of managing and administering his property and affairs (Family Proceedings Rules 1991, rule 9.1). Medical evidence will usually be required before the Official Solicitor can consent to act and his staff can provide a standard form of medical certificate. Where there are practical difficulties in obtaining such medical evidence, the Official Solicitor should be consulted.

Non-subject children
Again in the absence of any other willing and suitable person, the Official Solicitor will act as next friend or guardian ad litem of a child party whose own welfare is not the subject of family proceedings (Family Proceedings Rules 1991, r2.57, r9.2 and r9.5). The most common examples will be:

a   a child who is also the parent of a child, and who is a respondent to a Children Act or Adoption Act application. If a child respondent is already represented by a CAFCASS officer in pending proceedings of which he or she is the subject, then the Official Solicitor will liaise with CAFCASS to agree the most appropriate arrangements;
b   a child who wishes to make an application for a Children Act order naming another child (typically a contact order naming a sibling). The Official Solicitor will need to satisfy himself that the proposed proceedings would benefit the child applicant before proceeding;
c   a child witness to some disputed factual issue in a children case and who may require intervener status. In such circumstances the need for party status and legal representation should be weighed in the light of *Re H (Care Proceedings: Intervener)* [2000] 1 FLR 775;
d   a child party to a petition for a declaration of status under Part III of the Family Law Act 1986;
e   a child intervener in divorce or ancillary relief proceedings (r2.57 or r9.5);
f   a child applicant for, or respondent to, an application for an order under Part IV of the Family Law Act 1996. In the case of a child applicant, the Official Solicitor will need to satisfy himself that the proposed proceedings would benefit the child before pursuing them, with leave under Family Law Act 1996, section 43 if required.

Any children who are parties to Children Act or inherent jurisdiction proceedings may rely on the provisions of Family Proceedings Rules 1991 rule 9.2A if they wish to instruct a solicitor without the intervention of a next friend or guardian ad litem. Rule 9.2A does not apply to Adoption Act 1976, Family Law Act 1996 or Matrimonial Causes Act 1973 proceedings.

Older children who are also patients
Officers of CAFCASS will not be able to represent anyone who is over the age of 18. The Official Solicitor may therefore be the more appropriate next friend or guardian ad litem of a child who is also a patient and whose disability will persist beyond his or her 18th birthday, especially in non-emergency cases where the substantive hearing is unlikely to take place before the child's 18th birthday. The Official Solicitor may also be the more appropriate next friend or guardian ad litem in medical treatment cases such as sterilisation or vegetative state cases, in which his staff have particular expertise deriving from their continuing role for adult patients.

Advising the court
The Official Solicitor may be invited to act or instruct counsel as a friend of the

court (amicus) if it appears to the court that such an invitation is more appropriately addressed to him rather than (or in addition to) CAFCASS Legal Services and Special Casework.

Liaison with CAFCASS
In cases of doubt or difficulty, staff of the Official Solicitor's office will liaise with staff of CAFCASS Legal Services and Special Casework to avoid duplication and ensure the most suitable arrangements are made.

Invitations to act in new cases
Solicitors who have been consulted by a child or an adult under disability (or by someone acting on their behalf, or concerned about their interests) should write to the Official Solicitor setting out the background to the proposed case and explaining why there is no other willing and suitable person to act as next friend or guardian ad litem. Where the person concerned is an adult, medical evidence in the standard form of the Official Solicitor's medical certificate should be provided.

Invitations to act in pending proceedings
Where a case is already before the court, an order appointing the Official Solicitor should be expressed as being made subject to his consent. The Official Solicitor aims to provide a response to any invitation within 10 working days. He will be unable to consent to act for an adult until satisfied that the party is a 'patient'. A further directions appointment after 28 days may therefore be helpful. If he accepts appointment the Official Solicitor will need time to prepare the case on behalf of the child or patient and may wish to make submissions about any substantive hearing date. The following documents should be forwarded to the Official Solicitor without delay:

a   a copy of the order inviting him to act (with a note of the reasons approved by the judge if appropriate);
b   the court file;
c   if available, a bundle with summary, statement of issues and chronology (as required by President's Direction of 10 March 2000).

Contacting the Official Solicitor
It is often helpful to discuss the question of appointment with the Official Solicitor or one of his staff by telephoning 020 7911 7127. Inquiries about family proceedings should be addressed to the Team Manager, Family Litigation.

The Official Solicitor's address is:
81 Chancery Lane,
London WC2A 1DD.
DX 0012 London Chancery Lane
Tel: 020 7911 7127
Fax: 020 7911 7105
E-mail: enquiries@offsol.gsi.gov.uk

2 April 2001
Laurence Oates, Official Solicitor

APPENDIX K

Letter from Barbara Roche (Minister) to Lord Archer of Sandwell QC, 30 June 2000

To the Rt Hon The Lord Archer of Sandwell QC
House of Lords
LONDON
SW1A 0PW

Dear Peter

Thank you for your letter of 29 February enclosing this correspondence about xxxxxxx, a refugee who wants his family to join him here. I am sorry that you have not had an earlier reply.

Under the family reunion concession, a minor who has been recognised as a refugee can immediately apply for his parents and any of their other minor dependent children to join them in the United Kingdom. Any application must be made at a British diplomatic post abroad.

I will forward this correspondence to the Entry Clearance Officer in Islamabad so that he is aware of your interest.

Yours ever

Barbara Roche

APPENDIX L

Extracts from Marriages Handbook for Registration Officers (produced by General Register Office)

Extracts from Marriages Handbook for Registration Officers
General conditions for marriage

Reporting suspicious marriages

7   All marriages involving persons who are not British citizens or nationals of a European Economic Area state and which are entered into for the purpose of avoiding the effects of United Kingdom immigration law, fall within the definition of a sham marriage as defined in the Immigration and Asylum Act 1999.

8   A national of a European Economic Area state means a national of one of the following countries:

Austria	Greece	Netherlands
Belgium	Iceland	Norway
Denmark	Irish Republic	Portugal
Finland	Italy	Spain
France	Liechtenstein	Sweden
Germany	Luxembourg	United Kingdom

9   If, when taking a notice of marriage, or at any time before, during or after the solemnisation of a marriage, a superintendent registrar or registrar has reasonable grounds for suspecting that a marriage will be or is a sham marriage, the officer concerned must report his suspicions without delay to the Home Office.

10 The factors taken into account when considering reporting a suspected sham marriage must be obtained by direct observation or during the questioning of the parties. The criteria for the report might include:
   (i)   one party giving the impression of knowing very little about the other person
   (ii)   either party referring to notes to answer questions about the other person
   (iii) reluctance to provide evidence of name, age, marital status or nationality
   (iv)   parties unable to converse in the same language
   (v)   one of the couples may have exceeded their period of permitted stay in the UK
   (vi)   one of the couples is seen to receive payment for the marriage.

265

None of these reasons may in themselves necessarily indicate that the marriage is a sham, and indeed there may be other factors that arouse an officer's suspicions that are not listed. But it is generally expected that it will be a combination of factors, together with the officer's observations of the couple's behaviour, which indicate that the marriage may be a sham. Superintendent registrars or registrars should have reasonable suspicions that the marriage is a sham before reporting it to the Home Office.

11 Any report to the Home Office should be made using the form supplied by the General Register Office. The form should be sent either by post to Immigration and Nationality Directorate, Intelligence Section, Status Three, 4 Nobel Drive, Hayes, Middlesex UB3 5EY, by fax to 020 8745 1655, or by e-mail to INDIS.DutyOfficer@homeoffice.gis.gov.uk. At the same time, a copy should be retained in the records of the reporting officer and a copy of the report should be sent, by post, fax or e-mail to the General Register Office (Marriages Section) for information. The fax number for Marriages Section is 0151 471 4523 and the e-mail address is marriages.gro@ons.gov.uk.

12 The report of a suspected sham marriage to the Home Office should not prevent a marriage being solemnised, providing the parties are free, legally, to marry each other. Particular care must be taken to treat everyone equally and without discrimination. A person should not be treated less favourably on grounds of his or her race, colour, ethnic or national origins, nationality or citizenship when carrying out any function that involves providing a facility or service to the public.

13 Registration officers should be aware that any report of a sham marriage sent to the Home Office may be produced as evidence in a tribunal or appeal hearing. This should not deter registration officers from reporting their suspicions to the Home Office, but means that the use of inflammatory or derogatory language should be avoided.

14 A sham marriage should not be confused with a traditional arranged marriage that is usually organised by family members without any intent to circumvent immigration law.

15 Where a registration officer is in any doubt about whether or not to report a marriage to the Home Office, advice should be sought from the General Register Office (Marriages Section).

...

Re-marriage

17 Parties who wish to be re-married on account of some informality or supposed informality in the proceedings connected with their former marriage may do so, and notice of such re-marriage may be given to a superintendent registrar. Before taking the notice, the superintendent registrar should establish where the previous marriage ceremony took place, who was present at the ceremony and the reason why the couple wish to go through another marriage ceremony with each other.

Previous marriage ceremony in England or Wales

18 If the previous marriage ceremony took place in England or Wales, in the presence of a registrar, authorised person or other religious minister, eg,

Extracts from Marriages Handbook for Registration Officers 267

priest, Imam, in a building where marriages can normally take place, the ceremony may be capable of recognition, depending on whether or not the couple knew or believed the ceremony to be valid and whether or not they have lived together since the ceremony.

19 If the couple know or believed that their previous marriage ceremony was not valid and/or was required to be followed by a civil ceremony, it can be ignored and the marital status of the couple recorded as it was prior to that ceremony.

20 If, however, the couple believe the marriage ceremony to have been valid, regardless of the fact that it was outside the provisions of the Marriage Act, the couple should be advised to seek legal advice about the implications of going through another marriage ceremony. If, having sought legal advice, the couple still wish to marry, notice should be taken in the usual way, and the marital status of the parties recorded as 'Previously went through a form of marriage at ... on ...', including a reference to the previous marriage ceremony.

21 If the ceremony took place in England or Wales in the presence of a registrar, authorised person, religious minister, eg, priest, Imam, etc, in some place other than a building where marriages can normally take place, eg, a private house, the ceremony is not capable of recognition whether or not the couple believe it to be valid. In such cases, notice can be taken in the usual way and the marital status of the parties recorded as it was prior to that marriage ceremony.

Previous marriage ceremony outside England or Wales

22 If the parties claim to have been married outside England or Wales but suggest to the superintendent registrar that the marriage may not be valid in the country in which it took place, or if the superintendent registrar is in doubt for any reason about the validity of the former marriage, Marriages Section should be contacted for advice.

23 If the parties wish to re-marry and there is no apparent informality in the proceedings – they merely wish to go through another marriage ceremony with each other for whatever reason – they should be informed that if they are already lawfully married to each other, the ceremony they propose will have no legal effect and will inevitably case doubts upon the legal marriage which they have already contracted. While such a ceremony would be registered in the marriage register, the marital condition of the parties would be recorded therein as 'Previously went through a form of marriage at ... on ...'. It is, therefore, not a desirable step to take, especially where there are children of the marriage. If however, despite this warning, the parties still persist in their wish to proceed with the ceremony, notice may be accepted.

APPENDIX M

Useful resources

Useful resources
Useful books
DNA testing
Websites

Useful resources

The UK Advice Finder is a comprehensive data base of voluntary, community and statutory agencies across the UK. Available from

Resource Information Service (RIS)
The Basement
38 Great Pulteney Street
London
W1F 9NU

Tel: 020 7494 2408
Email: ris@ris.org.uk

Useful books

Macdonald's Immigration Law and Practice (5th edn, Butterworths, 2001).
The Law of Refugee Status by Professor James Hathaway of the University of Michigan (Butterworths Canada Ltd, 1991).
The Refugee in International Law: Professor Guy Goodwin-Gill, Professor of International Refugee Law at the University of Oxford (Clarendon Paperbacks, 1996).
Fransman's *British Nationality Law* (2nd edn, Butterworths).
Refugees and Gender Law and Process by Dr Heaven Crawley (Jordans, 2001).
Immigration Encyclopedia (Butterworths)
European Human Rights Law by Keir Starmer, (LAG, 1999)
Human Rights Practice edited by Jessica Simor and Ben Emmerson QC
Human Rights: the 1998 Act and the European Convention, Stephen Grosz, Jack Beatson and Peter Duffy (Butterworths, 2000).
UKCOSA Manual 2001 – a guide to Regulations and Procedures for International Students
UNHCR Handbook
RWLG Gender Guidelines 1998
IAA Gender Guidelines 2000

DNA Testing

Cellmark Diagnostics 1
PO Box 265
Abingdon
Oxon OX14 1YX

Tel: 01235 528 609
Email: cellmark@orchid.co.uk

The Forensic Science Service 2
109 Lambeth Road
London SE17 1LP

Tel: 020 7230 6282

University Diagnostics Ltd 1
LGC Building
Queen's Road
Teddington
Middlesex TW11 ONJ
Tel: 020 8943 8400
Email: udl@lgc.co.uk

Websites

Statutes, statutory instruments and orders
www.hmso.gov.uk/stats.htm

Immigration Rules
www.ind.homeoffice.gov.uk

Ministerial statements that can be found in Hansard
www.parliament.the-stationery-office.co.uk/pa

European Court of Human Rights
www.echr.coe.int

University of Minnesota Human Rights Library
contains many international treaties
www.umn.edu/humanrts/

Electronic Immigration Network
contains useful links to many websites containing international materials. A subscription service permits access to Immigration Tribunal Appeal Tribunal and higher court determinations.
www.ein.org.uk

The Times Law Reports
available as a paper subscription service or free on the web or you could buy the daily newspaper.
www.thetimes.co.uk

Casetrack
a web based service that provides access to all approved judgments of the High Court and Court of Appeal.
www.casetrack.com

Westlaw
contains an extensive database which provides access to statutory provisions, case-law and articles.
www.westlaw.co.uk

Lawtel
similar to Westlaw
www.lawtel.co.uk

LexisNexis Direct
similar to Westlaw and Lawtel.
www.butterworths.com

Justis
contains the reports of the Incorporated Council of Law Reporting.
www.justis.com

Europa
contains judgments and materials concerning European Community law.
www.europa.eu.int

Human Rights Watch
www.hrw.org

The Office of the United Nations High Commissioner for Refugees
www.unhcr.ch

US State Department
www.state.gov/www/global/human_rights/

Home Office Country Assessments (CIPU Reports)
www.ind.homeoffice.gov.uk

The Immigration Consortium Country Information Database ICCID produced by Injit Research
www.hjt-research.com

Immigration Appellate Authority
www.iaa.gov.uk/index.htm

The Legal Services Commission
www.legalservices.gov.uk

Civil Procedural Rules
www.open.gov.uk/lcd/civil/procrules_fin/crulesfr.htm

Expert Witness Institute
www.ewi.org.uk

Amnesty International
www.amnesty.org.uk

Advice Services Alliance
www.asamcmail.com

Asylum Aid
www.asylumaid.org.uk

Commission for Racial Equality
www.cre.gov.uk

Immigration Law Practitioners Association
www.ilpa.org.uk

Joint Council for the Welfare of Immigrants
www.jcwi.org.uk

Language Line
www.languageline.co.uk

Refugee Council
www.refugeecouncil.org.uk

Refugee Women's Legal Group
www.rwlg.org.uk

Refugee Women's Resource Centre
www.asylumaid.org.uk

Index

Abroad
    adoption 2.8–2.12
    divorce obtained 1.13, 5.55
    marriage taking place overseas 1.10
    removal of child looked after by local authority to live abroad 1.100–1.104

Accommodation
    local authority. *See* Local authority
    NASS, by 3.6–3.12
    unaccompanied minor, for 1.84, 3.19–3.21

Administrative removal and deportation
    children, of,
        child born in UK 6.122
        child with right of abode 6.110–6.112
        long residence in UK, child with 6.113–6.115, 6.123, 6.132–6.134
        parents in UK, with 6.125–6.127
        parents subject to deportation action, where 6.116–6.124
        unaccompanied, where 6.128–6.131
        See also marriage and children, cases involving *below*
    exercise of power 6.97
    factors taken into account 6.93
    family members, of 6.94
    generally 6.91–6.97
    marriage and children, cases involving,
        commencement of enforcement action 6.103–6.104
        conditions for remaining in UK 6.101
        EEA nationals 6.99
        marriages that post-date enforcement action 6.105–6.108
        policies to be taken into account 6.98
        right to remain in UK 6.99
        settled spouse leaving UK 6.102
        sponsor requirements 6.101
        See also children, of *above*
    powers 6.91–6.92
    psychiatric illness, powers where 6.72–6.75
    spouse, of 6.95–6.96
    terminally ill patient, policy as to 6.70

Adoption
    'adopted' abroad,
        designated country, in 2.9–2.10
        entry clearance requirements 2.8
        non-designated country, in 2.11–2.12
    adoption abroad not possible, where 2.13–2.14
    British citizenship and 2.1
    EEA nationals, adoptive children of 2.15
    Hague Convention on Protection of Children, compliance with 2.3
    non-British children by British parents, of,
        'adopted' abroad. *See* 'adopted' abroad *above*
        approval requirement 2.1

Adoption, non-British children by British parents, of, *continued*
  examples 2.2, 2.4
  Home Secretary, need to inform 2.4
  House of Lords tests 2.5–2.6
  UK, in 2.1–2.7
  welfare of child and 1.21
Age
  dependency, of 1.7
  disputed, of unaccompanied child 5.15
AIDS
  Home Office policy as to 6.60–6.71
Appeals
  alleged breaches of ECHR 4.12–4.15
  application of ECHR 4.16–4.24. *See also* European Convention on Human Rights
  effects of HRA 1998 4.11
  Immigration and Asylum Act 1999, effect 4.11–4.15
  prior to HRA 1998 coming into force 4.11
  right of 8.40
  s65 appeals 4.11
  s74 notice 4.12, 4.13
Application, making. *See also* Entry clearance, Exceptional leave to remain, Home Office policy, Indefinite leave to remain
  appeal rights 8.40. See also Appeals
  application, mixed 5.25–5.26
  assessment of claim,
    difficult issues 8.11
    Home Office records 8.10
    identification of issues 8.8
    information required 8.4–8.7
  child's own file 8.12
  ECHR, use of 8.28
  family court orders, use of,
    care proceedings 8.26–8.27
    generally 8.17–8.22
    section 8 orders 8.23–8.25
  generally 8.1–8.3

  international conventions, use of 8.28–8.29
  mixed application 5.25–5.26
  port application 4.13, 6.133, 8.31
  potential problem areas 8.9
  preparation of 8.33–8.39
  process 8.30–8.32
  time for Home Office decisions 8.2, 8.14–8.15
  when to approach Home Office 8.12–8.16
Army
  child recruitment into 4.35
Arrest
  power of, where domestic violence 1.17
  unlawful, prohibition under ECHR 4.42–4.47
Asylum-seeker
  accommodation provision by NASS 3.6–3.18
  appeal. *See* Appeals
  applications. *See* Application, making, Home Office policy
  dispersal,
    effects 3.11–3.12
    policy 3.9–3.10
    report on 3.13–3.14
  divorce. *See* Divorce
  domestic violence. *See* Domestic violence
  education 3.9, 3.10, 3.12, 3.15
  failed, and exceptional leave to remain or enter 5.47–5.48
  family issues, generally 5.1
  health and medical treatment. *See* Health matters
  housing benefit 3.3
  income support,
    from 4.2.96 to 5.12.99 3.4
    from 6.12.99 3.5
    prior to 4.2.96 3.3
  marriage. *See* Marriage
  mixed applications 5.25–5.26
  NASS, role of 3.5–3.9
  proposals for future 3.15–3.18
  public housing, availability of 3.40
  recognised as refugee in another country, where 5.44

s74 notice and 4.12, 4.13
separation. *See* Separation
sponsor. *See* Sponsor
unaccompanied children. *See*
  Unaccompanied minor
unmarried partners 5.45
vouchers 3.6, 3.8, 3.14, 3.27, 3.37

Birth family
  importance of 1.37

CAFCASS. *See* Children and Family Court Advisory and Support Service
Care. *See also* Local authority
  children leaving, preparation for 1.82
  children taken into,
    accommodation for 1.80–1.82
Care order. *See also* Court order
  application for 1.28, 1.45
  circumstances for 1.89–1.92
  effect 1.94–1.95
  indefinite leave, where 6.36
  interim 1.93, 1.94
  legal aid 1.42
  removal of child subject to, to live abroad 1.100–1.104
  right to family life and 4.52
Care plan
  contact with child and 1.97
  elements of, guidance as to 1.98
  requirements 1.98–1.99
Care proceedings
  example 1.91
  supervision order and, comparison 1.73
Child. *See also* Family, Home Office policy, Unaccompanied minor
  12 years,
    over, concession for 6.16
    under, concession for 6.13–6.17
  18 years,
    approaching 6.19, 6.21, 6.22
    Home Office policy for admission 6.37
    over 6.37, 6.38

  reaching, before applications decided 6.22–6.23
  abandoned, where very young 6.20
  administrative removal and deportation cases. *See* Administrative removal and deportation
  British citizen, registration as,
    criteria for 6.140–6.142
    factors considered 6.139, 6.143
    illegitimate child 6.138, 6.146–6.147
    minor, of 6.136–6.143
  children with different status, asylum and 4.54
  citizenship, determination of 6.136–6.137
  contact with,
    sustain family relationship, to 4.51
    where in care 1.96–1.97
    See also Contact order
  delay in reaching decision 1.24–1.25
  development of, meaning 1.77
  DNA testing 6.38–6.47
  domestic slaves, employment as 4.39
  enslavement of 4.35–4.41
  financial support for families which include children 3.27–3.31
  homosexual couple, of 1.4
  identity, proof of 5.22
  illegitimate,
    British citizenship of 6.112, 6.138, 6.146–6.147
    deportation 6.116
    DNA testing and 6.44–6.47
  in need,
    definition 1.76, 1.83
    local authority accommodation for 1.80–1.81, 1.83–1.88
    unaccompanied minors arriving in UK 1.84, 3.19–3.21
  interviewing 7.6–7.19. *See also* Interviewing a child

Child, *continued*
  law relating to children, generally 1.2
  local authority, looked after by. *See* Local authority
  meanings 1.6–1.7
  recruitment to serve in army 4.35
  same sex partners, of 1.4
  seven years or more in UK 5.9, 6.23, 6.33, 6.89, 6.109
  sex industry, employment in 4.36–4.38, 4.41
  welfare principle 1.20–1.23. *See also* Welfare of child
Children and Family Court Advisory and Support Service (CAFCASS)
  creation of 1.30
  reports 1.25
  role of 1.30
Children's guardian
  role of 1.31
Community Legal Service Funding
  availability 1.42
Confidentiality
  family proceedings, in 1.38–1.41
Contact order. *See also* Court order
  application 1.46–1.50
  circumstances for making 1.96
  effect 1.52, 1.69, 8.23
  requirements 1.68
  terms of 1.97
Contact with child. *See also* Contact order
  sustain family relationship, to 4.51
  where in care 1.96–1.97
Council for International Education (UKCOSA) 3.35
Court
  confidentiality and disclosure in 1.38–1.41
  representation of child's views in 1.30–1.36, 1.47
    immigration court, in 1.33
    right to fair hearing under ECHR, relevance to UK courts 4.48–4.50
Court order. *See also under specific orders, eg* Contact order

  age of dependency 1.7
  child, relating to, term of 1.6
  domestic violence, relating to 1.14–1.17
    effect 1.45, 1.106
    example 1.106
  non-molestation order 1.14, 6.49
  occupation order 1.14, 1.15
  presumption of no order 1.26
  section 8 order,
    application for 1.46–1.52
    effect, where making application 8.23–8.25
    nature of 1.46
  which can be made,
    generally 1.53
    parental responsibility and 1.54–1.60
Court welfare officer 1.32
Criminal offences
  effect 6.87
Custodianship 1.64

Death penalty
  return of asylum-seeker to country where used 4.25–4.28
Dependant. *See also* Child, Marriage
  adult, indefinite leave to remain 5.31
  sponsor of. *See* Sponsor
Deportation. *See* Administrative removal and deportation
Detention
  centre, education in 4.46
  family detention accommodation 4.45–4.46
  international terrorists, of, UK derogation in relation to 4.47
  minors, of, UK policy 4.43–4.47
  prohibition under ECHR 4.42–4.47
Disclosure
  family proceedings, in 1.38–1.41
Dispersal of asylum-seekers
  effects of policy 3.11–3.12
  nature of policy 3.9–3.10
  report on 3.13–3.14
Divorce. *See also* Separation

asylum and,
   family settled, where 5.7
   family with limited leave 5.5–5.6
   generally 5.3–5.4
validity,
   obtained abroad, where 1.13, 5.55
   UK, obtained in 1.12, 5.55
DNA testing
   action taken following 6.43–6.47
   assessment of report 6.42
   entry clearance requirement, as 6.39–6.40
   process 6.41
   prove parentage, to 6.38–6.47
Domestic slave
   child employed as 4.39
Domestic violence
   asylum and 5.8
   concession relating to 'one year' rule 6.48–6.54
      EU law and 6.55
   criminal proceedings 1.19
   injunctions 1.18
   non-molestation order 1.14, 6.49
   occupation order 1.14, 1.15
   orders, application for 1.16
   power of arrest 1.17

ECHR. *See* European Convention on Human Rights
Education
   access to 1.86–1.88, 3.12, 3.15, 3.32–3.35
   accommodation and 1.88, 3.9, 3.10
   detention centres, in 4.46
   funding 1.82, 1.87
   further and higher 1.86, 3.33, 3.34
   local authority accommodated children, for 1.86–1.88, 1.98
   needs 1.22, 7.3, 7.19, 7.25, 7.26
   return to country of origin and 7.28, 7.30, 7.33
   right to, under ECHR 4.63
   school trips 6.132, 6.142
   special needs 1.98
   UKCOSA 3.35
   unaccompanied minors, of 3.20–3.21
Education supervision order. *See also* Court order
   application for 1.45
EEA nationals
   adoptive children of 2.15
   AIDS or serious illness, having, Home Office policy 6.71
   NHS treatment for 3.39
   right to remain with spouse 6.99
   separated spouses and EU law 6.59
Emergency protection order. *See also* Court order
   application for 1.45
   nature of 1.72
Entry clearance
   adoption and 2.8, 2.14
   application 1.69, 5.50, 6.13–6.17, 6.22, 6.100, 6.135, 8.32
   spouse, for 5.50, 6.100
   where suffering from serious illness 6.64, 6.70, 6.71
   exceptional leave to enter 5.47–5.48
   general instructions 5.1, 5.17, 5.43
   granting 5.43
   human rights and 4.21, 4.56, 5.26
   refusal 4.14, 5.17, 5.42, 6.38, 6.44
EU law
   domestic violence concession and 6.55
   separated spouses and 6.56–6.59
European Commission
   decisions, relevance to immigration appeals 4.20
European Convention on Human Rights (ECHR)
   absolute rights 4.16, 4.17
   alleged breaches,
      immigration appeals for 4.12–4.15
      s74 notice and 4.12, 4.13
   appeals and. *See* Appeals
   application of 4.16–4.24, 8.28
   defence, use as 4.21–4.22
   detention, prohibition of 4.42–4.47

European Convention on Human Rights, *continued*
  domestic slaves, employment as 4.39
  education, right to 4.63
  evidence of post-decision facts 4.24
  extra-territorial effect of rights under 4.23
  fair and public hearing, right to 4.48–4.50
  family life, right to respect for 4.51–4.58. *See also* Family and private life
  history of application of ECHR in UK 4.5–4.10
  inhuman and degrading treatment, prohibition on 4.17, 4.29–4.33
  life, right to 4.25–4.28
  meaning of family under 1.4
  private life, right to respect for 4.51–4.58. *See also* Family and private life
  purpose of 4.4
  qualified right 4.16, 4.18–4.19
  slavery, prohibition of 4.17, 4.36–4.41
  substantive rights 4.25–4.63
  torture, prohibition on 4.17, 4.29–4.33
  types of rights 4.16
  unlawful arrest, prohibition of 4.42–4.47
  use of ECHR as defence 4.21–4.22
European Court of Human Rights
  decisions, relevance to immigration appeals 4.20
European Union. *See* EU law
Exceptional leave to enter
  failed asylum-seekers and 5.47–5.48
Exceptional leave to remain
  adult at decision time, initially minor 5.14
  application for child 5.21, 5.33
  child granted 4.38, 5.12, 5.14, 5.17–5.18, 6.20
  failed asylum-seekers and 5.47–5.48
  human rights grounds, on 4.51, 8.20
  public housing for those with 3.40
  relevance to assessment of application 8.4
  sick child 6.20
  sponsor having,
    dependants in UK 5.39–5.42
    dependants outside UK 5.43
    general factors 5.43
  support for refugees with 3.2
  unaccompanied child with 5.17–5.18
  unmarried partners 5.45
Experts
  medical and psychiatric, reports from 1.43–1.44

Family. *See also* Child, Family and private life, Family law
  aspects of immigration,
    divorce, validity of 1.12, 1.13, 5.55. *See also* Divorce
    marriage 5.52–5.54. *See also* Marriage
    policies 5.51. *See also* Home Office policy
    requirements 5.50
  birth family, importance of 1.37
  children, with, who have lived in UK for seven years or more 6.132–6.134
  court. *See* Court, Court order
  financial support 3.27–3.31. *See also* Financial support and public services
  interviewing family members. *See* Interviewing a child
  meanings of 1.2–1.5, 1.79, 4.57
  protection of 5.2
  reunion 1.5, 5.17–5.18, 5.21, 6.36
  sibling groups 6.15–6.16, 6.144–6.145
  units, removal of 6.135
Family and private life. *See also* Family
  children with different status, asylum and 4.54
  country where can be enjoyed 4.55

discretion of court 4.52
divorce, where 5.6
factors considered by court 4.52–4.53
interest of child, whether paramount 4.54
one partner obliged to leave country 4.56
respect for, under ECHR 4.51–4.58
same sex partners 4.57
unaccompanied minors 4.58
Family law. *See also* Family concepts,
  birth family, importance of 1.37
  Community Legal Service Funding 1.42
  confidentiality 1.38–1.41
  delay 1.24–1.25
  disclosure 1.38–1.41
  divorce 1.12–1.13
  domestic violence 1.14–1.19
  generally 1.2–1.8
  legal aid 1.42
  marriage 1.9–1.11
  medical and psychiatric experts 1.43–1.44
  persons who can make application 1.27–1.29
  presumption of no order 1.26
  private law and public law, distinction 1.45–1.52
  representation of children's views in court 1.30–1.36
  void/voidable marriages 1.12–1.13
  welfare principle 1.20–1.23
member, definition of 1.8
orders, use of, example 1.106
Financial support and public services
access to, generally 3.1
destitute, for,
  asylum-seekers 3.3–3.18
  destitute for particular reasons, where 3.26
  immigration control, those subject to 3.22–3.25
  leave to remain, those with 3.2
  notification of Home Office 8.16

refugees 3.2
separated children 3.19–3.21
unaccompanied minors 3.19–3.21
families which include children, for 3.27–3.31

Guardian
children's, role of 1.31
parental responsibility 1.55, 1.61
Guardian ad litem 1.31

Health matters
AIDS, Home Office policy 6.60–6.71
asylum-seekers' access to medical treatment 3.9, 6.60–6.71
health service provision for asylum-seekers 3.12, 3.15, 3.27
HIV positive status,
  Home Office policy 6.60–6.71
  human rights and 4.32
medical and psychiatric experts in court proceedings 1.43–1.44
National Health Service, treatment of immigrants under 3.36–3.39
psychiatric illness 6.72–6.75
serious illnesses, Home Office policy 6.62–6.66, 6.68–6.70
terminally ill, removal policy for 6.70
vulnerable adult, taking instructions from 7.1, 7.4
HIV infection
Home Office policy as to 6.60–6.71
human rights and 4.32
Home Office policy
administrative removal and deportation, as to. *See* Administrative removal and deportation
AIDS, as to 6.60–6.70
concessions and, generally 6.1–6.3
legal position of 6.9–6.11
sources of 6.4–6.8

Home Office policy, *continued*
  discretionary 6.132
  domestic violence, where 6.48–6.55
  generally 6.1–6.3
  HIV infection, as to 6.60–6.70
  Immigration Directorate's Instructions (IDI) guidance 6.4–6.8, 6.12
  long residence concessions,
    10-year 6.77–6.85
    14-year 6.86–6.90
    children, application to 6.113–6.115, 6.123, 6.132–6.134
    generally 6.76
  marriage,
    administrative removal and deportation cases. *See* Administrative removal and deportation
    concession relating to 'one year rule' 6.48–6.54
  policy outside rules regarding children,
    generally 6.12
    'looked after' by local authority, where 6.18–6.21
    'over-age' children and DNA testing 6.37–6.47
    reach 18 before applications decided, children who 6.22–6.23
    under-12 concession 6.13–6.17
    without parents in UK 6.24–6.36. *See also* Unaccompanied minor
  psychiatric illness, as to, power of removal 6.72–6.75
  separated spouses 6.56–6.59
  serious illness, as to 6.60–6.71
  sibling groups split by nationality, as to 6.144–6.145
  widowed partners 6.48–6.54
Homosexual couples. *See* Same sex partners
Housing benefit
  asylum-seekers, for 3.3
  public, availability 3.40

Human rights. *See also* European Convention on Human Rights Act 1998,
  function of 4.21
  immigration appeals, effect of 4.11
  European Commission, relevance of decisions of 4.20
  European Court of Human Rights, relevance of decisions of 4.20
  law, relevance of 4.1–4.3
Illegitimacy. *See* Child
Immigration
  appeals. *See* Appeals
  control,
    financial support for those subject to 3.22–3.25
    students subject to 3.35
    See also Asylum-seeker
  court, representation of children's views in 1.33
Immigration Directorate's Instructions
  Home Office policy in 6.4–6.8, 6.12
Immigration Rules
  application by Home Office 6.1–6.3, 6.9
  family issues, application to 5.1, 5.50, 6.100, 6.117
Indefinite leave to remain
  adult dependants, granted to 5.31
  application for, making 8.14
  child granted 1.65, 1.91, 1.106, 4.52, 5.31, 6.20, 6.21, 6.36, 6.44, 7.24
  divorce or separation where 5.7, 5.54
  domestic violence concession and 6.49
  hospital treatment and 3.38
  long residence concession and 6.76, 6.77, 6.82, 6.87, 6.88
  public housing for whose with 3.40
  refugee leaving before grant of 7.4
  right to family life and 4.52

support for refugees with 3.2
Injunctions
  domestic violence, relating to 1.18
Instructions
  taking, from child. *See*
    Interviewing a child
Interpreter
  availability and provision 3.10,
    3.12, 4.46, 4.63
  interviewing child through 7.14,
    7.15
Interviewing a child
  expert assessment,
    benefits if child stays in UK, as
      to 7.26
    child's future in UK, of 7.25
    child's parents in UK, where
      7.27
    developmental years in UK,
      where 7.29
    reports 7.30–7.35
    return to country of origin,
      effect on child of 7.28
  factors affecting child 7.3
  generally 7.1–7.3
  reports, consideration of 7.30–
    7.35
  taking instructions,
    child, from 7.6–7.19
    child subject to care order,
      where 7.24
    generally 7.4–7.5
    parents/carers, from 7.22–7.23
    persons from whom should be
      obtained 7.4

Legal aid 1.42
Local authority. *See also* Court order
  accommodation,
    meaning 1.83
    unaccompanied minor arriving
      in UK, for 1.84, 3.19–3.21
    under CA 1989, s20 1.80–1.81,
      1.83–1.88
  care orders. *See* Care order
  care plan,
    contact with child and 1.97
    elements of, guidance as to 1.98
    requirements 1.98–1.99

children leaving care of 1.82, 6.19,
  6.21
children looked after by,
  Home Office immigration
    policies as to 6.18–6.21
  removal to live abroad 1.100–
    1.104
  role generally 1.80–1.83
complaints procedure under CA
  1989 s26 1.105
parental responsibility 6.20
provision of education for
  accommodated children 1.86
responsibility for child,
  general duty as to 1.75–1.79
  looked after by local authority,
    where 1.80–1.83
  not British citizen, where 1.78
social services, role of 6.18, 6.21,
  6.30
Long residence
  children with, deportation and
    removal cases 6.113–6.115
  Home Office concessions,
    10-year 6.77–6.85
    14-year 6.86–6.90
    generally 6.76

Marriage. *See also* Dependant
  administrative removal and
    deportation cases. *See*
    Administrative removal and
    deportation
  certificate 5.53
  divorce. *See* Divorce
  domestic violence 'one year'
    concession 6.48–6.54
  indefinite leave on basis of 5.54
  'one year' rule concession and
    domestic violence, EU law
    and 6.55
  separation. *See* Separation
  'suspicious' 5.52
  validity,
    custom marriages 1.11
    overseas, taking place 1.10
    religious ceremonies and 1.11
    UK, taking place in 1.9, 1.11
  void/voidable 1.12–1.13

Medical treatment. *See* Health matters
Minor. *See also* Child, Unaccompanied minor

National Asylum Support Service (NASS)
  accommodation provision by 3.6–3.12
  application form 3.7
  creation of 3.5
  role of 3.5–3.9
National Health Service
  immigrants, for 3.36–3.39
Non-molestation order 1.14, 6.49. *See also* Court order

Occupation order 1.14, 1.15. *See also* Court order
Order. *See* Court order
Overseas. *See* Abroad

Parent. *See also* Adoption, Child, Family, Parental responsibility
  DNA testing 6.38–6.47
  in UK,
    administrative removal and deportation where 6.125–6.127
    assessment where 7.27
    subject to deportation action, where 6.116–6.124
    unmarried father, parental responsibility 1.56
Parental responsibility
  care order, where 1.94
  delegation of 1.60
  local authority, conferred on 6.20
  meaning 1.54
  non-biological parent, where 1.59
  person obtaining residence order 1.57
  persons who have 1.55–1.59
  wardship and 1.63
Private law
  proceedings,
    children's representation in 1.34, 1.36

  medical and psychiatric experts 1.44
  public law and, distinction 1.45–1.52
Private life, respect for. *See* Family and private life
Prohibited steps order. *See also* Court order
  application 1.46–1.50
  effect 1.52
nature of 1.70
Public law
  medical and psychiatric experts in proceedings 1.43
  private law and, distinction 1.45–1.52
Public services. *See* Financial support and public services

Refugee
  another country, in, applications from 5.44
  family reunion policy 1.5, 5.17–5.18, 5.21, 6.36
  NHS and 3.36–3.39
  sponsor, as,
    dependants in UK 5.27–5.34
    dependants outside UK 5.35–5.37
  support where destitute 3.2
Religious marriage ceremony
  UK, in, validity of 1.11
Removal. *See* Administrative removal and deportation
Residence order. *See also* Court order
  application for 1.46–1.51
  effect 1.52, 1.67, 8.24
  example 1.65
  nature of 1.65–1.66
  right to family life and 4.52
  use of 1.106
Return to country of origin. *See also* Administrative removal and deportation
  death penalty, where 4.25–4.28
  effect on child of 7.28, 7.29
  unaccompanied children, of 5.10–5.14

Same sex partners
  asylum-seekers 5.45
  children of 1.4
  right to private life 4.57
School. *See* Education
Section 8 order. *See* Court order
Secure accommodation order
  circumstances for 1.74
Separation. *See also* Divorce
  asylum and,
    family settled, where 5.7
    family with limited leave 5.5–5.6
    generally 5.3–5.4
  separated spouses and EU law 6.56–6.59
Sex industry
  children employed in 4.36–4.38, 4.41
Slavery
  children, of 4.35–4.41
  prohibition under ECHR 4.17, 4.36–4.41
Specific issue order. *See also* Court order
  application 1.46–1.50
  effect 1.52
  nature of 1.71
Sponsor
  asylum-seeker, where 5.23–5.24
  dependent children, of 6.13–6.14
  exceptional leave, having,
    dependants in UK 5.39–5.42
    dependants outside UK 5.43
    general factors 5.38
  refugee, where,
    dependants in UK 5.27–5.34
    dependants outside UK 5.35–5.37
  spouse for entry clearance 6.101
Supervision order. *See also* Court order
  application for 1.28, 1.45
  care proceedings and, comparison 1.73
  circumstances for 1.73
  legal aid 1.42
  removal of child subject to, to live abroad 1.100–1.104

Support
  education, access to 3.32–3.35
  financial. *See* Financial support and public services
Surrogacy arrangement
  parental responsibility 1.58

Terrorists
  international, detention 4.47
Torture
  country of origin, in 5.47
  ECHR prohibition on 4.17, 4.29–4.33
  Medical Foundation for the Care of Victims of Torture 3.9
Trafficked children 4.36–4.41, 5.16

UKCOSA (Council for International Education) 3.35
UN. *See* United Nations
Unaccompanied minor. *See also* Local authority
  abandoned,
    IDI guidance 6.24, 6.33–6.35
    where very young 6.20
  accommodation for 1.84, 3.19–3.21
  administrative removal and deportation of 6.128–6.131
  asylum,
    disputed age 5.15
    exceptional leave to remain, where child has 5.17–5.18
    generally 5.9
    refugee, where child is 5.17–5.18
    returnability of children 5.10–5.14
    trafficked children 5.16
    unknown immigration status 5.19–5.22
    See also Home Office *below*
  change of circumstances 6.29
  education 3.20–3.21
  enslaved 4.35–4.41
  Home Office,
    case-worker, role of 6.28, 6.30–6.32
    considerations 6.31

Unaccompanied minor, Home Office, *continued*
  general aim 6.25
  policy as to 6.24–6.36
  rejection of application 6.35
  social services' opinion 6.30
  IDI guidance as to 6.24, 6.26–6.29
  right to private life 4.58
  sex industry 4.36–4.38, 4.41
  trafficking 4.36–4.41, 5.16
United Nations Convention on the Rights of the Child (UNCRC) 1.35, 4.1, 4.41, 5.11, 8.29
United Nations High Commission for Refugees (UNHCR)
family, as to 5.2
Unmarried partners. *See also* Same sex partners
  asylum-seekers 5.27, 5.29, 5.39, 5.45

Vouchers 3.6, 3.8, 3.14, 3.27, 3.37
Vulnerable adult
  taking instructions from 7.1, 7.4.
    See also Interviewing a child

Wardship
  circumstances for 1.62
  parental responsibility and 1.63
Welfare of child
  adoption and 1.21
  checklist of factors 1.22
  delay in reaching decision 1.24–1.25
  importance of 1.20
  orders with respect to child 1.23
  persons who can make application 1.27–1.29
  presumption of no order 1.26
  principle 1.20–1.23
Welfare officer
  role of 1.32

LAG Legal Action Group

Working with lawyers and advisers to promote equal access to justice

Legal Action magazine
The only monthly magazine published specifically for legal aid practitioners and the advice sector.

2002 annual subscription: £79
Concessionary rates available for students and trainees – call the LAG office for details.

Books
LAG's catalogue includes a range of titles covering:

- community care
- crime
- debt
- education
- employment
- family
- housing
- human rights
- immigration
- personal injury
- practice & procedure
- welfare benefits
- LAG policy

Community Care Law Reports
The only law reports devoted entirely to community care issues. Compiled by an expert team and published quarterly, each issue contains:

- editorial review
- community care law update
- law reports
- guidance
- cumulative index
- full tables

Training
Accredited with the Law Society, the Bar Council and the Institute of Legal Executives, LAG provides topical training courses across a broad range of subjects.

Conferences
LAG runs major conferences to examine issues at the cutting-edge of legal services policy and to inform practitioners of their implications.

For further information about any of Legal Action Group's activities, please contact:

Legal Action Group
242 Pentonville Road
London N1 9UN

DX 130400 London (Pentonville Road)
Telephone: 020 7833 2931
Fax: 020 7837 6094
e-mail: lag@lag.org.uk
www.lag.org.uk